Atal Bihari Vajpayee
Prime Minister of India

ATAL BIHARI VAJPAYEE
PRIME MINISTER
OF
INDIA

Editor
Sujata K. Dass

KALPAZ PUBLICATIONS
Delhi-110052

Atal Bihari Vajpayee Prime Minister of India

Rs. 690

ISBN: 81-7835-277-X

Published in 2004 in India by
Kalpaz Publications,
C-30, Satyawati Nagar, Delhi-110052
E-mail : Kalpaz@hotmail.com

Laser Typesetting at : Shree Vaishnavi Creations, Delhi
Printed at : Mehra Offset Press, Delhi

Contents

Preface

In the long-drawn political struggle for the last more than six decades, Shri Atal Bihari Vajpayee has shown significant innings in public, Parliament and as Prime Minister of India. He is indeed a well-disciplined statesman, an orator for excellence, an eminent organizer, peaceful negotiator, and last but not the least a reputed poet. Born in a middle class family, he has struggled very hard to carve out his political career in his party. He is very well respected by one and all, even by the opposition leaders having different ideology. In the domain of foreign policy, he is the firm believer of maintaining friendly relations with the neighbouring countries as well as other powers in the world. Thus a firm believer in the policy of peaceful coexistence, he is instrumental in strengthening the dignity of our sub-continent in the eyes of the global powers. And whenever he happens to go abroad he brings back the goodwill of that country.

The theme has been well-weaved into twenty-one chapters having deep bearing on various aspects of his policy implemented during the period of his Prime Ministership. Commencing from his brief profile, this work advances systematically towards his successful years as Prime Minister having bearing on his socio-economic measures, role in Parliament including his participation in numerous debates, views on industry, particularly its development, speeches on the eve of Independence Day, National Commission on Population, the Kargil issue, launching of Agni II, views on terrorism, Indian Economic Summit-1998, speech at the FICCI, Forum, Concern on Brain Drain during the session of Indian Science Congress, address to NRIs offering them economic concessions in Indian-subcontinent, Conference with Chief Ministers and their problems, the labour problem, significant aspects of foreign policy, need to restructure Indo-US ties for the good of Global Democracy, key to peaceful World Order, flays attack on Christians, emphasis on Indianness, in General Assembly of the United Nations Organisation, views on child labour, India's participation in SAARC at Islamabad, 2004, signing of Social Charter by SAARC nations, India and Pakistan to start dialogue in February and the announcement in connection with the coming elections for the Lok Sabha.

It is thus a well-selected documentation of Shri Vajpayee's historic career as the Prime Minister of India. Indeed he has shown a deep sense of optimism of his policies and works undertaken by him with the cooperation of the National Democratic Alliance. In fact he is very optimistic about the bright future of India which he always mentions in his speeches and writings. This work will be useful for statesmen, Parliamentarians, teachers, researchers and students in India and abroad.

Sujata K. Dass

1
A Profile

Shri Atal Bihari Vajpayee has been Sworn-in as the Prime Minister of India

The President Shri K.R. Narayanan administered the oath of office and secrecy at an impressive ceremony in the forecourt of Rashtrapati Bhawan. Shri Vajpayee has assumed the august office of the Prime Minister of India for the third time.

Earlier, Shri Vajpayee was Prime Minister of India from May 16-31, 1996 and a second time from March 19, 1998 till date. With his swearing-in today as Prime Minister, he becomes the only Prime Minister since Jawaharlal Nehru to occupy the office of the Prime Minister of India through three successive mandates. He is also the first Prime Minister since Smt. Indira Gandhi to lead his party to victory in successive elections.

Born on December 25, 1924 at Gwalior, Madhya Pradesh to Shri Krishna Bihari Vajpayee and Smt. Krishna Devi, Shri Vajpayee brings with him a long parliamentary experience spanning over four decades. He has been a Member of Parliament since 1957. He was elected to the 5th, 6th and 7th Lok Sabha and again to the 10th, 11th and 12th Lok Sabha and to Rajya Sabha in 1962 and 1986. He has again been elected to Parliament from Lucknow, in Uttar Pradesh, for the fourth time consecutively. He is the only parliamentarian elected from four different States at different times namely—UP, Gujarat, MP and Delhi.

Elected leader of the National Democratic Alliance, which is a pre-election coming together of political parties from different regions of the country and which enjoys a comfortable backing and support of the elected Members of the 13th Lok Sabha, Shri Vajpayee was earlier elected leader of his own Bharatiya Janata Party (BJP) parliamentary party which has also again emerged as the single largest party in the 13th Lok Sabha as was the case in the 12th Lok Sabha.

Educated at Victoria (now Laxmi Bai) College, Gwalior and DAV College, Kanpur, Uttar Pradesh, Shri Vajpayee holds an M.A. (Political Science) degree and has many literary, artistic and scientific accomplishments to his credit. He edited *Rashtradharma* (a Hindi monthly), *Panchjanya* (a Hindi weekly) and the dailies *Swadesh* and *Veer Arjun*. His published works include "Meri Sansadiya Yatra" (in four volumes), "Meri Ikkyavan Kavitayen", "Sankalp Kaal", "Shakti-se-Shanti", "Four Decades in Parliament" (speeches in three volumes), 1957-95, "Lok Sabha mein Atalji" (a collection of speeches), "Mrityu Ya Hatya", "Amar Balidan", "Kaidi Kaviraj Ki Kundalian" (a collection of poems written in jail during Emergency), "New Dimensions of India's Foreign Policy" (a collection of speeches delivered as External Affairs Minister during 1977-79), "Jan Sangh Aur Mussalman" "Sansad Mein Teen Dashak" (Hindi) (speeches in Parliament - 1957-1992 - three volumes; and "Amar Aag Hai" (a collection of poems) 1994.

Shri Vajpayee has participated in various social and cultural activities. He has been a Member of the National Integration Council since 1961. Some of his other activities : (i) Assistant Station Masters Association (1965-70); (ii) Pandit Deendayal Upadhyay Smarak Samiti (1968-84); (iii) Deen Dayal Dham, Farah, Mathura, U.P.; and (iv) Janmabhomi Smarak Samiti, 1969 onwards.

Founder-member of the erstwhile Jana Sangh (1951), President, Bharatiya Jana Sangh (1968-1973), leader of the Jana Sangh parliamentary party (1955-1977) and a founder-member of the Janata Party (1977-1980), Shri Vajpayee was President, BJP (1980-1986) and the leader of BJP parliamentary party during 1980-1984, 1986 and 1993-1996. He was Leader of the Opposition throughout the term of the 11th Lok Sabha. Earlier, he was India's External Affairs Minister in the Morarji Desai Government from March 24, 1977 to July 28, 1979.

Widely respected within the country and abroad as a statesman of the genre of Pt. Jawaharlal Nehru, Shri Vajpayee's 1998-99 stint as Prime Minister has been characterised as 'one year of courage of conviction'. It was during this period that India entered a select group of nations following a series of successful nuclear tests at Pokharan in May 1998. The bus journey to Pakistan in February 1999 was widely acclaimed for starting a new era of negotiations to resolve the outstanding problems of the sub-continent. India's honesty made an impact on the world community. Later, when this gesture of friendship turned out to be a betrayal of faith in Kargil, Shri Vajpayee was also hailed for his successful handling of the situation in repulsing back the intruders from the Indian soil. It was during Shri Vajpayee's 1998-99 tenure that despite a global recession, India achieved 5.8 per cent GDP growth, which was higher than the previous year. Higher agricultural production and increase in foreign exchange reserves during this period were indicative of a forward-looking economy responding to the needs of the people. "We must grow faster. We simply have no other alternative" has been Shri Vajpayee's slogan focussing particularly on economic empowerment of the rural poor. The bold decisions taken by his Government for strengthening rural economy, building a strong infrastructure and revitalising the human development programmes, fully demonstrated his Government's commitment to a strong and self-reliant nation to meet the challenges of the next millennium to make India an economic power in the 21st century. Speaking from the ramparts of the Red Fort on the occasion of 52nd Independence Day, he had said, "I have a vision of India : an India free of hunger and fear, an India free of illiteracy and want."

He has served on a number of important Committees of Parliament. He was Chairman, Committee on Government Assurances (1966-67); Chairman, Public Accounts Committee (1967-70); Member, General Purposes Committee (1986); Member, House Committee and Member, Business Advisory Committee, Rajya Sabha (1988-90); Chairman, Committee on Petitions, Rajya Sabha (1990-91); Chairman, Public Accounts Committee, Lok Sabha (1991-93); Chairman, Standing Committee on External Affairs (1993-96).

He participated in the freedom struggle and went to jail in 1942. He was detained during Emergency in 1975-77.

Widely travelled, Shri Vajpayee has been taking keen interest in international affairs, upliftment of Scheduled Castes and Scheduled Tribes, women and child welfare. He has been a Member of the National Integration Council since 1961. Some of his other associations include : President, All India Station Masters and Delegation to Australia, 1967; European Parliament, 1983; Canada, 1987; Indian Delegation to Commonwealth Parliamentary Association meetings held in Canada, 1966 and 1994; Zambia, 1980; Isle of Man 1984; Indian Delegation to Inter-Parliamentary Union Conference, Japan, 1974; Sri Lanka, 1975; Switzerland, 1984; Indian Delegation to the UN General Assembly, 1988, 1990, 1991, 1992, 1993 and 1994; Leader, Indian Delegation to the Human Rights Commission Conference, Geneva, 1993.

He was conferred Padma Vibhushan in 1992 in recognition of his services to the nation. He was also conferred the Lokmanya Tilak Puruskar and the Bharat Ratna Pt. Govind Ballabh Pant Award for the Best Parliamentarian, both in 1994. Earlier, the Kanpur University honoured him with an Honorary Doctorate of Philosophy in 1993.

A man of the masses, firm in his political convictions. India has an inspiring leader in Atal Bihari Vajpayee.

On October 13, 1999, he took charge as Prime Minister of India for the second consecutive term at the head of a new coalition government, the National Democratic Alliance. He was Prime Minister for a short period in 1996.

A veteran Parliamentarian whose career stretches over four decades, Shri Vajpayee has been elected to the Lok Sabha (House of the People) nine times and to the Rajya Sabha (House of the States) twice, a record by itself. As India's Foreign Minister, Chairperson of various important Standing Committees of Parliament and Leader of Opposition, he has been an active participant in the shaping of India's post-Independence domestic and foreign policy.

His first connection with nationalist politics was in his student days when he joined the Quit India Movement of 1942, which hastened the end of British colonial rule. A student of political science and law, it was in college that he developed a keen interest in foreign affairs—an interest he has nourished over the years and put to skilful use while representing India at various multilateral and bilateral fora.

He had embarked upon a journalist's career, which was cut short in 1951 when he joined the Bharatiya Jana Sangh, the forerunner of today's Bharatiya Janata Party, the leading component of the National Democratic Alliance. A critically acclaimed poet, he still takes time off from affairs of state to indulge in music and in a bit of gourmet cooking.

Born in the family of a humble school teacher on December 25 1924, in the erstwhile princely State of Gwalior (now a part of the Indian state of Madhya Pradesh), Shri Vajpayee's rise in public life is a tribute to both his political acumen and Indian democracy. Over the decades, he has emerged as a leader who commands respect for his liberal worldview and commitment to democratic ideals.

An ardent champion of women's empowerment and social equality, he believes in a forward-looking, forward-moving India, a strong and prosperous nation confident of its rightful place in the comity of nations. He stands for an India anchored in 5000 years of civilizational history, ever modernizing, ever renewing, and ever re-energizing itself to meet the challenges of the next 1000 years.

India's second highest civilian honour, the Padma Vibhushan, was conferred upon him in recognition of his selfless dedication to his first and only love, India, and his more than half-a-century of service to society and the nation. In 1994, he was named India's 'Best Parliamentarian.' The citation read: "True to his name, Atalji is an eminent national leader, an erudite politician, a selfless social worker, forceful orator, poet and litterateur, journalist and indeed a multi-faceted personality...Atalji articulates the aspirations of the masses... his works ever echo total commitment to nationalism."

2

Successful Years as Prime Minister

The following Work may be Counted as the Government's Achievement which Indeed Deserve Appreciation

Youth Affairs and Sports

- Launching of the 'National Reconstruction Scheme' on 30.6.99 on a pilot basis in 80 selected backward districts of the country. The scheme provides an opportunity to youths to participate in the process of nation building.
- The National Sports Development Fund has been created with an initial corpus of Rs. 2 crore as contribution by the Government. Measures have been taken to involve the Industrial Houses, Chief Ministers of States and Public Sector Undertakings. The Fund will be used for betterment of sports.

Education

- Eight-fold increase in the budget for an Area Intensive Programme for educationally backward minorities.

Food and Consumer Affairs

- Involvement of Panchayats in PDS: In his Budget Speech 1999-2000, the Union Finance Minister announced strengthening of the TPDS in the rural areas with greater involvement of Gram Panchayats in the supervision and implementation of the programme so as to ensure proper coverage and increase its efficiency. In line with this policy declaration, detailed guidelines have been issued in June, 1999 for involvement of Gram Panchayats in supervision of the functioning of the Fair Price Shops. These guidelines include, inter-alia, the Right to Information regarding FPS, display of stock position and list of Below Poverty Line (BPL) beneficiaries, formation of the FPS

Committee by each Gram Panchayat, involvement of the Gram Sabha in running of the FPS, and redressal of grievances.

- Special allocation of foodgrains: Hitherto additional allocation of foodgrains under the TPDS had been made at rates applicable to the Above Poverty Line (APL) population. However, special additional allocations have been made at BPL rates for the first time in respect of the earthquake affected areas in Uttar Pradesh, for drought relief in Manipur, and for increasing the availability of foodgrains in the 8 KBK districts of Orissa.
- The Cabinet Committee on Prices has been reconstituted and is now headed by the Prime Minister. A High-Powered Price Monitoring Board was constituted in December, 1998 to review all aspects relating to prices and availability of essential commodities.
- A Special Study Group has been set up to identify measures required to meet the needs of North-Eastern States and Island Territories regarding the supply of essential commodities.
- Futures trading in jute goods commenced in March 1998 and in cotton in December, 1998. International Castor Oil Futures Contracts have been launched on May 10, 1999. The Cabinet Committed on Economic Affairs (CCEA) in its meeting held on March 23, 1999 has approved the proposal to introduce/resume the futures trading in rapeseed/mustardseed, groundnut, sunflower, ricebran, cottonseed, coconut, sesamum, safflower and their oils and oilcakes.

Women Reservation Bill

- The Government introduced a Bill, namely, the Constitution (Eighty-fourth Amendment) Bill, 1998 seeking to provide for reservation of seats for women in Lok Sabha and State Legislative Assemblies.

PIO Card

- A PIO card scheme has been launched on 31.3.1999. The PIO card will entitle the holder to visa free entry into India and also confer some special economic, educational, financial and cultural benefits. PIOs, both settled abroad and those staying in India on long term visa, have evinced keen interest in the scheme.

State Reorganisation

- Bills for re-organisation of the existing States of Bihar, Madhya Pradesh and Uttar Pradesh so as to provide for the new States of Vananchal, Chattisgarh and Uttarakhand/Uttaranchal, were introduced in the Lok Sabha in December, 1998. The Bills, however, lapsed with the dissolution of the Twelfth Lok Sabha.

Regulation of Lottery Trade

- The Lotteries (Regulation) Ordinance was replaced by the Lotteries (Regulation) Act, 1998 on July 7, 1998. Besides banning single digit and instant lotteries, the Act provides for regulating other kinds of State lotteries. The Act also empowers a State to prohibit, within the State, the sale of tickets of a lottery organised, conducted or promoted by every other State.

Administrative Reforms etc.

- The Lok Pal Bill, 1998 was introduced in Lok Sabha on 3-8-98. The Bill was subsequently examined by the Parliamentary Standing Committee on Home Affairs.
- The CVC Bill, 1998 was formulated in pursuance of the directives of Supreme Court and the Bill was introduced in the Lok Sabha on the 7th December, 1998. It was subsequently passed by Lok Sabha but could not be taken up for consideration by the Rajya Sabha.
- In pursuance of the recommendation of the Fifth Central Pay Commission, the age of retirement for Central Government employees (including the officers of All India Services) was raised from 58 years to 60 years with effect from 13th May, 1998. Similarly, the age of retirement of the employees of Central Public Sector Undertakings, Banks and Insurance Companies was raised to 60 years. The age of retirement of Armed Forces and Central Para-Military Forces was also raised by two years.
- The maximum age prescribed for eligibility to appear in the Civil Services Examination has been raised from 28 years to 30 years with effect from the Civil Services Examination, 1999. Similarly, the upper age limit for direct recruitment through other open competitive examinations for Central Civil Services and Civil posts has been increased by two years.
- In pursuance of the recommendation of the Fifth Central Pay Commission, it has been decided to step up the pension of all pre-1996 Pensioners to 50 per cent of the minimum of revised scale of pay as on 1-1-96 of the post last held by the pensioner subject to the existing provision in the rules relating to qualifying service and the family pension to 30 per cent of the minimum of the revised scale of pay as on 1-1-96 of the post last held by the deceased employee.
- The families of Central Govt. civilian employees who die in terrorist activities were earlier eligible to get a compensation of Rs.50,000/-. Government have since decided to enhance the rate of ex-gratia lump

sum compensation payable to families of Central Government civilian employees who die in harness in the performance of their bonafide duties to Rs. 5 lakhs and to those dying in action against terrorist to Rs. 7.50 lakhs.

- With a view to improving the quality of public services and making them more customer-friendly, an Award Scheme has been started from the year 1998-99. The Scheme is open for Central Government employees as well as members of the public. Under the Scheme, such suggestions which can lead to financial savings, enhance efficiency/ productivity or public satisfaction in Government offices would be considered for being awarded.

Review of Administrative Law

- A Commission was set up in May, 1998 to review the administrative laws. The Commission submitted its final report on 30th September, 1998. The Commission has recommended inter-alia repeal of over 1300 Central Laws and amendments to 109 Acts.

Foreign Affairs/ Strategic Dialogue

- Strategic dialogues were initiated with key countries including the US, Russia, France, Germany and UK during which the Indian position on strategic matters including CTBT etc. was clearly explained to the interlocutors. The result has been a much greater appreciation and understanding of India's strategic and security requirements after Pokhran-II, both in bilateral and in multilateral fora.

Jammu and Kashmir Affairs

- Operationalisation of Rs. 560.47 crores action plan to tackle militancy in the state of J&K which includes curbing infiltration, countering militancy in the hinterland, protection of minorities, greater interaction with the border population, enhancing intelligence capabilities, countering secessionist over ground base within J&K and greater functional integration, has led to perceptible improvement in ground situation.
- The norms for security related expenditure to be reimbursed to J&K has been broadened and a sum of Rs.273 crores has been reimbursed to the State Government during the year 1998-99.
- Steps have been initiated to strengthen the Village Development Councils in the State by providing arms and communication systems. The number of Special Police Officers have been increased from 7455 to 12855 which is proposed to be further raised to 19855.

- A provision of Rs. 150 crores has been made during the year 1999-2000 under the Debt Relief Scheme. So far Rs. 193.30 crores has been released to Banks/Financial Institutions to implement the scheme and pass on the benefits to the borrowers.
- An amount of Rs. 100 crores has been provided during the current year by the Ministry of Railways for Udhampur-Srinagar-Baramula Railway Project.

Initiatives for NE States

- Creation of Non-Lapsable Central Resource Pool: In order to implement some important infrastructure and economic development projects a Central Resource Pool was created in the central budget for development of North-East. A sum of Rs. 93.10 crores was released during 1998-99.
- Industrial Policy for the North-East: Under the new Industrial Policy, Government have exempted certain goods from payment of excise/ additional duty of excise in Assam, Tripura, Meghalaya, Mizoram, Manipur, Nagaland and Arunachal Pradesh and the notification issued on 7.7.99. The proposal to give exemption from income-tax for 10 years in the industrial growth centres and integrated infrastructure development centres in North-East has been incorporated in Finance Bill 1999-2000 to specified units or notified industries set up in North-East after 1.4.1998.
- The IFAD Project at a cost of Rs.159.40 crores aimed at socio-economic development in the States of Assam, Meghalaya and Manipur has been approved.
- Security related expenditure: The Government have approved guidelines to reimburse Security Related Expenditure to various State Governments. Reimbursements of Rs. 294.36 crore (Assam:210.77, Manipur:19.43, Tripura:28.55, and Nagaland:35.64) have already been made to these States.
- The peace talks with the NSCN (I.M) have been continuing and cease-fire has been extended for a further period of one year with effect from 1.8.99.
- With a view to making Mizoram self-sufficient in power by 2006 AD, sanction has been accorded for Tuirial Hydro Electric Project (60 MW) at a cost of Rs. 368.72 crores.
- A surrender-cum-rehabilitation scheme for North-East militants has been approved. 589 militants have surrendered upto 30.6.1999.
- Royalty rates for oil supplied by Assam have been revised upwards

w.e.f. 1.4.97. The arrears have been paid upto 31.3.1997 on account payments are being made regularly.

Petroleum and Natural Gas Sector

A Group on India Hydrocarbon Vision 2025 was set up on 31.3.1999 to work out a specific framework for creating an India Hydrocarbon Vision in which India becomes a major Hydrocarbon power of the world in future. This Group is headed by Finance Minister. This Group has set up six Sub-Groups with detailed terms of references. These Sub-Groups are at present holding meetings and doing detailed exercises for working out specific frameworks. The Group on India Hydrocarbon Vision 2025 is expected to give its report before middle of September, 1999.

- Prime Minister's Self-Employment Scheme of Oil Companies launched to set up one Retail Kerosene Dealership in every Development Block of the country to provide employment to educated unemployed youth.
- For the welfare of the Defence Personnel, the Government have earmarked 500 new Retail Outlets and LPG Distributorship for the widows/kith and kin of the personnel who sacrificed their lives.
- Phased dismantling of Administered Pricing Mechanism commenced since 1st April, 1998. Prices of all products except Petrol, Diesel, Aviation Turbine Fuel, Liquified Petroleum Gas, Kerosene Oil (Public Distribution System) decontrolled.
- Refining sector has been delicensed. Five Year Tax Holiday granted for new refineries set up after 1st October, 1998. Three new refineries at Panipat, Numaligarh and Jamnagar completed. Government approval accorded to refineries at Paradeep (Orissa), Bina (Madhya Pradesh) and Bhatinda (Punjab).
- A progressive and attractive New Exploration Licensing Policy (NELP) finalised and announced. Bids have been invited for 48 Exploration Blocks including 12 deep sea offshore blocks which hold large hydrocarbon potential under NELP.
- The Uttar Pradesh Petrochemicals Complex of Gas Authority of India Limited (GAIL) has been commissioned at Pata in Uttar Pradesh at a cost of Rs. 2500 crore and dedicated to the nation by the Prime Minister on June 10, 1999.

Planning Commission

- The major initiatives taken by Planning Commission are detailed in the Ninth Plan. Special Action Plans related to (i) Doubling of food production and making India hunger-free in 10 years; (ii) Rapid improvement in physical infrastructure; (iii) National Water Policy; (iv) Social Infrastructure: Rural Housing, Urban Housing, Health Care Services, Education, Urban Water Supply and Sanitation and Rural Water Supply and Sanitation and (v) Information Technology, have been incorporated into the Ninth Five Year Plan document.

- The Planning Commission has offered to assist the State Governments in preparing a Vision 2020 Document so as to have a Perspective Plan in place for the development of the States for the next 20 years or so.
- The Planning Commission has decided to support the preparation of the State Level HDRs which would be an important tool for identifying areas that are deficient in social infrastructure, with a view to increasing the flow of allocations to these areas and improving the delivery systems.
- A National Task Force on Information Technology and Software Development (headed by Deputy Chairman, Planning Commission) to formulate the National Informatics Policy (aimed at enabling the country to emerge as an Information Technology Superpower within the next ten years) has since submitted some of its Reports to make the adoption of information technology into a national movement.

Power Sector

- Electricity Regulatory Commission Act, 1998 has been passed and Central Electricity Regulatory Commission has been set up which has full power to fix bulk power tariffs. To encourage reforms in the power sector by the States, special incentives have been offered to States which have set up State Electricity Regulatory Commissions. These Commissions will fix power tariffs.
- To encourage private investment in transmission sector, Electricity (Law) Amendment Act, 1998 has been passed.
- New policy for development of Hydel Power Development has been approved to increase investment in the hydel sector. A long term comprehensive package for harnessing the Hydel Power potential and improving the Transmission and Distribution in North East States with concessional funding has been approved.
- To add large power generating capacities at competitive tariff rates. the Government has approved a new mega power policy for setting up multi-State mega power project.
- Under the revised procedure, Government of India has given counter-guarantee to three fast track power projects - Bhadravati, ST-CMS

and Visakhapatnam Power Project of Hinduja National Power Co. Ltd.

Railways

Initiatives for improving the Customer Interface the following steps has taken :

- In keeping with the Railways' dedication to the cause of passengers, 1999-2000 has been declared as the "Year of the Passenger".
- A Customer Care Institute has been set up in Delhi for making the Railways a customer-friendly organisation.
- With networking of the Computerised Passenger Reservation Systems at Mumbai, Delhi, Calcutta, Secunderabad and Chennai a passenger can book tickets on any train from any Passenger Reservation System (PRS) location in the country.

Initiatives for Backward Areas

- Sanction of new Railway line from Agra to Etawah.
- Gauge conversion of Kaptanganj-Siwan-Thave-Chhapra Metre Gauge line to Broad Gauge has been taken up.
- Electrification and doubling of Patna-Gaya line.
- Laying of optical fibre cable between Guwahati and Lumding in the North Eastern Region has been taken up.
- In addition to the above, a number of sanctioned projects for laying of new lines and gauge conversion on which work could not be started for want of requisite clearances, have been cleared by the Cabinet Committee on Economic Affairs.

Direct Tax Measures

- As a welfare measure for Senior Citizens, expenditure incurred by them or on their behalf, on certain diseases would be allowed as a deduction upto Rs. 60,000 per year. The deduction for medical insurance premium has also been raised from Rs.10, 000 to Rs.15, 000.
- As a fiscal incentive for women and child welfare, full deduction from income tax has been granted on payments to projects engaged in establishing and running educational institutions and hospitals in rural areas for women and children, and for creches and schools for children of workers employed in factories or at project sites.
- The income of members of Scheduled Tribes of Ladakh has been exempted.
- The standard deduction for salary earners having income upto Rs. 1 lakh has been raised from Rs. 20,000 to Rs. 25,000. A ceiling of tax-free reimbursement of medical expenses has been raised from

Rs.10,000 to Rs.15,000.

- In recognition of the contribution of Members of the Armed Forces, the pension received by the recipients of Param Vir Chakra, Mahavir Chakra and Vir Chakra and other notified gallantry awards has been made exempt from income-tax.
- Donations made to the National Defence Fund have been made fully deductible for tax purposes.
- A large number of fiscal incentives have been given to encourage house building activity. These include (i) housing projects to be treated as infrastructure facility and tax holiday announced for new housing projects that are completed before 31.03.2001; (ii) the amount of interest deductible for tax purposes in respect of borrowings for self-occupied properties has been increased to Rs.75,000 per year; (iii) deduction for repairs for let-out buildings has been raised from 20 per cent to 25 per cent; (iv) carry forward of loss from house property allowed for set-off against income from house property; (v) 50 per cent of the profits from World Bank aided housing projects allowed as a deduction; (vi) interest income on bad or doubtful debts of Housing Finance Companies is to be taxed on actual receipt basis; (vii) depreciation rates on certain dwelling units have been doubled; (viii) several incentives have also been given for residential properties under the Wealth Tax Act.
- For improvement of environment, complete tax holiday subject to a ceiling of Rs. 5 lakhs, is given to undertakings engaged in the collection or processing of bio-degradable waste. Payments made to eco-friendly projects or schemes producing bacteria-induced fertilisers are fully deductible.
- For promotion of sports and games, 100 per cent deduction is allowed on donations made to the National Sports Fund.
- To encourage infrastructure development, several incentives have been given. These include: (i) tax holiday benefits for Inland Waterways and Inland Ports; (ii) extension of tax holiday benefit to power generating, transmitting or distributing units; (iii) 7-year tax holiday for commercial production of mineral oil, has been extended to oil refineries set up after 1.10.1998. In addition to this, Petroleum Sector is also allowed certain additional expenses such as expenses for site restoration and assignment expenses, to be deductible from tax.
- Telecommunication Sector has been given fiscal incentives by extending the tax holiday benefits to radio paging, trunking and ED

Network and Domestic Satellite Service.

- Information Technology Sector has been given incentives by way of enhanced depreciation on computers, extension of export benefits to supporting developers on export of software and exemption from with holding tax on interest payable by computer software manufacture undertakings. Complete deduction for Y2K expenses has also been allowed.
- The Capital Market plays an important role in the socio-economic well being of the country. To encourage the Capital Market. income from Unit Trust of India and Mutual Fund has been exempted in the hands of the investors. The rate of long-term capital gains tax on transfer of shares/securities for residents has also been pegged at 10 per cent. Fiscal incentives to Venture capital have been rationalised.
- Special measure for socio-economic development of backward areas. Two-tier fiscal incentives are available to industries set up in backward districts and backward States, in the form of tax holiday for initial five years, and 25 per cent deduction from profits for subsequent five years. These benefits were available to industries set up on backward States during the period from 01.04.1993 to 31.03.1998. This period has now been extended to 31.03.2000. Similarly, industries set up in backward districts between 01.10.1994 to 31.03.1998 were eligible for this benefit. This period has been extended upto 31.03.2000.
- Further, with a view to encourage industrial development in North Eastern Region, any industry set up after 01.04.1998 in Industrial Infrastructure Development Centres and Industrial Growth Centres located in Assam, Arunachal Pradesh, Manipur, Meghalaya, Mizoram, Nagaland, Sikkim and Tripura have been allowed exemption from Income Tax for ten initial assessment years. Similary, 100 per cent deduction from profits of specified industries set up in North Eastern States after 01.04.1999 has been provided.

Indirect Tax Measures

- A special additional duty of customs of 4 per cent has been imposed on imports to provide level playing field to the domestic industry. Its total incidence is almost equal to the incidence of local taxes on domestically produced goods.
- Customs duties on electronic sector have been reduced considerably to encourage use of information technology.
- The existing 7 major ad valorem rates of basic customs duty have been reduced to 5 rates.

- Additional duty of customs on high speed diesel oil has been imposed @ Re.1 per litre for development of highways.
- Deeper concessions have been granted to the Information Technology sector. A Special Advance Licensing Scheme has been notified to promote export of electronic hardware.
- Customs duty exemptions have been granted to mega power projects. Export Promotion Capital Goods Scheme providing full exemption from payment of customs duty, has been extended to hotel, tourism and bio-tech sectors. This Scheme has been further relaxed for 9 products of engineering sector by reducing the threshold limit to Rs.1 crore from the earlier Rs. 20 crore; the same limit has been reduced from Rs. 20 crore to Rs.10 lakhs for software products.

Excise

- The limit for excise exemption to SSI units has been raised from Rs.30 lakhs to Rs. 50 Lakhs. SSI units allowed to pay duty on monthly basis.

  The existing 11 ad valorem rates of excise duty, have been brought down to three ad valorem rates, i.e., 8 per cent, 16 per cent and 24 per cent.
- Additional duty of Re.1 per litre has been imposed on petrol and high speed diesel oil to mobilise resources for development of roads.
- Reduction has been announced in excise duty for cold chain equipments for the benefit of food processing industry.
- Special measures for socio-economic devleopment of backward areas: Full exemption from excise duty has been provided to excisable goods manufactured by units located in growth centres/Integrated Infrastructure Development Centres (IIDCs)/Industrial areas etc. in the North Eastern region. These exemptions are available to new units set up in these centres after 24.12.1997 or units undertaking substantial expansion after that date. These exemptions would be available for a period of 10 years.

Agriculture Sector

- Watershed Development Fund (WDF): For effective operationalisation of the Watershed Development Fund, the Planning Commission will have to provide an additional plan allocation of Rs. 100 crores as a matching contribution by GOI over and above a corpus of Rs. 100 crores already created by NABARD.
- New Crop Insurance Scheme, viz. Rashtriya Krishi Bima Yojana: The Government has decided to introduce a new Crop Insurance Scheme

entitled Rashtriya Krishi Bima Yojana in the country from the ensuing Rabi season. The basic objective of the scheme is to provide a safety net for farmers in the event of failure of their crops due to various kinds of natural disasters, pest attacks and disease. The scheme will cover loanee as well as non-loanee farmers, and a number of additional crops.

- New Credit linked capital subsidy scheme for constructing cold storages: Based on the recommendations of the High Level Committee set up by the Government of India, a new back-ended capital subsidy scheme has been proposed for providing concessional finances/ soft loan for the construction of 12 lakh tonnes of new cold storage capacity, modernisation of 8 lakh tonnes for potatoes and construction of 4.5 lakh tonnes of storages for onions in the next three years. The capital subsidy scheme will be implemented by the National Horticulture Board. This scheme would help to mitigate the serious losses suffered due to inadequate post-harvest storage infrastructure.

Chemical and Petrochemical Sector

- Government have allowed foreign direct investment (FDI) upto 74 per cent of equity shareholding under the automatic route in the pharmaceutical sector.
- Government have approved setting up of a Centre of the Central Institute of Plastic Engineering and Technology (CIPET) at Guwahati at a cost of Rs. 10.35 crores. This will enable training in the plastic processing industry in the North Eastern Region.

Civil Aviation

- Improvement in Airport Infrastructure and Airlinks in the North Eastern Region: One of the major initiatives, taken by this Ministry with regard to development of backward areas, relates to improvement in airport infrastructure and airlinks in the North Eastern Region. In this regard a Task Force headed by the Secretary(Civil Aviation) was set up on 28th December, 1998 to examine and make recommendations for improving airport infrastructure and better airlinks in the Region. The Task Force has since submitted its report in April, 1999.
- Private Sector Participation in Airport Infrastructure Development: With a view to promote Private Sector participation in the upgradation and development of airport infrastructure, initiative was taken, as per the decision of the Task Force on Infrastructure to offer selected airports to reputed investors on long term.
- Disinvestment Commission of India recommended disinvestment of

Air India involving infusion of funds immediately, followed by disinvestment to a strategic partner as also to domestic investors. Ministry of Civil Aviation agree with the need for disinvestment including to a strategic partner. Inter-Ministerial consultations are in progress. Disinvestment is expected to lead to a better-brand image, improved product, modernisation/expansion of Air India's fleet with greater reach and better connectivity, and to turn Air India into a profitable company.

Water Resources Sector

- Resolution of the Cauvery Water Dispute: A consensus was arrived at between the Chief Ministers of the Cauvery Basin States following discussions in the meetings chaired by the Prime Minister on 6-7 August, 1998. As a result, a scheme could be finalised for implementation of the Interim Order of the Cauvery Water Disputes Tribunal dated 25.6.91, and all the related consequent orders of the Tribunal. This scheme was notified on 11.8.98. Under the scheme, a Cauvery River Authority has been constituted with the Prime Minister of India as the Chairman and the Chief Ministers of Karnataka, Kerala, Tamil Nadu and Pondicherry, to monitor the progress of the implementation. A Monitoring Committee of the Cauvery River Authority has also been constituted under the Chairmanship of the Secretary (Water Resources) for reviewing the progress made from time to time.
- Modifications in the guidelines under the Accelerated Irrigation Benefit Programme (AIBP): The Accelerated Irrigation Benefit Programme (AIBP) was launched during 1996-97 for providing Central Loan Assistance (CLA) to those major and medium irrigation projects which are in an advanced stage of construction. The CLA was provided to the States on matching basis, except in the North-Eastern and hilly States, which were provided CLA in the ratio of 2:1 (Centre/State). The guidelines under AIBP have recently been relaxed to bring the 8 chronically drought-prone KBK districts of Orissa at par with the North-Eastern and hilly States of Himachal Pradesh, Sikkim and J & K in respect of the funding pattern. Moreover, CLA to this Special Category States including the KBK districts will now be provided in the ratio of 3:1 (Centre/States). Minor irrigation surface schemes of KBK districts and the Special Category States have also been brought under the ambit of the AIBP. These modifications are expected to remove the uneven distribution of funds in AIBP of the

States.

- The Saraswati Project: Studies for confirming the existence of the lost courses of ancient rivers in western Rajasthan (Jaisalmer district) have been undertaken. Preliminary evidence of the existence of buried palaeo-channels is available. Confirmation of the existence of the channels shall open the possibility of transporting water from the waterlogged areas of north-eastern parts of the State to the water-scarce areas of western Rajasthan.

Rural Development

Jawahar Gram Samridhi Yojana (JGSY)

- The Scheme of Jawahar Rozgar Yojana has been modified to ensure that all funds are placed at the disposal of the Gram Panchayats for creation of rural infrastructure. Under the revamped scheme of the JGSY, the DRDAs/ Zilla Parishads will release the funds directly to the Village Panchayats. The Annual Action Plan prepared by the Village Panchayat will have the approval to the Gram Sabha and the priority of works to be taken up will also be decided by the Gram Sabha. The emphasis of the scheme would be on creation of durable assets at the village while taking due care of need based wage employment generation. Village Panchayats will have the.power to execute works/schemes up to Rs.50,000 with the approval of the Gram Sabha.

Employment Assurance Scheme (EAS)

- The Government has decided to restructure the EAS which would continue as the single wage-employment programme to be implemented at the district/block levels throughout the country. The funds to the States would be allocated in accordance with the criteria to be decided by the Government/National Development Council from time to time, and to the districts on an index of backwardness. Seventy per cent of the funds flowing to the districts would be allocated to the blocks and 30 per cent reserved for at the district level to be utilised in the areas of distress. Selection of the works under the scheme would be decided by the Zilla Parishads.

Swaranjayanti Gram Swarozgar Yojana (SGSY)

- Government have restructured the self-employment schemes of IRDP, TRYSEM, DWCRA, SITRA, Million Wells Scheme and Ganga Kalyana Yojana by merging them into one comprehensive programme known as Swaranjayanti Gram Swarozgar Yojana (SGSY). This will be a holistic programme covering all aspects of self-employment such as organisation of the poor into Self-Help groups, training, credit, technology, infrastructure and marketing. The objective of the scheme is to bring every assisted family above the poverty line in a period of 3 years. Thirty per cent of the rural poor will be covered in the next 5 years.

Rural Housing

- Government have announced a National Housing and Habitat Policy which aims at providing "Housing For All" and facilitating construction of 20 lakh additional housing units annually with an emphasis on extending benefits to the poor and the deprived. Of these, 13 lakh additional houses are to be constructed in the rural areas. It has also approved the Action Plan for Rural Housing which includes conversion of unserviceable kutcha houses into semi-pucca houses, change in the criteria of allocation under Indira Awas Yojana, a new credit/subsidy scheme for rural housing, equity support to the HUDCO, setting up of Rural Building Centres, and introducing Samagra Awas Yojana on pilot basis in one block each of 25 districts in 24 States and one UT, to ensure integrated provision of shelter, drinking water and sanitation. A National Mission for Rural Housing and Habitat has also been set up.

Watershed Development Programme

- All area development programmes of the Ministry, viz., Drought Prone Areas Programme (DPAP), the Desert Development Programme (DDP) and Integrated Wastelands Development Programme (IWDP) have been unified and placed under the newly created Department of Land Resources.

Annapurna Scheme

- The Finance Minister had announced a new scheme entitled "Annapurna Scheme" to provide food security to the indigent senior citizens who do not get old age pension. 10 kgs of grains per month are to be provided free of cost under the scheme to all indigent senior citizens through the PDS. The Ministry of Rural Development will be implementing the scheme and the number of beneficiaries to be covered under the scheme is estimated to be 13.76 lakhs.

Social Justice and Empowerment

Scheduled Caste

- The scheme of Post Matric Scholarships to students belonging to

Scheduled Castes and Scheduled Tribes has been reviewed in view of the financial constraints and their inability to provide adequately in the State Budget towards the requirements of Committed Liability in the case of North Eastern States. Their committed liability has been dispensed with. This decision will give a relief of Rs. 20.83 crores per year to the North Eastern States and enable provision of scholarships to about 2.11 lakh Scheduled Castes and Scheduled Tribes students of these States during each year of the Ninth Five Year Plan.

Other Backward Classes (OBC)

- Recognising that educational advancement is the key to economic and social progress, Government have launched the following new schemes during 1998-99: (a) Pre-Examination Coaching; (b) Hostels for OBC Boys and Girls; (c) Pre-Matric Scholarships for OBCs and (d) Post-Matric Scholarships for OBC students for studies in India. In addition, a scheme of Assistance to Voluntary Organisations to improve the educational and socio-economic conditions of OBCs has also been launched.

Children

- Child Help Line has been launched through a toll free 24 hour dedicated telephone line (Tel: 1098) which is being implemented through NGOs in 9 cities. The scheme for Street Children has been expanded to provide vocational training, nutrition and healthcare programme for street children through NGOs.
- The Central Adoption Resource Agency (CARA) has been converted into an Autonomous Body. The procedure and norms for adoption have been simplified to have thousands of children adopted.

Senior Citizen

- National Policy for older persons has been announced.
- 18 mobile medi-care units, 46 new old-age homes and 176 new day care centres have been opened for senior citizens. Doctors and Nurses are being trained for the first time in medical colleges in geriatric care. A National Council for Older Persons (NCOP) has been constituted.
- The Older Age Social and Income Security (OASIS) Project has been initiated as a part of which the Dave Committee has made recommendations for strengthening Old Age Income Security Provisions in the country. Pension schemes are on the anvil.

Welfare of Disabled

- The Government has identified more than 1600 new NGOs working in the area of disability so that a much larger number of disabled can be provided rehabilitation services.
- The scheme for providing aids and appliances to disabled persons has been revised to make it more liberal and expand its scope to include corrective surgery.
- Rehabilitation Council of India has undertaken two major programmes, viz. Upgrading the skills of existing untrained personnel through bridge course and orientation training of medical officers on rehabilitation.

Prevention of Drug Abuse

- National Centre on Drug Abuse Prevention (NCDAP) has been established to train service providers working in Alcohol and Drug Demand Reduction Sector.
- The Ministry has recently launched a major project for implementation in collaboration with the UNDCP (United Nations Drug Control Programme). The Project has three components: (1) Community Based Rehabilitation Programmes and workplace prevention for the country, (ii) Comprehensive Rehabilitation Programme for the North Eastern States and (iii)Development of National Centre of Drug Abuse Prevention. These projects developed on the initiative of the Minister for Social Justice and Empowerment, are being perceived as a landmark in the Government-UNDCP collaboration for drug demand reduction in the country.

Tribal Development

- A new Central Sector Scheme for the development of Primitive Tribal Groups has been introduced from financial year 1998-99. Under this scheme, cent per cent assistance is available to Integrated Tribal Development Projects (ITDPs), Tribal Research Institutes and NGOs for undertaking activities for awareness generation and confidence building, training for skill development of tribal youth organisation of self-help groups and provision of services/inputs not covered by any existing scheme.

Surface Transport

Highways Sector

- Prime Minister announced a major highway development programme, comprising the Golden Quadrilateral and North-South and East-West corridors to provide a major thrust to the development of the road sector in the country.

- A Task Force on Infrastructure has been established to operationalise the announcement on development of the Golden Quadrilateral and North South and East-West corridors. It has submitted two interim reports to the Prime Minister and a number of its decision have been implemented.
- A total length of 4732 kms. will be upgraded on the Golden Quadrilateral by 2003-04 at an estimated cost of Rs. 20,000/- crores and a further length of 6672 kms. will be upgraded by 2008-09 at a cost of Rs. 30,000 crores. At present, 31 projects are under implementation by NHAI involving a total length of 845 kms. with a proposed investment of Rs. 2500 crores.
- A cess on petrol and diesel has been imposed w.e.f. 1st April, 1999, the proceeds of which will flow into a dedicated fund. Part of these proceeds will be used for the development of highways in the country.

Ports Sector

- A corporate port will be developed at Ennore with private sector participation and a company has been registered for this purpose.
- A decision has been taken to corporatise major ports, beginning with Jawaharlal Nehru Port and Haldia. Necessary preparations for implementing this decision are in process.
- The approach channel and Harbour Basin of Tuticorin Port are being dredged under a major project costing Rs. 202.16 crores, with external assistance from OECF, Japan. The project will be completed by May, 2000.

Transport Sector

- A bilateral agreement was signed between the Govt. of India and Govt. of Pakistan in February, 1999 for a regular bus service between Delhi and Lahore to promote social, cultural and economic relations between two countries.
- A bilateral agreement was signed between the Govt. of India and Govt. of Bangladesh in June, 1999 for a regular bus service between Calcutta and Dhaka to promote social, cultural and economic relations between two countries.
- An amendment has been made in the Central Motor Vehicle Rules in March, 1999 to standardise various critical automotive components to bring them at par with international standards.
- Following the directives of the Supreme Court, India 2000 vehicle emission norms have been notified for the National Capital Territory region w.e.f. 1.6.99 for private non-commercial vehicles (cars). This is

expected to bring about an improvement in the air quality of this area.

Prime Minister Atal Bihari Vajpayee, whose first government collapsed in 13 days, on Wednesday completed five years in office.

The landmark comes after years of instability of non-Congress governments and almost four decades of uninterrupted Congress rule.

The earlier non-Congress prime ministers, who all had Congress upbringing, fell like nine-pins with only the late Morarji Desai remaining at the helm for two-and-a-half years as the head of the Janata Party government in the late seventies.

While V P Singh, H D Deve Gowda and Inder Kumar Gujral lasted for around 11 months each, Chandra Shekhar was around for four months and Charan Singh for three months.

Once dubbed a *mukhauta* (mask) of the Bharatiya Janata Party by party ideologue Govindacharya, Vajpayee wove a combination of political parties, many of them regional, to keep the Congress at bay.

By cobbling up the National Democratic Alliance, Vajpayee ended the 'untouchability' of the BJP.

With a political career spanning five decades, Vajpayee became the natural leader of the NDA due to his image as a sober politician with a liberal aura surrounding him despite reservations over his party.

The backing of Lal Kishenchand Advani, who was instrumental in the BJP's phoenix-like rise by leading the Ram Janambhoomi movement in the 1990s, was another factor that catapulted Vajpayee to the top political post.

It was Advani who had first publicly proposed Vajpayee's name for the prime ministership much before the 1996 elections.

The rise of Vajpayee coincided with a period when the Congress failed to get its act together in the 1996 and 1998 polls, first under P V Narasimha Rao and then the late Sitaram Kesri.

The Pokhran nuclear tests in 1998 were the high point of Vajpayee's prime ministership, but it failed to pay him any political dividends vis-a-vis his allies.

Perpetual pulls and pressures marred his first 13 months in power by the likes of AIADMK leader J Jayalalithaa and Trinamool Congress leader Mamata Banerjee.

In 1999, just one vote caused his government's downfall.

In his third tenure, Vajpayee's leadership suffered a severe setback when the BJP met its Waterloo in Madhya Pradesh, Rajasthan and Delhi as rising prices of onions brought tears to the eyes of the saffron party.

If there has been a dominating theme in Vajpayee's stint at the top, it is the three Ks — Kargil, Kandahar and Kashmir.

It is a measure of the shrewd politician in him that he successfully returned to power in 1999 by projecting the unsuccessful Pakistan-sponsored intrusion in Kargil as a victory for the Indian armed forces.

When Indian Airlines' flight IC-814 was hijacked to Kandahar, it marked a low point in Vajpayee's third tenure in contrast to the bus journey to Lahore, which was one of his bold initiatives.

The terrorism menace continued to trouble Vajpayee's government and things came to such a pass that the heart of Indian democracy — Parliament — was attacked on December 13, 2001.

The attack was preceded by a terrorist strike on the Jammu and Kashmir Assembly and the failed Agra summit, which was one more attempt to mend fences with Pakistan in the post-Kargil period.

The NDA rule witnessed matters worsening in the sensitive border state with no sign of any letup in Pakistan-sponsored terrorism.

The aftermath of December 13, 2001 saw India's relations with Pakistan touch a new low and the armed forces of the two countries in an eyeball-to-eyeball confrontation for several months.

Earlier, in a bid to disentangle the Kashmir imbroglio, Vajpayee had declared a unilateral ceasefire (by the security forces) in J&K, but with no success.

However, credit goes to Vajpayee for the successful conduct of assembly elections in the strife-torn state, which independent observers found to be free and fair.

On the domestic front, Vajpayee's leadership could not save the BJP from losing citadel after citadel to the Sonia Gandhi-led Congress, which now rules in 16 states.

The BJP emerged a poor third in the politically sensitive Uttar Pradesh and the party had to once again align with the Mayawati-led Bahujan Samaj Party to retain power.

Despite the setbacks, his leadership remained unscathed.

A Narendra Modi-inspired BJP victory in Gujarat last year proved a major morale booster for the BJP ahead of the Lok Sabha polls next year.

A highlight of his third tenure has been the gradual sidelining of the coalition partners.

Now there is a certain stridency in the BJP's Hindutva talk as well as in the rantings of the Sangh Parivar outfits.

The biggest crisis for the Prime Minister came with the Tehelka expose, which tainted the BJP's image of being a 'party with a difference' as its president Bangaru Laxman was caught on camera accepting money from journalists masquerading as arms dealers.

Vajpayee's tenure also saw members of the Sangh Parivar adopt a more strident pose what with the likes of K C Sudershan, Pravin Togadia and Dattopant Thengdi constantly breathing down his neck.

Though the septuagenarian leader had left Delhi twice for knee replacement surgery two years back, he did not formally name a second in command during his absence.

But in July 2002, he elevated Advani to the post of Deputy Prime Minister thereby putting at rest all speculation about an internecine struggle at the top. Observers say he has virtually named his successor.

Notwithstanding stiff opposition from the Sangh Parivar, Vajpayee continued the process of economic reforms, including divestment, but opted for the middle path of non-confrontation.

His pet initiative is the National Highways Project, and he has also taken initiatives for interlinking rivers for better distribution of water resources across the country.

Despite doubts among economists, Vajpayee talks of ensuring an eight per cent annual GDP growth

Will Vajpayee Survive this 13?

Enough has been written in the past about Prime Minister Atal Bihari Vajpayee's association with the number 13. This time again, we can't help but remember that today is March the 13th. It's exactly one year since the Vajpayee government was rocked by the Tehelka bombshell. A year has passed and the matter has died down to a great extent. This time, its a bigger bombshell, the Ayodhya issue that Vajpayee has to grapple with.

Centuries ago in 1528, Mir Baqi, a noble under Mughal emperor Babri, build a mosque. The Hindus claim the mosque has been built on a 11th century temple marking the birthplace of Lord Ram in Ayodhya. The first reported Hindu-Muslim clashes on this issue had claimed around 75 lives way back in 1853. Last month's Godhra incident, which is linked with the Ayodhya issue has claimed around 1,000 lives so far. Gujarat still has to recover from the drought, cyclone effect, earthquake and now communal violence.

The 75-year-old Atal Bihari Vajpayee, who leads the NDA government has received some setback with today's developments. The Supreme Court has rejected plans for a *bhoomi pujan* near the disputed site at Ayodhya on March 15. The Court has further said that no religious activity would be permitted on the acquired land. The government on its part has assured it will uphold the Supreme Court verdict. In 1992 too, the UP government led by BJP's Kalyan Singh had given a similar assurance. However, kar sevaks succeeded in entering the disputed site and demolishing part of the Babri Masjid.

Some NDA allies and the Opposition have expressed their displeasure after Attorney General Soli Sorabjee had submitted to the three-judge bench hearing the case that a symbolic *bhoomi pujan* could be allowed on the undisputed land in Ayodhya.

Terming the government stand as objectionable, the TDP and Trinamool Congress say the government has taken its *bhoomi puja* decision without informing or consulting the allies. The NDA allies are expected to meet and hold discussions on the issue of the government's stand. For the time being, the prime minister started a damage control exercise and held meetings with Trinamool Congress leader Mamata Banerjee, Telugu Desam leader K Yerrannaidu, RLD leader Ajit Singh and Lok Janashakti leader Ram Vilas Paswan.

Popular Prime Minister

Many Indians said they voted for Vajpayee and his Hindu-nationalist Bharatiya Janata Party because of his track record.

"I believe he has a sense of integrity," said Indian novelist Shobha De. "Relatively speaking, he has a cleaner record than most politicians in office."

His popularity soared in May 1998 when his government exploded several nuclear devices, drawing criticism from the international community. In fact the whole world took notice of India after it exploded the bomb.

He was also credited for pushing back Pakistani intruders from Indian territory during a summer border conflict in Kashmir. Now, many Indians want their prime minister to seek a lasting peace with their neighbouring nuclear rival.

India's financial markets also cheered the news of Vajpayee's victory, closing the day up more than 5 percentage points. Moody's Investor Service upgraded India's rating from stable to positive, saying the new government is likely to pursue aggressive economic restructuring.

With such a large majority, Vajpayee's alliance stood a better chance of lasting a full five-year term than previous governments. The new government will be India's fourth in three years.

3
Role in Parliament

Suo Motu Statement by Prime Minister Shri Atal Bihari Vajpayee in Parliament on 27th May, 1998

Sir,

I rise to inform the House of momentous developments that have taken place while we were in recess. On 11 May, India successfully carried out three underground nuclear tests. Two more underground tests on 13 May completed the planned series of tests. I would like this House to join me in paying fulsome tribute to our scientists, engineers and defence personnel whose singular achievements have given us a renewed sense of national pride and self-confidence. Sir, in addition to the statement I make, I have also taken the opportunity to submit to the House a paper entitled "Evolution of India's Nuclear Policy".

In 1947, when India emerged as a free country to take its rightful place in the comity of nations, the nuclear age had already dawned. Our leaders then took the crucial decision to opt for self-reliance, and freedom of thought and action. We rejected the Cold War paradigm and chose the more difficult path of non-alignment. Our leaders also realised that a nuclear-weapon-free-world would enhance not only India's security but also the security of all nations. That is why disarmament was and continues to be a major plank in our foreign policy.

During the 50's, India took the lead in calling for an end to all nuclear weapon testing. Addressing the Lok Sabha on 2 April, 1954, Pt. Jawaharlal Nehru, to whose memory we pay homage today, stated "nuclear, chemical and biological energy and power should not be used to forge weapons of mass destruction". He called for negotiations for prohibition and elimination of nuclear weapons and in the interim, a standstill agreement to halt nuclear testing. This call was not heeded.

In 1965, along with a small group of non-aligned countries, India put forward the idea of an international non-proliferation agreement under which the nuclear weapon states would agree to give up their arsenals provided other countries refrained from developing or acquiring such weapons. This balance of rights and obligations was not accepted. In the 60's our security concerns deepened. The country sought security guarantees but the countries we turned to were unable to extend to us the expected assurances. As a result, we made it clear that we would not be able to sign the NPT.

The Lok Sabha debated the issue on 5 April, 1968. Prime Minister late Smt. Indira Gandhi assured the House that "we shall be guided entirely by our self-enlightenment and the considerations of national security". This was a turning point and this House strengthened the decision of the then Government by reflecting a national consensus.

Our decision not to sign the NPT was in keeping with our basic objectives. In 1974, we demonstrated our nuclear capability. Successive Governments thereafter have taken all necessary steps in keeping with that resolve and national will, to safeguard India's nuclear option. This was the primary reason behind the 1996 decision for not signing the CTBT, a decision that also enjoyed consensus of this House.

The decades of the 80's and 90's had meanwhile witnessed the gradual deterioration of our security environment as a result of nuclear and missile proliferation. In our neighbourhood, nuclear weapons had increased and more sophisticated delivery systems inducted. In addition, India has also been the victim of externally aided and abetted terrorism, militancy and clandestine war.

At a global level, we see no evidence on the part of the nuclear weapon states to take decisive and irreversible steps in moving towards a nuclear-weapon-free-world. Instead, we have seen that the NPT has been extended indefinitely and unconditionally, perpetuating the existence of nuclear weapons in the hands of the five countries.

Under such circumstances, the Government was faced with a difficult decision. The touchstone that has guided us in making the correct choice clear was national security. These tests are a continuation of the policies set into motion that put this country on the path of self-reliance and independence of thought and action.

India is now a nuclear weapon state. This is a reality that cannot be denied. It is not a conferment that we seek; nor is it a status for others to grant. It is an endowment to the nation by our scientists and engineers. It is India's due, the right of one-sixth of humankind. Our strengthened capability adds to our sense of responsibility. We do not intend to use these weapons for aggression or for mounting threats against any country;

these are weapons of self-defence, to ensure that India is not subjected to nuclear threats or coercion. We do not intend to engage in an arms race.

We had taken a number of initiatives in the past. We regret that these proposals did not receive a positive response from other nuclear weapon states. In fact, had their response been positive, we need not have gone in for our current testing programme. We have been and will continue to be in the forefront of the calls for opening negotiations for a Nuclear Weapons Convention, so that this challenge can be dealt with in the same manner that we have dealt with the scourge of two other weapons of mass destruction – through the Biological Weapons Convention and the Chemical Weapons Convention.

Traditionally, India has been an outward looking country. Our strong commitment to multilateralism is reflected in our active participation in organisations like the United Nations. This engagement will continue. The policies of economic liberalisation introduced in recent years have increased our regional and global linkages and my Government intends to deepen and strengthen these ties.

Our nuclear policy has been marked by restraint and openness. We have not violated any international agreements either in 1974 or now, in 1998. The restraint exercised for 24 years, after having demonstrated our capability in 1974, is in itself a unique example. Restraint, however, has to arise from strength. It cannot be based upon indecision or doubt. The series of tests recently undertaken by India have led to the removal of doubts. The action involved was balanced in that it was the minimum necessary to maintain what is an irreducible component of our national security calculus.

Subsequently, Government has already announced that India will now observe a voluntary moratorium and refrain from conducting underground nuclear test explosions. We have also indicated willingness to move towards a de-jure formalisation of this declaration.

The House is no doubt aware of the different reactions that have emanated from the people of India and from different parts of the world. The overwhelming support of our citizens is our source of strength. It tells us not only that this decision was right but also that our country wants a focussed leadership, which attends to their security needs. This, I pledge to do as a sacred duty. We have also been greatly heartened by the outpouring of support from Indians abroad. They have, with one voice, spoken in favour of our action. To the people of India, and to Indians abroad, I convey my profound gratitude. We look to the people of India and Indians abroad for support in the difficult period ahead.

In this, the fiftieth year of our independence, we stand at a defining moment in our history. The rationale for the Government's decision is based on the same policy tenets that have guided us for five decades. These policies have been sustained successfully because of an underlying national consensus. It is vital to maintain the consensus as we approach the next millennium. In my statement today and in the paper placed before the House, I have elaborated on the rationale behind the Government's decision and outlined our approach for the future. The present decision and future actions will continue to reflect a commitment to sensibilities and obligations of an ancient civilisation, a sense of responsibility and restraint, but a restraint born of the assurance of action, not of doubts or apprehension. Avoiding triumphalism, let us work together towards our shared objective in ensuring that as we move towards a new millennium, India will take its rightful place in the international community.

Vajpayee's Five Years in Office

The last five years have been a period of challenges and assurances for India and the Prime Minister, Atal Bihari Vajpayee. The nation was able to weather the storms that rose at home and abroad because of the determination of its people and the leadership of Vajpayee. This compliment may seem strange but one has to take one's mind back to 1998 when Vajpayee assumed office. Three governments at the Centre had been formed and had fallen in less than two years. One of them headed by Vajpayee had to resign in just thirteen days because a political party switched its allegiance at the last minute and the government lost the vote of confidence in the Lok Sabha by one vote. Frequent changes and the resultant instability created doubts in the minds of the people about the very utility of democracy for the country. It created doubts in other countries about any decisions that were taken by the Indian government. Both were dangerous because they not only hampered the march for the eradication of poverty and ignorance but threatened the very fabric of the political system as well.

Functioning

The Government of the National Democratic Alliance headed by Vajpayee, which came to power in 1998, reversed this dangerous trend of instability. It won the mandate of the people in the elections to the 13th Lok Sabha in 1999. What was more, India began marching ahead because of the ambitious programmes launched by the Government in all spheres of the economy. It becomes difficult at times for a political period, which has a majority of its own to push through all the measures that it wants. The task becomes Herculean when an Alliance which has parties of diverse and sometimes divergent political ideologies is in power. It is a tribute to Vajpayee's leadership that he was able to keep his flock together. As the senior partner in the Alliance, Vajpayee's Bharatiya Janata Party had to agree to more adjustments than the others. Hardliners within his party have often criticized him for giving up on some contentious issues. But he has so far been able to convince them that like the other parties the BJP has to honor the pledges given in the manifesto of the Alliance.

He has had often to compromise so as to reach a consensus and win the support of the others for his views. It has, however, to be remembered that the compromise has been on the degree of emphasis and the priority to be given, in the form and not the substance. He has tried to give the maximum concessions to win over the critics. He persuaded the Finance Minister to give in to the demand of the farmers' lobby and not raise the prices of fertilizers. But it has to be remembered that he has not allowed anyone to hold him to ransom. Whenever any minister has threatened to resign on an issue and the Prime Minister has found it difficult to agree to his demand, Vajpayee has bid him good bye with a smile on the face. What is more, though he has not allowed such a person to stage come back, he has kept the best personal relations with him.

Style

To work towards a consensus to the maximum extent possible and to meet the challenge when a consensus is impossible has been the hallmark of his approach not only with those in the Alliance but also those in the opposition. It was because of the understanding reached with the opposition parties that the two Houses of Parliament passed 42 bills during the winter session. All of them have received the assent of the President. The Government was able to bring forward several pieces of legislation last year. Out of them 93 bills have been passed. This is the highest number of pieces of legislation enacted in a single year in the last 25 years and the third highest since Independence. This number assumes significance when one remembers that the work of legislatures in the country is often disturbed by members who want to discuss other issues, which they consider important. Legislative work, therefore, gets derailed. Viewed in this background, the progress of legislative work last year is indeed remarkable. It was possible because of the rapport established between the ruling Alliance and the Opposition. Even when patently false allegations were made against him, Vajpayee rarely lost his cool and replied to the charges in a dignified manner.

Traditionally, India has had good relations with its neighbours. The only exception is Pakistan. In a bid to normalize relations with it, Vajpayee undertook a bus journey to Lahore after taking over as Prime Minister. He also had a summit meeting with President Pervez Musharraf in Agra. But it was soon clear that Pakistan was not interested in friendship with India. Even when Vajpayee was shaking hands with the then Pakistan Prime Minister, Mr. Nawaz Shareef, Gen Musharraf, then the Army Chief, was planning a large scale incursion in the sensitive Kargil area. He used the summit in Agra for a tirade against India. This was understandable because President Musharraf has himself confessed that no ruler of Pakistan can continue in office unless he rakes up anti-India feelings by raising the Kashmir issue. Successive Indian leaders have recognized this compulsion of the Pakistani leadership. Rarely, therefore, have they replied in kind to Pakistan's vituperations. So has Vajpayee. As he once observed one could choose one's friends but whether one likes it or not one has to accept one's neighbours. Hence, his effort to win over Pakistan to the path of peace and friendship. He tolerated the oral diatribe but it was impossible for him or for the people to tolerate the incursion in Kargil intended to cut off Indian troops in Ladakh. More important still, no one could tolerate the proxy war that Pakistan has been waging against India, first in Punjab and now in Kashmir.

This proxy war has now been going on for more than 20 years. Pakistan has been training, arming, equipping and financing terrorists for operations against India. According to one estimate nearly 50,000 people—innocent, men, women and children—have been killed by these terrorists. It is ironic that most of them were Muslims who were killed by men sent by a country which claims to be Islamic. India has been trying to persuade Pakistan to stop this cross-border terrorism but it has had no effect. The terrorists targeted centres of India's political authority like Parliament House in New Delhi, and the Jammu and Kashmir State Legislative Assembly building in Srinagar. For a time, India ordered its armed forces to take up positions on the forward line on the border with Pakistan and the line of control in Jammu and Kashmir. The terrorists killed innocent pilgrims in the Akshardham temple in Gandhi Nagar, Raghunath Mandir in Jammu and innocent women and children sleeping in an army camp in Kaluchak near Jammu. It became clear that Pakistan would not stop sending the terrorists to India.

This forced India to take up the stand that till Pakistan stopped this cross-border terrorism India will not take part in any talks with it. The Prime Minister, Vajpayee and other leaders have reiterated this stand. This must have been a bitter pill to swallow for someone that made every effort to win over Pakistan to the path of peace and friendship but failed.

President Musharraf has since confessed that raking up the Kashmir issue and fanning the flames of hatred against India were essential for any ruler who wanted to continue in power in Pakistan.

Vajpayee has given expression to his disappointment that while the United States talks about ending terrorism everywhere in the world, it does not put enough pressure on Pakistan to end the cross-border terrorism against India. Washington's reaction to terrorism seems to be selective – it is terrorism only when targets in the United States or its embassies are hit. Otherwise, the US Government would rather turn the blind eye to the menace of terrorism elsewhere.

Development

It is remarkable that while the people of Jammu and Kashmir were fighting the menace of terrorism, elections were held to the State Legislative Assembly last October. By their active participation in the exercise, the people of the State replied to the threat of the bullet fired by Pakistan-trained terrorists with the power of the bullet. There have been protests in many places against the terrorists for the their wanton killing of innocent people. The Central Government is totally committed to working closely with the present government in the State, elected by the people to bring peace, normalcy and economic development. The Prime Minister has announced projects and schemes worth Rs. 6000 crore covering various spheres of development. The thrust will be on providing employment opportunities to the youth, relief to migrants affected by militancy and building the infrastructure. When the State acceded to India in 1947, the railway line stopped at Pathankot, 100 kms from Jammu. The railway line now goes to Udhampur and beyond in Jammu province. A major project costing Rs. 3500 crore is being implemented to extend the railway line to Baramula in South Kashmir. This will not only help in the development of the area but also act as an integrating force with the rest of the country. The first train is expected to roll into Kashmir Valley before August 15, 2007.

Diplomacy

Since India was fighting the menace of terrorism single handedly, it was only natural for it to take a keen interest in the campaign to oust the Taliban regime in Afghanistan, which had usurped the rights of the people and tried to push the country back to the Middle Ages. India's interest was all the more great because the people of Afghanistan have had great respect for Indian leaders and friendship with its people. The approach was, however, low-key. India gave Afghanistan whatever help it could in fighting the menace of Taliban and continues to do so in its reconstruction.

The Gulf region is of great importance to India. Much of the crude oil that India imports comes from there. India and the countries in the region are major partners in trade and investment. More than 35 lakh Indians work in the Gulf countries. These countries may have differences among themselves but all have friendly ties with India. It is, therefore, only natural that India should be concerned about the unhappy situation concerning Iraq. Iraq has been a staunch friend of India but India cannot ignore the demands of truth. The Prime Minister put the Indian viewpoint succinctly when he told Parliament that whatever action was taken should be taken only under the authority of the United Nations. Any action taken unilaterally by any country will mean the end of the world body. He also stated that no country can impose a government on another and if there has to be a change of government it can be only according to the wishes of the people of the Country.

Some members of Parliament wanted that the Government should be more categorical and the country threatening unilateral action should be named. They forget two important facts. Firstly, India is not a member of the Security Council and though it may be interested in the happenings in the area so are many others. Secondly, India can only go thus far in criticizing the world's only superpower. What India wants about everything else is that there should be no war in the region. A war in the Gulf area will push up the price of crude oil, affect supplies, push up prices and once again throw the country back into a recessionary trend from which it is emerging. War may also mean lakhs of refugees fleeing back to the country as they did during the Gulf War in the nineties. India, therefore, does not want a war.

The war in Afghanistan, the threat posed by terrorism and a severe drought in 14 States of the country cast a shadow on the Indian political and economic scene during the last five years. Also in the background was the persistent threat of a war in the Gulf region. There were genuine fears that all these factors would affect the growth of the Indian economy. Despite the general slowdown of the economy in most countries, the financial year 2002-03, the last of the five-year period of Vajpayee's years in office, was a fairly good year for India. India continued to be rated amongst the world's fast-growing economies. In the first nine months of the financial year, India's exports grew by more than 20 per cent to reach 38 billion US dollars, i.e., Rs. 181, 300 crore. The total revenues from excise and customs rose by over 15 per cent during this period. Inflation remained at a moderate level. India's foreign exchange reserves rose to 73 billion US dollars, i.e., Rs. 348, 429 crore. Though the Centre had to release foodgrains for relief of the people living in areas affected by the drought, the stocks of foodgrains continued to be comfortable and prices continued to be relatively stable.

Economy

After a period of gloom in the first four years, there was a turnaround in the economy last year. Though the country had to make contingency planning in the event of a war in the Gulf, the picture was no longer as gloomy as was once feared. This ray of hope is reflected in the Tenth Five-Year Plan approved by the National Development Council. The Plan aims at achieving faster economic growth with a stronger thrust on employment generation and equity. To the surprise of many, the Plan document set a target of an annual rate of growth of 8 per cent in the Gross Domestic Product during the Plan period. What is more important, this growth rate is expected to generate five crore employment and self-employment opportunities.

These targets are certainly ambitious and skeptics have expressed doubts if they can be achieved. But the Document argues the case for these ambitious objectives by pointing out that unlike previous Plans, the Tenth Five-Year Plan is not merely a resources plan. It is a Reforms Plan. The area of reforms in the economy is to be widened. State Governments are to be given incentives to carry out reforms. Non-financial barriers in the way of economic growth are to be removed by carrying out reforms in the civil service, judiciary, education but, above all, governance at all levels – the Centre, the States and the Panchayati Raj institutions. This last area of administration is of particular importance for the people living in the countryside. The Plan document does not leave things vague. It gives a detailed list of the legislative and administrative measures needed for transforming the goals and targets into ground realities.

What is envisaged is a total revolution of life at all levels and spheres—agriculture, industry, education and power generation. National security is high on the agenda and so is expansion and strengthening of the infrastructure. In the first 50 years of Independence only 556 kms. of four and six-lane highways were constructed in India. At present, five kilometres of such highways are being built every day. The Golden Quadrilateral of world class highways to connect the four metropolitan cities of Delhi, Kolkata, Chennai and Mumbai is progressing ahead of schedule. Besides generating employment and giving a boost to the country's cement and steel industries, the 6000 kms of highways will also mean an annual saving of Rs. 8000 crore on fuel and vehicle maintenance costs. Side by side with the development of roads, a Rail Vikas Yojana has been launched at a cost of Rs. 15,000 crore to put the country's premier transport infrastructure on the fast track. The incredible growth of telecom services in India has made the telephone an affordable tool of empowerment for the common man.

What is the guiding spirit behind the efforts of the last five years and the Tenth Five-Year Plan? In his address from the ramparts of the Red Fort on the last Independence Day, the Prime Minister had given a call to the people to lift India from the ranks of developing countries to the rank of a developed nation by the year 2020. It is a stupendous task no doubt but the impressive achievements of the past, a proper management but, above all the determination of a hundred crore people will make it possible. President A.P.J. Abdul Kalam has said that the concentration should be on two *mantras*: effective implementation with people's participation and effective communication for people's participation.

Vision

The years since Independence have seen a steep rise in the population of India's cities. The population of the cities increased from 15.9 crore to 21.8 crore between 1981 and 1991, and has further increased since. People from the villages rush to the cities in search of employment and a better life. The cities are bursting at the seams and are not able to provide basic amenities like housing, health, education, drinking water, or electricity. Slums therefore grow in the cities while villages are impoverished because of the flight of the youth, particularly the educated and skilled youth to the cities. It was at first believed that heavy industry would act as an engine of development and lift the surrounding areas from poverty to prosperity by promoting ancillary industry and other activity. This has not happened to the extent that it should have. In most cases the centres of heavy industry have become pockets of prosperity in a sea of poverty. Disparities have increased, giving rise to social tensions and despair. Successive Plans have tried to solve this problem but have been only partially successful — the countryside continues to be impoverished and the cities continue to grow into large clusters of slums.

The problem has so far defied solution. The answer lies in providing amenities available in the cities to the villages as well where two-thirds of the people live. Nearly 26 million people living there are mostly below the poverty line and want to join the mainstream of national life. They do not want doles or spoon–feeding. They are prepared to work hard to lift themselves from poverty to prosperity. What is needed is a mega mission for their empowerment. Pointing this out, President Abdul Kalam said in his address to the joint session of the two Houses of Parliament in February that the people living in the villages need four critical connectivities. First, they want good roads, transport services and quality power. Secondly, along with this physical connectivity, the people in the villages should have electronic connectivity. They should have reliable communication facilities. Thirdly, most professional institutions and vocational training centres should be opened in the countryside so as to give them knowledge connectivity. Lastly, market connectivity should help them to realize the best value for the products and services of the people and provide them ever-growing employment opportunities.

Vision 2020 is an assertion of the confidence of the people of the country and so is the 8 per cent annual growth in the Gross Democratic Product envisaged in the Tenth Five-Year Plan document. The determination of the people can make the vision a reality. Both give a concrete shape to the dream that Vajpayee has in mind :

Wonder years...NDA govt completes five years

PM Calls on Party to Reach out to Minorities

Indore, April 5 (NNN) : The Bharatiya Janata Party (BJP) on Saturday ended its two-day brainstorming session of the National Executive here with a hard-hitting political resolution against Pakistan for its continued abetment of terrorism and criticism of the Congress-PDP government in Jammu and Kashmir, amid a clear attempt to reach out to the minorities and weaker sections of the society as the party prepared for a crucial round of Assembly elections in several states, culminating in the general elections next year.

Even as Prime Minister Atal Bihari Vajpayee called upon the party to reach out to the minorities and weaker sections, the National Executive, in a political resolution, asked the NDA government to act in a manner that Pakistan pays a "price" for its continued sponsorship of cross-border terrorism while it maintained the US has not been able to rein in Islamabad.

"The government must now act in a manner that shows that Pakistan has paid a price for its continued sponsorship of cross-border terrorism. The United States has not been able to rein in Pakistan," said the political resolution adopted at the two-day national executive of the party here.

The resolution criticised the PDP-Congress coalition government in Jammu and Kashmir, saying it must stop its "laxity towards terrorists and anti-India elements".

The eight-page resolution, moved by party general secretary Pramod Mahajan, said the massacre of 24 Kashmiri Pandits in Nadimarg in Jammu and Kashmir last week was a "grave and intolerable" development.

In the resolution, the party told the government that the Constitution

Amendment Bill for reservation of women in Lok Sabha and state assemblies should be passed without any delay.

Steps should also be initiated to introduce in the current session of Parliament a bill for evolving financial and administrative powers on Panchayat Raj institutions, it said, while demanding the scrapping of the Illegal Migrant Detection Act which it said has been proved to be detrimental in throwing out illegal migrants from Bangladesh.

The resolution said, "today our (NDA) alliance is stronger and more cohesive than ever before. Atalji's tenure is an era of statesmanship, stability and development. It marks the evolution of India as a global force, as an economic power, crucial diplomatic player and a nuclear power."

Asserting that the party had defeated Congress' destabilisation game, it said the leadership of the main Opposition party had still not learned the right lessons from its defeats.

"On more than one occasion, its blind anti-BJP stand, coupled with its habitual reliance on vote-bank politics, has led the Congress to take positions that are detrimental to our national security. This was evident from its criticism of Pokhran-II, its stand during the Kargil war, its hypocritical opposition to POTA and its continued opportunism on the Ayodhya issue," it said.

The resolution listed out the party's achievements and initiatives in the past five years and said many of them were "unprecedented and of historic significance".

Earlier, setting the tone for the BJP's agenda for the forthcoming Assembly polls in several states and the general elections next year, Prime Minister on Saturday called upon the party to reach out to the minorities and weaker sections.

Apparently worried by the growing alienation of the BJP from these sections, Vajpayee said, "We will have to establish a live communication with the people and I am confident that the party will come out with flying colours in the four states."

The party will have to expand its base in the society especially among Scheduled Castes, Schedules Tribes, minorities and women, said Vajpayee, and added, "We will have to expand and expedite our work."

Asserting that the outcome of coming assembly elections would be decisive, the Prime Minister told the second and concluding day of the BJP National Executive that the poll result would set the direction for the country's future politics.

"The elections in Madhya Pradesh, Chhattisgarh, Rajasthan and Delhi are very crucial," Vajpayee told the second and concluding day of the BJP National Executive, adding that the result would set the trend for politics in the days to come.

BJP workers would have to reach out to the people in these states, said the Prime Minister, adding that the media could be of some help in the matter but that alone would not suffice. "We will have to establish a live communication with the people and I am confident that the party would come out with flying colours in the four states," he added.

Stressing that the performance of the government would be the ultimate barometer, the prime minister said while manifestoes and speeches were important, it was eventually the people's experience with the government that would play a significant role in deciding the future of the government.

"We will have to expand and expedite our work. The Party President M Venkaiah Naidu has brought momentum in the party and we will have to keep it up to achieve success," Vajpayee said.

Vajpayee, who did not touch any contentious issues like Ayodhya, POTA etc., said that the party's victory in Gujarat and its subsequent defeat in Himachal Pradesh had sent out a definite message to the party to remain prepared for the coming polls.

The BJP-led government had not only completed five years in office but had also tried to bring the country in the fast track of development by serving the people, said Vajpayee.

Statement in Rajya Sabha Regarding U.N. Security Council Resolution on June 8, 1998

Sir,

Hon'ble Members are aware of the resolution adopted on 6th June, 1998 by the United Nations Security Council. I would like to take the House into confidence on our position on this matter.

We regret that the Security Council has acted in a manner in which it has and produced a Resolution which is completely unhelpful in respect of the objectives it seeks to address. The Resolution contains a number of references to nuclear non-proliferation. As I had mentioned in my earlier statement in the House, we are a responsible and committed member of the international community. The Resolution urges us not to carry out any nuclear weapons test explosions. For India, such an urging is redundant because we have already instituted a voluntary moratorium. We have also indicated our willingness to explore ways and means of converting this undertaking into a de jure obligation. Further, we have made clear our readiness to engage in multilateral negotiations on a Fissile Material Cut-Off Treaty in the Conference on Disarmament in Geneva.

We cannot, however, be expected to commit ourselves in advance of these negotiations, to unilaterally restrain production of fissile materials. In keeping with our commitment to non-proliferation, we maintain the strictest controls over exports of nuclear materials and technologies. Our record in this regard has been impeccable and better than that of some countries who are parties to the NPT or members of the Nuclear Suppliers' Group or even Permanent Members of the UN Security Council.

However, the call made in the Resolution that we should stop our nuclear programmes or missile programmes is unacceptable. Decisions in this regard will be taken by the Government on the basis of our own assessments and national security requirements, in a reasonable and responsible manner. This right, which we claim for ourselves is not something new; it is the right of every sovereign country, and a right that every Government in this country has strongly upheld for the last 50 years.

A glaring lacuna in the Resolution is the total absence of a recognition that the non-proliferation issue is not a regional issue but has to be dealt within a non-discriminatory global context. We find it unfortunate that the UN Security Council Resolution does not reflect on the judgment of the highest international judicial body – the International Court of Justice, which has questioned the legitimacy of nuclear weapons and called for urgent negotiations for their elimination. In the paper on the Evolution of India's Nuclear Policy laid on the Table of this House, we have reiterated our commitment to nuclear disarmament. Let me categorically state that unlike other nuclear weapon states have sought to retain their exclusive hold over their nuclear arsenals, India has no such ambition. Government is committed to initiatives that can open negotiations for a global convention for the elimination of all nuclear weapons. The attempt to project the recent tests by India as a threat to peace and security is totally misguided and grossly out of focus. Such a portrayal of our policy ignores the positive steps announced by Government to which I have already referred, both in the global disarmament framework and the regional context. Our tests were necessary because of the failure of a flawed non-proliferation regime, and, therefore, we categorically reject the notion that these have adversely affected either regional or global security.

Government have indicated willingness to engage in a meaningful dialogue with key interlocutors on the whole range of nuclear disarmament and non-proliferation issues. Last week, Special Envoy Shri Brajesh Mishra visited Paris and London in this regard. He had meetings at the senior most levels in the two capitals. Dialogues with other countries are also planned. These dialogues have to be seen as part of a process, a process that will lead to a better understanding of India's position.

Hon'ble Members are aware that India has always desired a peaceful, friendly, and mutually beneficial relationship with Pakistan based on confidence and respect for each other's concerns. I have already said on the floor of both Houses, and I would like to reiterate, that a secure and prosperous Pakistan is in India's interest. Our vision of our bilateral relationship is not confined to a resolution of outstanding issues, but is also directed to the future by seeking to building a stable structure of cooperation, which will benefit the people of both countries. As I wrote recently to Prime Minister Nawaz Sharif, we must not remain mired in the past, prisoners of old contentions. And I say to him today, let us put the past behind us, let us think of the welfare of our children and grandchildren.

We have remained committed to a path of direct bilateral dialogue with Pakistan. This reflects the nation's conviction and confidence that it is only through direct discussions in a sustained and constructive manner that we can move ahead in our bilateral relationship. I would again like to reiterate our desire for the earliest resumption of the official talks with Pakistan. The subject for discussions including peace and security, (along with confidence building measures) Jammu & Kashmir, economic and commercial cooperation and cross-border terrorism have been identified. Our proposals for the modalities of these talks have been with Pakistan since January this year. We await their response. We have also made it clear once again that there is no place for outside involvement of any nature whatsoever in our dialogue process with Pakistan.

Hon'ble Members have expressed strong reservations against attempts to internationalise the Kashmir issue. There is simply no question of India ever agreeing to such internationalism. UN Security Council has chosen to mention Kashmir in its Resolution. This is unacceptable and does not change the reality that the state of Jammu and Kashmir is an integral part of the Indian Union. I would also like to draw the attention of the Hon'ble Members to the terms in which Kashmir finds mention in the resolution. The UN Security Council has recognised that bilateral dialogue has to be the basis of India-Pakistan relations and mutually acceptable solutions have to be found for outstanding issues including Kashmir. This is in keeping with our position.

Prime Minister's Reply to the Discussion in Lok Sabha on Nuclear Tests on May 29, 1998

Sir,

As this long discussion comes to a close, I wish to thank the honourable members who have participated in the debate. The House is unanimous in felicitating the scientists, engineers and defence personnel who contributed to the success of the tests. There is almost total unanimity that if there are economic sanctions, if loans from International Financial Institutions are stopped or if there are other attacks on India's economic sovereignty, we will face them together.

A question has been raised—why? I recall the discussion on the first test in 1974 and Indrajit Gupta would remember it as well as he was also present. There is no difference between what I said then and what I say now. Mrs. Gandhi gave the go ahead and we welcomed it along with the entire nation. It was not a collective decision nor was the Opposition consulted formally. But it was a decision based on considerations of national security and provided an opportunity to our scientists. She did not even make a statement, some other minister did so and we were not dissatisfied.

There is an indication from Pakistan that in 1974 they could not respond as they were not ready. Some members say that Pakistan's tests were in response to our tests. I ask them: Can you do these tests in 16 days? You can not and there are people here who know that this is not possible. Preparations for these have gone on for years. Today there is a news that a long range missile has been tested. All this has been going on for quite some time.

I did not take a decision to test one fine day. 50 years of hard work and determination are behind these tests. Our scientists and jawans have toiled in the scorching heat of Pokhran with only one feeling--national security and pride. There can be differences in a democracy but on vital matters of national security we are all together. Rajiv Gandhi said in his remarks at the Press Club on 11 October 1985: "As I have said on a number of occasions, we would not let New Delhi or any other city be flattened out .... Pakistan's nuclear programme is partly financed from abroad and if nuclear weapons are developed, they will be shared....we are not going to wait a number of measures can be taken without actually producing nuclear weapons." This shows that the Government was concerned about these developments. Meanwhile, the great powers continued stockpiling nuclear weapons and did not heed our calls for a time-bound elimination of nuclear weapons and tried to impose a discriminatory treaty on us. We decided together not to sign the CTBT and keep our options open.

In addition to what we learnt later, inputs came from consultations with scientists on what steps to take. Nuclear weapons are weapons of mass destruction. They are meant for self-defence. Let our adversaries know that we have them and that they should not dare attack us. In 50 years, this country which has always given message of peace and has never sought anybody's territory has been attacked thrice. A nation of 100 crores cannot depend on charity for its national security.

We are for friendship but on the basis of justice and mutual respect. We have never sought to take undue advantage of our size, the Gujral doctrine is partly based on this. But this doctrine did not work with Pakistan. They did not let it happen. Their support to terrorism in India continued. We are ready to take the talks forward and resolve outstanding issues but the Dhaka understanding has not been honoured. Prime Minister Nawaz Sharif's offer of yesterday is good. As I said once to a Pakistani politician, we can change history but we cannot change geography. India and Pakistan are bound together by geography. I want to make one thing very clear to my friends in Pakistan. One often hears from people who come back from a visit to Pakistan that there is a sense of insecurity that India has not accepted Pakistan's existence. There is no basis for this feeling. We want Pakistan to prosper. India and Pakistan should work together to eliminate poverty, disease and illiteracy not only from this region but throughout the world.

I told reporters yesterday that the news of the Pakistani tests did not come as a surprise and this vindicates out decision to test. We have other problems but their tests are India specific. When we call for a nuclear-weapon-free world, our motives are questioned. We would like Pakistan to join us in working towards this end. There is support for our position-stated or unstated - in the countries of the Third World. The majority of mankind wants peace in a world without nuclear weapons. We do not differentiate between domestic security and global security. But we should not be taken for a ride ("Should not burn our hands while performing a yajna").

I want to refer Mr. Deve Gowda to the 1996 JD Manifesto. "We will formally give a pledge of no first use of nuclear capability to Pakistan." I say to him that you have to first develop this capability before you can offer this pledge. There was a general consensus on developing this capability. The question was "when". After yesterday's events, this should no longer be an issue.

If some of my own colleagues did not know about our decision, it does not mean that I do not have confidence in them. We could not consult widely and very few people knew about it. As somebody said that everything is leaked here, including entire reports of inquiry commissions. That we were able to maintain secrecy is a sign of national strength and shows that on vital matters we can sacrifice and we can be responsible. I was distressed to hear accusations of politicisation. I have never kept party before nation in my 40 years in the Opposition and will never do it as Prime Minister. Nobody should doubt my intentions. I did not ask such questions either in 1971 or in 1974. I called the liberation of Bangladesh "epoch-making". Mrs Gandhi called for elections, we lost. Elections are fought and lost governments come and go but the nations interests should be paramount.

I am glad that people are carefully reading the National Agenda for Governance and keeping a watch on our performance. But this agenda should not be misinterpreted. The agenda talks of preparedness of the armed forces, the proposed NSC and the review of the nuclear policy but it does not say that the review will wait till the armed forces are better equipped or the NSC is formed.

We are disappointed that US has displayed a lack of appreciation of India's legitimate security concerns. I wish to reiterate Government's commitment to engage with all principal interlocutors in a responsible dialogue. We remain ready to discuss and explain our position. Since 11 May, Government have taken certain initiatives:

- A moratorium is in place which we are ready to consider and discuss converting into a de-jure commitment.
- We have volunteered to engage in negotiations on an FMCT.
- India will undertake stringent export controls on nuclear and missile related technologies as well as those relating to other weapons of mass destruction.
- We have offered to discuss a no-first-use agreement with Pakistan, as also with other countries bilaterally, or in a multilateral forum.

These initiatives address substantially, a number of concerns expressed by other countries.

Concern has been expressed by some Hon'ble Members regarding China's reaction to our decision. Let me assure this House that we seek good relations with all our neighbours, including China, our largest neighbour. India and China are two of the world's largest and most populous countries. We are linked through history and geography. We believe that the Five Principles of Peaceful Co-existence, jointly enunciated by India and China, are of continuing relevance to the development of our relations.

India, like China, is engaged in the task of economic development and realisation of the legitimate aspirations of her people. Our bilateral trade and economic cooperation has grown significantly. There is considerable potential to expand our economic and commercial cooperation.

But we have some concerns. We would like the Chinese side to appreciate that our concerns need to be addressed in a meaningful manner with a view to finding early resolution. There are issues relating to India's sovereignty, territorial integrity and security that have been reflected at various levels, including highest levels. The Indian people must feel assured that friendship with China will be a factor for peace and stability and will contribute to enhancing our security. On the boundary question, we recognise that a resolution requires time and patience. But progress can, and should, be made. Our concerns regarding China's defence cooperation with Pakistan remain. Unlike India-China relations, which have shown improvement despite the difficulties of the past, Pakistan remains unreconciled to good relations with India. Our view in regard to external military assistance to Pakistan has been consistent over the last fifty years. Given Pakistan's approach to India, assistance in the defence field to Pakistan affects India's security directly and adversely. The Chinese side should pay attention to the depth of feeling on the Indian side.

On our part, we do not seek a confrontation with China. We seek a relationship in which both sides are responsive to each other's concerns. We believe that dialogue is the key to understanding; understanding is the key to resolution of differences; and resolution of differences is the key to good relations. We remain committed to the process of dialogue to resolve outstanding differences and to the development of friendly, cooperative, good neighbourly and mutually beneficial relationship with China.

I am sure that even those who oppose actions would understand our position.

We are a multi-religious and multi-linguistic nation. I was listening to Prime Minister Nawaz Sharif's provocative speech on TV last night. He does not realise that India has millions of Muslim citizens who enjoy equal rights. There is no need to create such an atmosphere. If I were to be forced to do such thing, I would prefer to resign.

Home Nuclear Tests

Speech at International Parliamentary Conference to Mark the Golden Jubilee of Parliament of India

New Delhi, January 22, 2003

A great occasion has brought all of us together today. The Golden Jubilee of our Parliament is no doubt a proud event for us in India, for people as well as their elected representatives. However, without sounding immodest, I would like to believe that it is also an important milestone in the onward march of democracy worldwide.

Which is why, the Lok Sabha secretariat has taken the commendable initiative to organize an international conference to mark the occasion. I am indeed heartened by the presence of participants from a large number of countries around the world. In just one Sanskrit word that carries the warm greetings of one billion people of India, I would like to say to our foreign guests: *Suswagatam*! Welcome!

Democracy is that system in which there can be opposition without hatred, and power can change hands without resort to violence. It disallows discrimination on any ground. In this sense, democracy has deep roots in India's national ethos and our ancient culture, which teaches respect for divergent and even dissenting points of view.

Like our Freedom Movement, the birth and evolution of Parliamentary Democracy in India was one of the momentous developments in the history of the world in the 20th century. The Indian mind has cherished Freedom and Democracy as two indivisible ideals. Hence, when one-sixth of humanity walked into freedom with one step in 1947, with the very next step India also strode into Parliamentary democracy. This gave a big fillip to the march of democracy around the world.

Just as the international community has cherished India's successes along the path of democratic development since our Independence, we too have greatly valued the victorious march of democracy around the globe. The closing decades of the last century have seen totalitarian systems collapse. The dogmas that sustained dictatorships of various stripes, and advertised their superiority over democracy in development and human welfare, have crumbled. Coups, bloody power struggles and military take-overs have come to be seen as anathema to the ethos of our times. Even rulers in *khaki* have felt the need to seek some kind of democratic legitimacy.

If the 20th century saw the global growth of democracy, the new century should see its further expansion and enrichment. Especially, we should develop democracy as an effective instrument for fulfilling people's aspirations and resolving conflicts and contentious issues. History has proved time and again that free and democratic societies are the ones that are creative, self-corrective and self-regenerative. The holding of regular elections, the victories and defeats of individuals and parties, and the periodic change of governments have many benefits. These make elected representatives accountable; keep the rulers in check if they develop hunger for power; prevent rigidity in governance; and dislocate social and economic interests that would otherwise get vested.

At the same time, we cannot overlook the many ways in which the Parliamentary system, including ours, needs to be strengthened. All democracies, especially in developing countries that have considerable diversities and carry the burden of developmental imbalances, have had to grapple with one paramount challenge. And that is: how to harmonise the legitimate self-assertion of communities that suffered deprivation and disempowerment in the past with the imperatives of good governance?

One obvious answer lies in the need to protect and further strengthen the institutions of democracy. Our ancient seers taught a *guru mantra: Dharmo Rakshati Rakshitah. Dharma*, protected, protects. In the same way, institutions, protected, protect. They can function well only if each of us adheres to the norms that are the essence of each institution. If we adhere to the norms of our institutions, the effectiveness of democracy would go up ten fold, even a hundred fold. If we don't, it is imperiled.

There is a second imperative. Our economies are becoming increasingly integrated. The demands of our people are ever more pressing. Thereby governance has become more complex, demanding newer competencies from elected representatives. All parliamentary democracies, therefore, face a common challenge: how are we to ensure that the rough and tumble of electoral politics brings such persons to office who can actually handle the complex tasks of governance?

In a democracy, there are bound to be differences among political parties, and there is bound to be vigorous debate among divergent viewpoints in Parliament. Differences and their well-researched, articulate expression both inside and outside Parliament is the very stuff of democracy. It is what lends vibrancy to democracy. But the vitality of democracy also demands discipline, constructive approach, and a readiness to contribute to consensus-building on pressing issues before the nation — and adherence to rules. A river flows well only if the banks are sturdy.

Distinguished delegates, each of us comes from a different version of the Parliamentary system. In that sense, we are the repositories of diverse experiences. Each of our systems has thrown up some particular problem, and each of our countries has devised some particular solution to that particular problem. Together we have a wealth of experience from which to devise solutions to the challenges before us.

For instance,

- Should our Parliaments be allowed to run their full term?

- Are there ways to ensure stability of governance and policies, while retaining the vibrancy of a multi-party democracy?
- Today in several of our countries we are kept from taking firm decisions because at all times some election or the other is taking place. Should we, therefore, schedule elections for all tiers simultaneously?
- Some of our legislatures are not always the fora they should be for deliberating on policy and crafting legislations; can presiding officers do more to ensure that our Houses function efficiently and get more work done?
- How can Parliamentarians strengthen mutual cooperation in the fight against terrorism and extremism, which have become a big threat to peace, democracy and civilized world order?

I, therefore, suggest that this conference be a beginning. We should make it a practice to meet often – and not only ceremonially. We should meet often and engage in substantive exchanges about our diverse experiences so that all of us together strengthen Parliamentary democracy in each of our countries.

My best wishes for the success of the conference.

Thank You.

Friends, let me conclude by stating once again that India is proud of your achievements. More and more Indians—both in India and abroad—are succeeding.

In the New Century that has just begun, let us together resolve to make India succeed.

Thank You.

The Prime Minister's message on Republic Day

New Delhi, January 26, 2000

The Golden Jubilee of our Republic is a major milestone in the nation's journey along the path of democracy which the nation adopted on January 26, 1950.

At this defining moment, India looks at her past with pride and to her future with confidence. In the last 50 years, India has achieved many successes, but there are many unfinished tasks ahead of us. Together, we should strive to make India a prosperous nation, free from poverty, hunger, disease and illiteracy. Above all, we have to remain ever-vigilant against threats to our country's unity and integrity.

Let the glorious legacy of our freedom struggle continue to guide us in the new century. Let our commitment towards the principles of secularism, social justice, egalitarianism and non-violence remain firm as ever.

On this day, let us rededicate ourselves to the noble principles of justice, liberty, equality and fraternity on which the Republic of India was founded.

Jai Hind.

Address the Function to Mark the Golden Jubilee of Republic Day in, Central Hall of Parliament

New Delhi, January 27, 2000

Respected Rashtrapatiji, Upa-Rashtrapatiji, Honourable Speaker of the Lok Sabha, Disti.guished Colleagues,

On January 26 India celebrated the Golden Jubilee of Republic Day. Today we have gathered here to commemorate this historic occasion. Fifty years ago, in this very hall, our Constitution was adopted.

That event was a culmination of our people's long suppressed aspiration for freedom; of an arduous, protracted struggle for self-governance.

The journey of the creation of our Constitution has closely paralleled the journey of our Freedom Movement in the early half of the last century.

Members will recall that the 'Commonwealth of India Bill', prepared by Indians in 1924, was an important initial milestone. This was followed by the preparation of the 'Swaraj Constitution'. A new dimension was added to that effort with the Fundamental Rights Declaration in 1931.

Following many ups and downs, the Non-party Conference prepared a comprehensive Constitutional scheme in 1944-45. Unfortunately, that was nipped in the bud. At last, the Constituent Assembly was set up.

Thereupon, the Constitutional Advisor to the Constituent Assembly prepared the Draft Constitution. The Draft was subjected to a clause-by-clause consideration in Committees—headed by Pandit Nehru, Sardar Patel, and other luminaries.

From the discussions in the Drafting Committee headed by Dr. Babasaheb Ambedkar to the deliberations—as intense as they were intensive—in the Constituent Assembly as a whole, it was one unbroken quest for perfection.

Indeed, it was a saga. Even as they were being lashed by riots, killings, oppression and imprisonment, our leaders kept at the task decade after decade.

To read the deliberations of the Constituent Assembly and its committees even today, even after 50 years, is to be overwhelmed by:

The earnestness with which they approached the task;

The insight they brought to bear on each Article;

The farsightedness with which they anticipated the situations and problems that were likely to arise;

The singular touchstone by which they judged every provisions – always guided by the interest of our country and our people;

How, engulfed as they were by the aftermath of Partition, by riots, by an invasion, by the urgent task of integrating the States – how they would abstract themselves from this tumult, gather in this very hall, and weigh, and deliberate, and fashion, and refashion, clause after clause.

We are beneficiaries of their sacrifice: we should never forget that.

We are heirs to that legacy – of exclusive, overarching devotion to the national interest; of reasoned, civil discourse; of harmonizing disparate views.

We should never forget that.

There is one great test for a Constitution, for any system of Governance. It must deliver and it must be durable.

Our Constitution has stood this test. And one reason it has been able to do so is that it embodies a masterly balance: between the rights of the individual and the requirements of collective life; between the States and the Union; between providing a robust structure and flexibility.

Our Constitution has served the needs of both India's diversity and her innate unity. It has strengthened India's democratic traditions.

But even in the mightiest fort one has to repair the parapet from time to time, one has to clean the moat and check the banisters. The same is true about our Constitution.

Five decades after the adoption of the Constitution, India is faced with a new situation. The need for stability, both at the Centre and in the States, has been felt acutely.

The people are impatient for faster socio-economic development. The country is also faced with a pressing challenge to quickly remove regional and social imbalances by reorienting the development process to benefit the poorest and the weakest.

That is the purpose for which a Commission to review the Constitution is proposed to be set up. The basic structure and the core ideals of our Constitution, however, will remain inviolate.

Let us not forget that in the end a Constitution is only as good as the ones who work the institutions which it has set up.

Participating in the Constituent Assembly debates, Dr.Ambedkar had said:

"I feel, however good a Constitution may be, it is sure to turn out bad because those who are called to work it, happen to be a bad lot. However bad a Constitution may be, it may turn out to be good if those who are called to work it, happen to be a good lot. The Constitution can provide only the organs of State such as the Legislature, the Executive and the Judiciary. The factors on which the working of those organs of the State depend are the people and the political parties they will set up as their instruments to carry out their wishes and their politics".

There is widespread apprehension today that our institutions are not working as the Constitution intends, that the conduct of those of us who run them is not what the proper functioning of those institutions requires.

Let this be our resolve today:

- We shall leave institutions – above all, our Parliament and our State Legislatures – for the coming generation in a condition vastly better than the condition in which we found them;
- In discharging our duties in them, our conduct will be such as would have done the Founding Fathers proud.

That would be a fitting way to repay our debt to them. That would be the one tribute worthy of them.

Statement in Lok Sabha Regarding Jammu & Kashmir

February 22, 2001

As Hon'ble Members would recollect, Rashtrapatiji during his address to the Joint Sitting of both the Houses of Parliament had given voice to the Government's approach to the whole question of Jammu & Kashmir. He had then, amongst other things, shared with the Hon'ble Members of Parliament that:

"The Government is pursuing a multi-pronged strategy to bring peace and normalcy in Jammu and Kashmir. As part of this, it launched 'ajor peace mission on November 19, 2000, by announcing a unilateral non-initiation of combat operations in the State during the holy month of Ramzan. This bold initiative was extended twice up to February 26, 2001. As anticipated, this was warmly welcomed by the people of Jammu & Kashmir, who are longing for an end to militancy and violence in their beautiful State. The international community has also given overwhelming support, because it sees in it yet another demonstration of India's sincere commitment to a peaceful and permanent solution to the Kashmir issue."

Rashthrapatiji had also then informed the Hon'ble Members that:

"Militancy in Jammu & Kashmir is now increasingly confined to foreign mercenary groups. This has widened the scope for democratic activity in the State. The people of the State participated enthusiastically in the recent Panchayat elections. I reiterate the Government's readiness to have talks with every group in the State that abjures violence."

The Government has decided to pursue this path by initiating talks with various groups in J & K.

The Government has seriously addressed the question of continuing with the peace process and further extending the period of non-initiation of combat operation by our security forces. In this regard, the Government has benefited by the detailed briefing of and consultations with all political parties that it had on February 21, 2001.

Having examined all aspects of the question in its totality, the Government has decided to further extend the period up till the end of May. Let this opportunity not be missed by all those that desire peace, for our patience is not infinite.

I wish to make it abundantly clear that the peace process is only for those that wish to benefit from it. We will not let this process be derailed, diluted or misused. For such organisations or elements, as have vowed to disrupt the peace process, or intend to continue with violence and the killing of innocents in J & K, my message is unequivocal and clear. If you inflict injury on any Indian citizen in the State of Jammu and Kashmir, or elsewhere, or commit any act of violence or terrorism then the security forces have clear instructions to act decisively and to defeat such intentions. Law and order shall be maintained. Those who think that our security forces are less determined today to put an end to terrorism are only deluding themselves.

It is my hope that Pakistan will act, even now, and adjure violence, give up their continuous hostile propaganda against India, stop promoting and aiding cross-border terrorism, take the path of peace through bilateral talks as enshrined in the Simla Agreement and the Lahore Declaration, thus creating a conducive atmosphere so that the comprehensive dialogue process can be resumed resulting in a lasting solution to the problems.

The process of peace is to enable our citizens in Jammu & Kashmir to live peacefully. It is their voice that has to be heard, not of the militants or foreign mercenaries.

4
Views on Industry

Inaugural address of at the National Conference and Annual Session of the Confederation of Indian Industry on April 28, 1998

In the recently concluded general elections, the people have given a mandate to the BJP and its allies to govern. At the same time, it is a fractured mandate. The challenge before us is to do full justice to our job even though we have a fractured mandate. I assure you, that in spite of some teething problems, the people's desire to see a stable, strong and action-oriented Government in New Delhi will be fulfilled. We have accepted the challenge.

The theme for this conference — "Bringing Growth Back: Economy, Education and Employment" — captures in a nutshell, the main thrust of our alliance's National Agenda for Governance, which is the blueprint for our policies. And as such there is a happy convergence of the concerns of the Government and the Indian industry. Such a participative relationship will enable India to realize her full potential o[illegible]nic growth, and the well being of our people. I have good reason to be emphatic on this point. Today, not only the global standing of a nation, but also its security, integrity and stability — indeed its very existence as a nation — is dependent on its economic strength.

I firmly believe, therefore, that the time has come to insulate the nation's economy as much as possible from the turmoil in its democratic polity. It is high time all sections of our society, including those in business, industry and politics, sank their partisan obsessions and focused their attention on the all-important national imperative: Growth. Let the common patriotic mantra for one and all be: Growth, More Growth and Still More Growth. With the Union Budget due for presentation in early June, this is an opportune time to spell out our philosophy of growth. The National

Agenda has stated in clear and unambiguous terms that my Government "shall strive to develop a national consensus on all major issues confronting the nation".

The problems facing the Indian economy are too many, too complex and far too important to be subjected to a partisan approach. We simply cannot afford to play politics with the nation's economy anymore. This indeed will be the real test of patriotism on the economic front. This point demands candid and even self-critical elaboration. The first phase of economic liberalization was launched in 1991. Some of the reforms brought about positive changes. Unfortunately, the measures taken to free the economy were not matched by checks and balances. And we have paid a price for those lapses. Also, the liberalization process suffered from inadequate attention to the eradication of unemployment and to many critical issues in the social sector such as health-care, education and housing. Importantly, it failed to give a momentum to infrastructure development, which is now choking growth.

In our view, the reasons lie in the failure of the Government to effectively address the core concerns of the Indian industry. They lie in the failure of the Indian industry to appreciate the core concerns of the Government. They also lie in the failure of both the Government and the Industry to convince the Common Man that he too has a stake — a vital stake — in the reform process. That is why, during the election campaign, I repeatedly stressed that India urgently needs to reform the reform process. To explain what we mean by this, let me first enumerate what I think are the three main complaints of the Industry against the Government, the three main complaints of the Government against the Industry, and also the three main complaints of the Common Man against both the Government and the Industry.

The three main complaints of the Industry against the Government are:

One: Industry thinks the Government is the root cause of avoidable delays owing to excessive controls.

Even after seven years of reforms, a typical industrialist is forced to spend considerable time in management of the Government than in management of his own business.

Two: Industry complains that the Government takes too much, but provides too little and that too haphazardly.

Three: The Government is in all those areas of business in which it had no business to be there in the first place.

Now let us look at the three main complaints of the Government against the Industry:

One: Government feels that the Industry does not share its social objectives.

Two: Government thinks the Industry wants the Government to abide by the canons of Good Governance such as transparency, accountability and fiscal prudence. Fair enough.

But does the Industry itself follow transparent accounting and strict norms of disclosure? Does it meet its obligations towards consumers, workers, shareholders, bankers, the environment and the society in general?

Three: Many industrialists want competition — but in other industries. In their own industry, they want protection.

Now, what are the Common Man's perceptions of both the Government and the Industry? He thinks that —

One: The top people in both the Government and the Industry are hand-in-glove to make the system work for their own self-enrichment.

Two: Neither the Government nor the Industry cares for the real needs of the people.

Three: There are two separate sets of laws in this country: one for the ordinary people and the other for the 'Big People' in the Government and the Industry.

Now, let us ask ourselves:

- Are any of the above perceptions wrong? No.
- Isn't it a fact that no genuine reform process is possible without squarely addressing these valid perceptions? Yes.

That is why I say that India urgently needs to reform the reform process.

We need to reform the Government, which is the engine in any nation's development strategy. The Government must become a helper, and not a hurdle. Therefore, I urge each and everyone in the Government - from the minister to the lowest clerk — to recognize their duty and responsibility flowing from this commitment.

We need to reform the Industry. Broadly speaking, every industry and industrialist is entitled to grow to their fullest potential. But without recourse to unethical practices or evasions of dues to the State.

We need to also reform the mentality of the Common Citizen. He must realize the imperatives of hard work, quality work, and discipline. Responsible citizenry demands no less.

And barring those who belong to the weaker sections of society — and hence deserve all the support of affirmative action that we can render unto them — the others should begin to respect the laws which fashion and govern a sound economy. Which means, they must pay for what they use. And, yes, they must also get what they pay for. In short, the nation as a whole needs to reform itself in order to be able to effectively face the new challenges, and seize the new opportunities, of the 21st Century.

Let us together create a Mindset Revolution to harmonize the objectives of Economic Liberalization and Social Liberation. Let us together build a strong, prosperous and self-confident India, freed from the curses of mass unemployment, illiteracy and other manifestations of underdevelopment. And let us make India a global economic power in the 21st Century.

The key to translating this Vision into Reality is Growth: Growth with employment and equity. In our National Agenda, we have pledged to bring sustainable GDP growth into the 7 per cent- 8 per cent bracket, from the present level of 5 per cent. Many people doubt if it is an achievable target. I would say that this is a moderate target, given both India's capacity and necessity. Even at this rate of 7 per cent-8 per cent, India has to wait for well over half a century to catch up with the developed world.

Can we afford to be slower than this?

We must grow faster. We can grow faster. We simply have no other alternative. In the sphere of the economy, I should tell you plainly that I have inherited a weak, deficit-ridden economy. But I am not complaining. My job is not to harp on the past but to look to the future, not to complain but to lead.

Ladies and Gentlemen,

I would Like to Utilize this Occasion to Tell you and the Nation what My Government will do in the Next Three Months

1. All of us are legitimately concerned about the prolonged downturn in the economy. Industry, especially, is looking to the Government to take necessary steps to kick-start the economy.

   This is no doubt dictated by the objective of faster economic growth. But it is also necessitated by my own Government's stated goal of creating at least ten million new jobs each year in the economy. We shall soon announce a series of schemes to mobilize investible funds from idled resources existing in the country but unavailable to the exchequer. In consultation with trade and industry we will take all necessary steps to reduce the currently untenable level of NPAs of banks and financial institutions. We will also devise machinery for resolving disputes between the revenue departments and trade and industry to speedily obtain for the Government what is legitimately the State's. Also, suitable policy measures will be taken to tap new and unconventional sources of funding, such as debt market instruments and pension and insurance funds, for infrastructure projects.

II. The Government is committed to broaden, deepen and speed up the process of internal liberalization.

In the case of globalisation, we will adopt a carefully calibrated approach, for reasons most of you appreciate. The Government will play the role less and less of an active player in the economy, and more and more of a legislator, facilitator and regulator. Where necessary, it will be the protector of India's commerce and industry. My Government's relationship with Industry will be based on trust, not marred by mistrust.

I come from a political tradition that does not look upon commerce and industry with suspicion. When it was conventional political expediency to decry entrepreneurship, we championed their cause.

As a government, we will do more. As a concrete proof of this approach, we will soon appoint a commission to comprehensively review in a short time frame all the administrative laws, rules and regulations governing industry and trade. Such of them which have outlived their utility will be either totally scrapped or radically simplified. With this move, we aim to enable Indian entrepreneurs—small, medium or big—to create more wealth for themselves and for the nation.

III. The Companies Act will be drastically overhauled. The Foreign Exchange Regulation Act (FERA) will be replaced with legislation consistent with current needs.

We will ensure that crucial Government Orders are not passed without first ascertaining their consequences on domestic industry. Many of the problems faced by Industry are at the State and local level. The process of internal liberalization will be widened to reach those operational levels. With this in view, we have recently appointed a Special Task Force, headed by Shri Bhairon Singh Shekhawat, to advise the Government on devolution of financial and administrative powers to the States.

IV. Infrastructure development is the very backbone of any strategy aimed at achieving higher growth and large-scale employment generation.

With this major success behind us we shall now embark on such other financial sector reforms as will further improve the efficiencies in our banks, financial institutions and stock markets. Our Government will also move decisively in other important areas such as the power sector, telecom sector, ports, airports and highways. We are determined to speedily increase the size of the export basket and also to diversify its contents. Our emphasis now will be improving decision-making and implementation of policies and projects to make all these sectors more attractive to private sector and foreign investment. Towards this end the Government shall radically simplify rules and procedures that cause delays.

Our Government has identified Information Technology as an area of immense promise for wealth creation and hence needing special focus. The world today fully recognises the potential as well as the performance of Indians in software development. Many of their success stories have so far been written abroad. But, of late as you know, they are being scripted in India as well. Our Government is determined to create the necessary conditions that will enable bright and enterprising young Indians to re-create the Magic of Silicon Valley while living and working in India.

Distinguished buissinessmen, I can sum up the brief narration of the Government's multi, faceted initiatives in the economic sphere in just five words: INDIA IS ON THE MOVE. The experience of the last decade of this century has given us many useful tips on how India can move faster in the first decade of the next century. The world will soon see the emergence of a strong and prosperous India, in which the basic needs of all her one billion children will have been fully met.

As economically resurgent India will be a source of stability and long term growth for the world economy. It will also contribute significantly to the emergence of a fair and equitable system of global trade and business serving reliable basis for universal peace and prosperity tomorrow.

In this endeavour to achieve self-growth and global growth, India actively seeks the participation of the international business community. If India is already a good business proposition I can assure you that it will be even better one in the times to come.

Thank you.

Speech at the Conference on Small Scale Industries

New Delhi, 30th August, 2000

My Colleagues, Shri L.K. Advani and Smt. Vasundhara Raje, Representatives of Small Scale Industries Sector, Ladies and Gentlemen:

It gives me great pleasure to be here with you today. Two years ago, Laghu Udyog Bharati had invited me to their conference in this very hall. Several measures were then suggested for strengthening the Small Scale Sector.

In these two years, various initiatives have been taken to address your concerns and strengthen the Small Scale Industries sector. These include the decision to lower investment limit to Rs. 1 crore from Rs. 3 crore and the setting up of a separate Ministry for Small Scale Industries.

I am happy to note that the Small Scale sector has responded to our initiatives by improving their performance. The growth rate registered by you is higher than that of the overall industrial sector.

No less important is the fact that the Small Scale sector has registered steady growth in employment generation. Indeed, this sector continues to lead the way in generation of employment opportunities.

As you are aware, a Group of Ministers, headed by Shri L.K. Advani, was constituted by the Cabinet to recommend measures to strengthen Small Scale Industries.

I am glad to inform you that based on the recommendations of the Group of Ministers, Government has decided to implement a set of measures which will substantially strengthen the Small Scale sector. These include:

The Small Scale sector has suffered due to inadequate access to credit availability. We have, therefore, loans from Rs. 10 lakhs to Rs. 25 lakhs. Entrepreneurs will now be able to secure term loans and working capital form the same agency.

Industry related service and business enterprises with a maximum investment of Rs. 10 lakhs will qualify for priority lending. These services are essential for the proper functioning of the Small Scale sector. These services also provide employment in rural and semi-urban areas.

Bearing in mind the urgent need for technology upgradation, Government is happy to announce a capital subsidy of 12 per cent for investment in technology in select sectors. We will set up an inter-ministerial committee of experts to define the scope of technology upgradation and sectoral priorities.

Government is alive to the grievance that frequent inspections by multiple agencies are a source of harassment to the Small Scale sector. We will set up a Group to recommend, within three months, means of streamlining inspections. These would include repeal of laws and regulations applicable to the sector that have since become redundant. I would urge you to submit your suggestions in this regard to the Ministry of Small Scale Industries.

The last census of Small Scale Industries was conducted 12 years ago. For effective policy-making and implementation, we need to update our data. Therefore, we have decided to go in for a fresh census that will cover, inter-alia, the incidence of sickness and its causes. I request industry associations to cooperate with the census authorities so that a true picture emerges.

I am happy to note that more and more Small Scale units are opting for ISO 9000 certification. To encourage total quality management, we have decided to continue, for the next six years, granting Rs. 75,000 to each unit that obtains ISO 9000 certification.

We have also decided to give one time capital grant of 50 per cent to Small Scale associations who wish to develop and operate testing laboratories, provided they are of international standard.

The SSI sector already enjoys some special fiscal incentives. However, for quite some time, this sector has been requesting for an increase in the loans from Rs. 10 lakhs to Rs. 25 lakhs. Entrepreneurs will now be able to secure term loans and working capital from the same agency.

I am happy to announce that in response to your requests, we are increasing the exemption limit from Rs. 50 lakhs to Rs. 1 crore.

This will be the second increase made by our Government, the first one having been in 1998 when the limit of Rs. 30 lakhs was increased to Rs. 50 lakhs. There are certain other requests relating to customs duties. The Finance Minister will be announcing suitable measures in due course.

Development of Khadi and Village Industries is a critical component of the strategy to achieve a balanced and integrated development. This segment is an important link not only to the informal economy, but it fosters skills, promotes entrepreneurship at a micro level and is integral to our growth process.

Khadi is environment friendly. It provides jobs to millions of people. With upgradation of skills and quality of Khadi products, it can be marketed globally. We are committed to further strengthening the viability of this sector.

A rebate on sale of Khadi products has been continued. Beyond this, we are working out a new comprehensive package to strengthen Khadi and Village Industries that will further upgrade the skills of the Khadi workers. These will cover.

Provision for 20 per cent of projected annual turnover to be given as working capital loan.

Continuation of concessional lending facilities; and, preference for loans for technology upgradation.

Government is conscious of the problems faced by the handloom sector. This sector represents a rich heritage and craftsmanship that needs to be protected and promoted.

I am happy to announce that yesterday, Government has approved a Deendayal Hathkargha Protsahan Yojana. This is a scheme aimed at supporting the handloom sector through finance, design and marketing inputs.

The scheme, to be implemented by the Centre and States, has a total financial implication of Rs. 447 crores. This scheme provides comprehensive financial and infrastructural support to weavers and handloom organisations that will substantially strengthen this sector.

I have broadly touched on some of the measures to strengthen the Small and Medium Industries. The Ministry of Small and Medium Industries will be separately announcing some other measures to further strengthen this sector.

The global environment is changing rapidly. The Small Scale sector has an important contribution to make in enhancing the competitive strength of our industry, provide an avenue for new employment and harness the entrepreneurial skills available in abundance in this country.

You must accept the challenge of globalisation and improve your product quality to effectively deal with the forces of competition. We will support your endeavours to meet this challenge on a sustainable basis.

I congratulate today's prize-winners for their outstanding achievements. Small entrepreneurs, rural artisans and cottage industry have done the country proud in the last 50 years. They form one of the pillars of our national economy.

Let us together strengthen this pillar so that our national economy can take off for newer heights.

Thank you.

Illustrative List of Small Scale Units that Could be Set Up Depending upon Local Requirements and Resource Endowments

I. Agro-Forest Based and Food Preservation

1. Fruit and Vegetable Preservation/Processing/Dehydration
2. Oil Mills/Expellers
3. Animal/Poultry Feeds
4. Processing of Spices
5. Cereal Processing
6. Bakery and Confectionary Products
7. Dairy Products Processing
8. Hatcheries/Nurseries
9. Cold Storage
10. Meat and Fish Processing
11. Pickles/Squashes/Juices etc.
12. Leaf Plates/Cups
13. Soap Nut Powder
14. Handmade Paper
15. Extraction of Essential Oils
16. Herbs Collection/Processing

17. Mushroom Production/Processing
18. Potato/Tomato Products
19. Starch
20. Brushes/Brooms
21. Silk Worm Rearing and Silk Processing
22. Papad and Vadi
23. Bee-keeping

II. Chemical/Plastic/Rubber Products

1. Soap and Detergents
2. Dhoop and Agarbatti
3. Paints/Varnishes/Distemper
4. Chalk Crayons
5. Candles
6. Hydrated Lime
7. Allopathic/Ayurvedic Medicine Formulations
8. HDPE/PVC Rigid Pipe/Polythene Pipes
9. Plastic Sheets
10. Plastic Bags
11. P.P. Granules
12. Plastic Container/Storage Tanks
13. Consumer Plastic Products
14. Plastic Shoes/Chappals/Hawaii Chappals
15. Rubber Footwear
16. Thermoplastic Rubber Products
17. FRP Products
18. Injection Moulding Plastic Products
19. Consumer Rubber Products
20. Hair Oils
21. Gums/Resins
22. Charcoal
23. Plastic Ropes

III. Leather Products

1. Leather Shoe Uppers Closed
2. Leather Shoe (Indian type-Desi jute)
3. Leather Sandals/Chappals
4. Leather-cum-Rubber Chappals/Sandals
5. Leather/Rexin Handgloves
6. Leather Suitcases and other products
7. Handbags and Purses (Leather/Rexin)
8. Leather Straps/Belts

9. Chrome Tents/Sole
10. Village Leather Processing
11. Leather Garments
12. Leather Washers and Laces
13. Leather Travel Goods

IV. Mechanical Engineering Industries

1. Agriculture/Horticulture Implements
2. Fabrication Unit
3. Storage Bins/Sheet Metal Products
4. Ploughs
5. Hoes
6. Mowers
7. Hand Pumps
8. Hand Shovels
9. Kudalis
10. Persian Wheels
11. Chaff Cutters
12. Disc Harrows
13. Levellers
14. Insecticides Sprayers
15. Seed Bins
16. Wheat and Rice Threshers
17. Seed Drills
18. Winnowers
19. Ghamelas
20. Seed Cleaners
21. Harvester Grader
22. Oil Crusher
23. Shell Huskers
24. Dal Mill

V. Electronics and Electrical Products

1. AM/FM Radio
2. Audio Tape Recorder and Combination with Radio
3. Public Address Amplifier
4. Assembly of Loud Speakers
5. TV Booster Amplifiers
6. Electronic Fan Regulators
7. Electronic Gas Lighter
8. Electronic Lantern/Emergency Lamp
9. Battery Eliminator/Power Packs

10. Electronic Calculators
11. Assembly of Audio Cassette (Blank)
12. Monochrome T.V. Receivers
13. Colour T.V. Receivers
14. Assembly of Blank Video Cassette
15. Invertors and Convertors
16. Solid state Voltage Stabilizers
17. Moisture Meter (Electronics)
18. Soil Testing Meter
19. Water Analyser
20. Electronic Milk Analyser
21. CRT, DATA/Display Monitor (Monochrome/Colour)
22. G.L.S. Lamps
23. Auto Lamps
24. Lamp Fittings
25. Miniature Lamps
26. Conductors, Cables and Wires
27. Electrical Measuring Instruments
28. Small Transformers
29. Household Electrical Appliances
30. Room Coolers/Desert Coolers
31. Electrical Wiring Accessories
32. Plugs, Sockets and Switches

VI. Hosiery and Textile

1. Powerloom
2. School Bags/Holdals/Shopping Bags
3. Cotton Durries
4. Readymade Garments
5. Cotton Hosiery :
   (i) Vests/Knitted
   (ii) Socks
   (iii) Under Garments
6. Woollen Hosiery :
   (i) Socks, Shawls, Muffler, Pullovers, Blankets
7. Nylon Socks
8. Rain Coats
9. Bed Sheets
10. Canvas Shoes
11. Shoe Laces
12. Tags/Wicks

13. Surgical Bandage
14. Canvas Shoes
15. Pranda/Ribbon
16. Cotton Niwar

Introduction of Existing Scheme

In accordance with the Industrial Policy Statement for promoting and strengthening small scale and tiny industries announced in August, 1991, a scheme for providing Central Government grant-in-aid to Industries Associations for establishing Quality Counselling and Common Testing Facilities was introduced in January, 1995 with a view :

(i) to encourage tne Industries Associations to establish and offer testing facilities in area of testing of raw-materials/components and of final products as per relevant standard specifications so that small scale units could be helped in improving quality of their products and become licensed users of ISI quality marking logo.

(ii) to offer Consultancy Services to SSI units in improving quality, standardization and provide necessary information relating to specifications of raw materials and final products.

Assistance Available

Under the above scheme, one time Central Government grant-in-aid is given to the registered Associations to meet the expenditure on plant and machinery not exceeding Rs. 20 lakhs or 50 per cent of the cost of machinery and equipments (whichever is lower) provided State Government also commits itself to release matching funds to the Associations. It is also stipulated under the scheme that Associations will provide fully developed infrastructure to accommodate Testing Centres and will meet the recurring cost of running the Testing Centres. The above scheme was modified to extend the benefit of this scheme for modernisation and expansion of the existing Quality Marking Centres run by Industries Department of the State Governments.

Proposed Scheme

As part of the Comprehensive Policy Package for promotion and development of SSIs, the Prime Minister on 30th August, 2000 announced, "..........we have also decided to give one time capital grant of 50 per cent to Small Scale Associations who wish to develop and operate testing laboratories, provided they are of international standards".

In pursuance to above announcement, the presently operative scheme is being modified and will cover testing laboratories established by Industries Associations including Chambers of Commerce, Industrial

Co-operatives representing the SSI and registered under the Societies (Registration) Act or under any statute and would be eligible to avail the benefits under the scheme. The scheme would provide for re-imbursement of the cost of the testing machinery and equipments purchased and installed at the testing laboratory. It will also cover expansion/ modernisation of the existing centres under the aegis of State Governments or State Government funded autonomous bodies. New centres set up or existing centres after modernisation would undertake testing as per international standards for which they will give an undertaking.

Objectives

The objective of the testing centres would be to establish and offer facilities mainly to the SSI units located in the state for testing quality of raw-materials, components and the end products as per the relevant standard specifications within the ambit of testing facilities available within the centre.

- To help the SSI units in obtaining ISI marks for their products.
- To offer consultancy services and improving the quality of products.
- To promote standardisation and provide necessary information in regard to material specifications and specifications for end products.
- To extend quality assurance and assist the promotional institutions of testing laboratories such as the Bureau of Indian Standards, Export Inspection Agency, National Productivity Council, Govt. and Non-Governmental Organizations in the region.
- To promote the Total Quality Management concept in the small scale sector units and to assist the units in obtaining accreditation for ISO-9000/BIS 14000.

Eligibility Criterion

All willing Industry Associations including Chambers of Industries and Industrial Co-operatives representing the Small Scale Industries interested in availing one-time grant-in-aid under this scheme would be registered under the Societies Registration Act, 1860 or any other statute.

(i) The applicant constitutes an exclusive Governing Council to look after the working of the Testing Centre.

(ii) All employees of the Testing Centre will have full functional freedom.

(iii) The Testing Centre should have accreditation from any of the agencies viz; (i) Bureau of Indian Standards, (ii) National Accreditation Board of Laboratories and Calibration and (iii) Accreditation to any of the reputed international agencies or their authorized representatives. This accreditation should be valid atleast for a minimum period of 5 years after release of grant-in-aid.

(iv) The new Testing Centre would have been set up after 1.4.1998.

(v) The beneficiary Association would not have availed any other Government grant-in-aid from State/Central Governments for the Testing Centre including assistance under the existing scheme.

Maximum Amount Payable under Re-imbursement

It is felt that with a cost of approximately Rs. 1 crore, a Testing Centre with reasonable modern facilities for a few products can be set up. Therefore, maximum amount to be re-imbursed under this scheme would be 50 per cent of the cost of equipment and machinery installed in the laboratories of the Testing Centre subject to an upper limit of Rs. 50 lakhs on one-time grant basis.

Implementation of the Scheme

The Registered Associations will appoint Chief Executive Officer and other required staff to establish the Testing Centre for products manufactured by their member units and will extend to them full functional freedom. After installing and commissioning the equipments and machinery, the CEO will approach any one or more of the agencies to get the accreditation. After obtaining the accreditation, a request in the prescribed form will be submitted to the Office of the DC(SSI) to claim the 50 per cent of the cost as re-imbursement. The request will accompany all the prescribed papers relating to cost of land, civil works, machinery etc. and photo copies of the documents, bills etc. showing the expenditure incurred to obtain accreditation. The cost incurred will be certified by a Chartered Accountant. The firm will also enclose a photostat copy of the accreditation.

Conditions for the Release of Funds

Re-imbursement in the form of grant-in-aid from the Govt. of India to the maximum amount of Rs. 50 lakhs or 50 per cent of the cost whichever is less shall be considered for release if the following conditions are satisfied :

1. The Industry Association will constitute the Governing Council comprising Executive Members of the Association. State Government will also be given representation in this Governing Council.
2. Association will provide details of all the documents pertaining to the expenditure incurred to establish the Testing Centre and thereafter to acquire accreditation.
3. Association will not dispose of any of the assets created out of the

grant-in-aid received from Government without the written permission of the Central Government. In case the Associations fail to abide by this condition, necessary proceedings to recover the same as land revenue will be initiated against it and its office bearers.

4. Central Government grant-in-aid is only for purchase of items of capital nature and will not be utilized to meet the recurring expenditure.

5
Independence Day Speeches

"My dear Sisters, Brothers and Children:

I greet all of you on the occasion of the 51st Anniversary of our country's Independence. Half a Century has passed still it appears as if it happened yesterday. Pandit Jawaharlal Nehru had unfurled our beloved tricolour from this very spot for the first time. Since then it has been a tradition to unfurl the National Flag from the historic Red Fort. I had never imagined that I shall have this good fortune one day. It is a symbol of strength and potential of the Indian democracy that the son of a school teacher hailing from the dusty and smoky environs of a village has the privilege of unfurling the National tricolour from the ramparts of Red Fort on this auspicious Independence Day.

We all know that independence did not come to us easily. On the one hand, while tens of thousands of our countrymen and women suffered in jails during the non-violent freedom struggle under the leadership of Mahatma Gandhi, on the other hand, thousands of revolutionaries sacrificed their lives on the gallows. We owe our independence to these known and unknown martyrs and freedom fighters. Let all of us together pay homage to them and take a pledge that we shall defend our freedom, even if we have to sacrifice everything for this.

Our country has been subjected to foreign aggressions. In this short period of 50 years, we had to face four aggressions. But we have safeguarded our independence and integrity. The highest credit for this undoubtedly, goes to our soldiers. Away from their homes and dear ones, braving dangers all the time, they guard our frontiers day and night. This is why we are always reassured about our security. Be it the snowy expanse of Siachen with minus 32 degree Celsius temperature Or the thick forests of the North-East, the deserts of Kutch or Jaisalmer.

However, we also want to make one point clear. India is a great country and its people are powerful.

The brave people of our country are always ready to face any danger to defend their honour. Our history bears testimony to this.

No force on earth can deflect us from our chosen path. I am saying this not out of arrogance but with humility and self-confidence. We are willing to make any sacrifice to uphold the unity, integrity and sovereignty of our country.

We wish to improve relations with our neighbours. We know that the easiest way to win a war is not to let it happen. We are ready to hold talks with Pakistan on any subject, at any level and at anytime.

You all know that I had taken the initiative during the SAARC Conference in Colombo. I am somewhat unhappy that we did not get the desired response. Still I have not given up. I will make another effort at reviving the dialogue during the Conference of the Non-Aligned countries in South Africa at the end of this month.

I believe that all problems of the world can be solved through talks. Therefore, whether it is Pakistan or China, we will endeavour to solve our mutual problems through friendly talks.

In the last few days, terrorist activities have increased in Jammu & Kashmir. The massacre in Himachal Pradesh appears to be part of a bigger conspiracy. Such terrorist activities every day, from across the border, are like a proxy war.

Government has taken these incidents very seriously. We are facing them with all our might and we will not rest content until we have defeated these.

Whether in personal or national life, the fifty first anniversary is always a golden opportunity to assess the past fifty years. It is also the time for retrospection and preparation for a leap into the Twenty-first Century.

While making an assessment we most often commit mistakes, tend to underrate our achievements and magnify our shortcomings which results in gloom.

Sometimes, I see a growing tendency of pessimism in the country. There may have been aberrations here and there but things have not gone that bad so as to defy solutions. Our scriptures say that only fools indulge in self-praise. But unnecessary self-condemnation is also like suicide. I want that a realistic assessment of the last fifty years should be undertaken. When we attained Independence, some Western experts had forecast that we were unfit for being a democracy and did not deserve freedom. They said, we would soon disintegrate. But, today, we can say with pride that we have not only safeguarded our integrity and independence but have also shown to the world how the biggest democracy can be governed. Almost all the countries which gained freedom along with us have fallen prey to dictatorship or military at one time or the other, but we have kept the democratic tradition alive. This is our Twelfth Lok Sabha and I am the Eleventh Prime Minister of India. We have seen over the years transformations taking place from the tiniest village assembly to the Parliament. You all deserve credit for this. Your political maturity in all these elections have baffled political Pundits. I congratulate you for this. Our democracy is safe as long as you remain vigilant. On the occasion of the Golden Jubilee celebrations of our Independence, the Nation has to address itself to the important fact that Independence, National Integration, Democracy and Secularism are complementary to each other. We have to remain independent under all circumstances. An essential condition for this is national unity. Democracy is necessary for national unity. Secularism and democracy are inseparable parts of national unity. I and my Government are committed to all these four elements. We oppose communalism in any form. We will ensure full security of the minorities and guarantee their participation in development. We should never forget that we are the citizens of one country. The boundaries of this country extend from Ladakh to Nicobar, from Garo Hills to Gilgit. Ours is a country whose civilization and culture is more than five thousand years old. Such a big country replete with varieties of languages, faith, living and food habits has resolved to achieve social and economic justice within the framework of democracy. Simultaneously, we cannot forget that we have to strive to rid this democracy of aberrations. Our legislators behave in such a way in Legislatures that even a school teacher would not tolerate such kind of behaviour in his class. Democracy is a system of Governance through free debate. The Opposition has the right to criticise and Government has the right to implement. The Opposition and the Government are complementary to each other and adversaries. Fearless and impartial voting has to be further strengthened. The electoral system has to be reformed to free it from casteism, violence, money power and other ills so that in the next century our system of governance is further refined.

Once upon a time this country was a land of prosperity. The situation deteriorated and we began to be counted among the poor nations of the world. In the past few years our farmers and agricultural workers have worked very hard to make the country self-sufficient in foodgrain production. An army with an empty stomach cannot fight and a hungry nation cannot have a restful sleep. Our farmers have made the country self-sufficient to justify their being called "Food Providers". I can only pray to God that He showers happiness on the "Food Providers".

There is a shadow of sorrow in this happiness. Today the condition of our "Food Providers" has become difficult. I feel very pained that this year in some States some farmers have had to commit suicide because they could not bear the burden of their debts. I offer my condolences to the bereaved families. As a tribute to these farmers I have taken a decision. The Crop Insurance scheme will be broadened, new crops will be brought within its purview and its geographical reach will be increased. A High-powered Commission will be formed to look into the real financial condition of farmers, improve their economic condition. I want to assure our farmer brothers who are the backbones of the nation that they will never suffer under this Government.

In Orissa, hunger still stalks the people in places like—Bolangir, Kalahandi and Koraput. It is unimaginable that even 50 years after Independence some people are still stalked by hunger. I have told the Planning Commission that the outlay on the Employment Assurance Scheme in these areas should be doubled. My efforts will be to ensure that no one dies of hunger.The country has made commendable progress in business, industry and services. Some of our industries are making their mark on the international scene. I congratulate all the workers, employees, managers, industrialists and businessmen for this achievement.

But we know that this achievement is only a stepping stone. It is not the attainment of the final goal which is to see the rise of India as an economic superpower. I know that saying this is much easier than doing it. For this, we will need to follow the path of hard work, establish high standards and depend on self-reliance. We will have to produce goods of international standard which can compete in the global markets. Economic reforms will have to be speeded up. But we will not allow others to take undue advantage of our liberalisation. We will implement infrastructure projects with speed.

'Swadeshi' does not mean an inward looking policy. The world has become a global village. Each one is dependent on the other. In this open market system we can use our inner strength to stand up to global competition and I have faith that we will!

This 51st Independence Day is being celebrated not only in India but also round the world. Every person of Indian origin in every country is celebrating this sacred occasion with joy and enthusiasm. I give my good wishes to every person of Indian origin round the globe on this occasion. In some countries our brothers and sisters are watching it live on television.

Non-Resident Indians have brought strength to the economies of the nations where they have settled. Now they have an opportunity to strengthen India's economy. We have floated the Resurgent India Bond. Non-Resident Indians around the world are taking benefit of this opportunity. So far, the scheme has brought in Rs. 5,000 crore. I am confident that Non-Resident Indians will take further advantage of this scheme.

We will have to solve these problems.I know that all of you, especially our sisters, are feeling the pinch of the rising prices of some commodities. I understand your problem. Nature is to be blamed more for this than the Government. But I know that by saying this your burden will not be lightened. The Finance Ministry and the State Governments will work together to combat the price rise. I also ask for the cooperation of traders. They should not indulge in hoarding or profit-making. We will not hesitate in taking strong measures against such elements. I know that a number of festivals are coming up in the next few days. My effort will be to see that rising prices do not dampen your festive spirit.

The country faces another problem that of corruption which is eating into the vitals of the country like cancer. We have decided to fight it. We have begun the fight from the top. I have not even left out the Prime Minister from the ambit of the Lok Pal Bill which was recently introduced in the Lok Sabha. This has made clear our intentions to fight corruption at the highest level.

Along with this, we wish to fight corruption in the bureaucracy. Very soon, I will initiate action to speed up work in the cell in the Prime Minister's Office which is looking into corruption cases against officials. Removal of unemployment is an important pledge in our National Agenda. It is affecting the lives of everyone. Employment is the only way of fulfilling the basic needs of the people. Creation of schemes for total employment is difficult, but not impossible. But there will be a need to change the planning process. The basic needs and services will have to be produced by the masses. Science and technology will have to be applied for this.

Government has decided that ten crore people should get employment opportunities over the next ten years. This means that every year one crore people should get employment opportunities. A Task Force will be set up for this purpose and it will present its report soon.

The status of women is a good indicator to judge the progress of a modern society.

We had promised to give women 33 per cent reservation in Parliament and the Assemblies. We are sorry that we have not been able to fulfil this so far. We have already decided to provide free education to girls up to Graduation levels. Now we are going to take another major initiative. All girls at the primary level will be provided books in their curriculum free of cost. This will cost Rs. 550 crore to the Government.

A new Insurance Scheme, 'Rajrajeshwari' will be started to provide women economic security. Another Insurance scheme, 'Bhagyashree' will be started for girls. Both schemes will begin on Diwali Day this year. The premium for the scheme will be Re. 1 per month. and the policy holder will be able to get Rs. 25,000 in case of emergency. The full details will be announced soon.

Reservation in jobs has already been provided to the Scheduled Castes, Scheduled Tribes and Other Backward Classes. However, implementation of these provisions is very slow. My Government's efforts will be to speed up the implementation process and to fill the reservation quotas as quickly as possible. The administration will be made more sensitive and accountable to these classes.

Youth power is the strength of the nation. It is also the future of the nation. Many years ago I had read the words of Baba Amte "*Haath lage nirman mey, nahin mangne, marne.*" (Use your hands to create, not to ask or hit). This is also our wish. The young girls and boys of India do not have to extend their hands before anyone, nor do they have to use their hands against anyone. They should only dedicate themselves to the task of national reconstruction. For this purpose, we have decided to form the National Reconstruction Force (*Rashtriya Punarnirman Vahini*) which will involve youth from 18-35 years of age. This force will focus on basic services in the rural and agricultural sectors, protection of environment, mass movement for population control, fight against drugs, spread of education, uplift of Dalit and tribal women and in the field of sports, art and culture.These youth will also get honorarium for their work. Initially this scheme will be implemented in some districts and finally extended all over the country.

This scheme will be launched on the 12th January, which is the Birth Anniversary of Swami Vivekanand and which is celebrated as the Youth Day. I call upon the young men and women of this country to donate one year of their youth to rejuvenate the Nation.

The next millennium is beckoning us. It will be century of Information Technology. The greatest strength of India is its intellect. India has the third largest trained manpower in the field of Science and Technology. We will have to tap this strength. My Government has taken several new initiatives in the field of Information Technology. It is our ambition that the country should become a super power in this field.

Keeping this in view I am announcing a new initiative. Space is a new challenging area which has provided the human race an opportunity to look for innumerable possibilities in the coming century. Space technology has many advantages which India can utilise to meet the aspirations of its younger generation. On the basis of the slogan 'Jai Vigyan', my Government wants to fulfil the dreams of our youth. In this direction we will start programmes on a new satellite named Swaran Jayanti Vidya Vikas Antariksh Upagraha Yojana (Golden Jubilee Education Development Space Satellite Scheme).

The first satellite of this programme INSAT 3-B will be assembled and launched before the 15th August, 1999 by the Indian Space Research Organisation (ISRO) within a record time of less than twelve months.

Six transponders of this satellite will be available exclusively to execute 'Operation Knowledge' which aims to provide computer, Internet and computer based education to all the students of the country. All Universities, engineering and medical colleges, research laboratories and other centres of higher learning particularly will be linked to the Information Technology network before the next Independence Day. This programme will also fulfil the development related information needs of the States.

Today 125th birth anniversary celebrations of Mahrishi Aurobindo are coming to a close. He visualized the spiritual, moral and cultural renaissance of the country. Today we should pledge to fulfil his dreams.

Bharat Ratna Baba Saheb Ambedkar once said that political freedom is incomplete without economic and social freedom. Today, on our political Independence Day we cannot forget this moot point. In the half-century gone by, we have been able to keep intact our political Independence but could not win the battle of economic and social independence.

We have not been able to free the country from the clutches of poverty and unemployment. The stigma of illiteracy could not be erased. The monsters of casteism and communalism still are raising their ugly head.

Today on India's 51st Independence Day, let us pledge to win economic and social independence.

In the short tenure of my Prime Ministership, I have made an effort to take everybody along and I have practised the politics of consensus. Take the example of Cauvery. There was dispute for years on sharing of Cauvery water among Karnataka, Tamil Nadu, Kerala and Pondicherry. On some occasions, this dispute took a serious turn. Water is used to extinguish fire but if water itself is on fire, what could be done. There is a solution. The solution lies in maturity, harmony, tolerance, patriotism and a willingness to keep others' interest in mind. The recently concluded Cauvery accord epitomises all this.

Is it not surprising that a large amount of water of our rivers flows away into the ocean, while we fight over our share of water? These disputes have been going on for years. This situation has to be changed. Our rivers which link the States of the country have to link the hearts of the countrymen too. There is a need to formulate a National Water Policy. We have promised to formulate such a policy. However, it is possible only with everybody's cooperation and patience.

My Government has been seriously endeavouring to fulfil the promises made in the National Agenda for Governance. Ours is a coalition and such Governments have their own character which has to be faithfully adhered to. We have prepared a common programme that is the National Agenda for our alliance. We have kept all contentious issues out of this arrangement. Whatever we have done till today has been in National interest. We have always held National interest to be above party and personal interest.

The country is passing through a transitional phase today. Our political and administrative system is facing a serious challenge. In such a situation every party and every leader has to conduct himself with a sense of responsibility. History will not forgive us for any action which hurts the Nation. The common man should also ponder over the existing political and administrative set up. We are faced with some basic issues. Are frequent elections in the interest of the country? Is it in the Nation's interest to incur heavy expenditures on frequent elections?

I have been Prime Minister only for five months. We have a very thin majority in the Lok Sabha. I am aware of the limitations of the coalition Government. I am also aware that in today's system an innocent sage can be hanged by the power hungry.

I can assure you that I have never compromised on principles in pursuit of power and I will never do it. Being in power or out of power is the same for me. I had been in opposition for forty years and faithfully performed my duties. My opponents have also commended it. Today, a poem of Dr. Shiv Mangal Singh Suman comes to mind -

'Kya har main kya jeet main!
Kinchit nahin Bhaybhit main!
Kartavya path par jo milen!
Yeh bhi sahi, wah bhi sahi!
Vardan mangoonga nahin'!

(I am not afraid of victory or defeat; whatever comes my way on the path of duty, I will accept it as it is and would not ask for any favours).

Friends, I wish to assure you that till my last breath I will neither ask for favours nor give up the path of struggle. I only need your support. I only need the blessings of one billion of my countrymen.

There comes a moment in life when one stands at crossroads and ponders over the path to take.

Sisters, Brothers and Dear Children,

Accept my greetings on the sacred occasion of Independence Day. This is a day of hallowed remembrance for us. This is a day of dedication for us.

This year's Independence Day has special significance for all of us. The present century is coming to an end. The world will have entered the next century by the time of the next Independence Day.

As we stand at the sunset of the 20th century, and look back at the events of the era that has passed, we see the end of colonialism from Indian soil to be the most important development. Our great leaders, and many generations of our countrymen, waged a powerful struggle for independence. By doing so, they paved the way for the independence of other countries, too.

We pay our homage to those self-sacrificing and devoted leaders and patriots who struggled for freedom throughout their lives, and, when necessary, even laid down their lives as *aahuti* (offering) in the great *yagya* of freedom.

Come, all my countrymen, let us strive to become worthy heirs to those great leaders. We dedicate today's sacred day to their memory.

In the same way, I offer my condolences to the valiant jawans, officers and others belonging to the Army and the Air Force, who displayed magnificent heroism and the spirit of sacrifice in recapturing that part of our Motherland in Kargil from the enemy. All of us bow our heads in gratitude for those who were martyred in the Kargil war.

Almost all our countrymen have seen on television glimpses of the impossible summits, which our heroes overcame and pushed out the enemy. To gain victory at such heights is not only to surmount the sky-piercing peaks, it displays the full might of the nation. It is a symbol of the bravery of our Armed Forces.

How can we forget such heroes?

How can we forget those wounded soldiers whose only wish was: how fast can we get well and rejoin our battalion to repulse the enemy?

How can we forget the members of the families of those brave martyrs, who, on receiving the body of their beloved, said, "We do not have tears in our eyes, we have pride in our heart"?

How can we forget the mother whose lament was that she had had only one son, and therefore, could not send another to fight for our country?

I know that mere words of solace are not enough. We have to take concrete measures for the families of the martyrs and wounded soldiers so that they may live a life of comfort and dignity.

It has been said that we remember and honour soldiers during a war, and in the immediate aftermath. But as the days pass, we forget them. And it is a sad fact that many who sacrificed their life and limb in previous wars were often forgotten. I give you my personal pledge that this will not happen again.

This Red Fort and its world-renowned ramparts are not merely a geographical spot. The very heartbeat of India's freedom struggle is linked to this fort and its ramparts. In the First War of Independence of 1857, this is where Bahadur Shah Zafar was held as prisoner.

Netaji Subhash Chandra Bose made this very fort the target of his campaign in 1943 and, blowing the bugle of Independence, gave the stirring call to his countrymen: "*Dilli Chalo, Chalo Lal Kile*".

It is from this very fort that our first Prime Minister, Pandit Jawaharlal Nehru hoisted for the first time, the tricolour of Free India in 1947.

More than half a century has passed. Today, we stand at the threshold of a new era.

Come, let us enter this new era united in step and united in resolve.

When I addressed you from this rampart last year, there was uncertainty and cynicism in the atmosphere. It was being asked:

- Will we be able to withstand economic sanctions?
- To what extent will we be able to ward off the economic crisis, which had struck the Tiger economies of Southeast Asia?
- Will the Government be allowed to carry on its work?

Today, speaking to a self-confident India, I declare:

- Sanctions have lost their effect. They have become a thing of the past. We have dealt with them in such a way that they hardly had any effect on our economy;

- We kept the South-East Asian economic crisis at bay;
- Yes, the Government was brought down, but the country was not. It continued to march ahead, fulfilling the mantra of *Charaiveti, Charaiveti* (Move on, Move on). The Government continued to discharge its duty;
- Most important, a war was imposed on us.

We have not just triumphed over difficulties, we have achieved much. In spite of obstacles that were put in our way,

- Our National Income has grown by 6 per cent;
- Having crossed 200 million tonnes, production of foodgrains is higher today than ever before;
- Food stocks are higher today than ever. For this our kisans deserve our felicitations. Our agricultural scientists are also worthy of our praise;
- Industrial production is reviving at an energetic pace;
- The new initiatives which have been taken in infrastructure have infused a new purposefulness right across the economy.

At over 30 billion dollars our foreign exchange reserves are higher than ever before;

My heartiest congratulations to all of you on the anniversary of our Independence. Wherever you may be — at the highest mountain peaks of the Himalayas or on the shores of the Indian Ocean; on the desert sands of Rajasthan or in the green jungles of the North East, may my greetings reach all of you.

Today is also the festival of Raksha Bandhan. The power of friendship can transform even a simple hand-spun thread into an unbreakable relationship. On this auspicious occasion, I extend my good wishes to all of you, especially to all my sisters.

This is the first Independence Day of the new century. While looking back at the century just past, we must work hard to convert the challenges of the new century into opportunities.

We must make our Independence last forever. We must reiterate, today, our resolve to defend our nation.

Today is a day of sacred remembrance. It is a moment for introspection. We offer our heartfelt gratitude to all the known and unknown martyrs. The memory of their martyrdom will forever live on in our hearts. Their sacrifices will always inspire us.

Today, we especially remember Mahatma Gandhiji. He was not only the foremost leader of our Freedom Struggle, but he was also among the greatest personalities of the 20th century.

On today's auspicious day, we extend our greetings to the people of all the countries in the world. We wish that the 21st century would bring the message of peace, fraternity, cooperation, and steady progress for the entire world.

Today, we send our best wishes to millions of Non-Resident Indians and Persons of Indian Origin living in other countries. Wherever they may live, they are always emotionally attached to India. We wish all of them success and prosperity.

Today, I extend my felicitations to the people of the three new States that have found their place on the map of India after the reorganisation of Madhya Pradesh, Uttar Pradesh, and Bihar. We are confident that the new States of Chhattisgarh, Uttaranchal, and Jharkhand will soon earn their rightful place in the Union of India.

We have succeeded in our commitment of creating these three new States. After the formation of these states, we have to work together for their development so that they become shining examples of success.

The new century is a Century of the Youth. India, too, which has lived for thousands of years, has now become a young nation. Nearly seventy per cent of our population is less than the age of 35. These young men and women are more ambitious, more aware, and more active than their predecessors. They not only think big, but they also work hard to realise their dreams.

I have full faith in India's youth. It is our responsibility to fully support our young men and women in building a bright future for themselves and their Motherland.

Dear Countrymen, last year when I had addressed you from the ramparts of this very Red Fort, our country was going through an extraordinary situation. The Lok Sabha had been dissolved and fresh elections announced. It was in these circumstances, that we had to face the aggression in Kargil. And India emerged victorious in this war.

One year later, democracy has become stronger in the country. India's international standing has risen. Our voice is being heard attentively in the capitals of the world.

India is on the move. An India full of self-confidence is marching forward on the path to progress.

It is an India that is as determined to win against all adversities as were our brave jawans and airmen who drove back the enemy's forces.

Our hearts are filled with ever-lasting gratitude towards the brave soldiers of the Kargil and all previous wars.

Pakistan would be committing a terrible folly if it thinks that it can secure anything through the undeclared war that it has been waging against India. Kashmir has been an unbreakable part of India, and it will remain so.

Our neighbour must realise that the clock cannot be turned back. I would advise the rulers and also the people of Pakistan to pay heed to the following verse from the lyricist, Sahir Ludhianvi:

वह वक्त गया, वह दौर गया,
जब दो कामों का नारा था,
वे लोग गए इस धरती से
जिनका मकसद बटवारा था!
अब एक है सब हिन्दुस्तानी,
अब एक है सब हिन्दुस्तानी
यह जान ले सारा हिन्दुस्तान
रूह जान ले सारा जहान!
यह जान ले सारा जहान!

Gone is that time, gone is that age,
When "Two Nations" was the slogan;
Gone are those people—
Whose purpose was Partition!
One, now, are all Indians,
One, now, are all Indians,
Oh India, know this!
Oh World, know this!
Oh World, know this!

The 21st century does not permit the redrawing of borders either in the name of religion or on the strength of the sword. This is the age for resolving differences, not for prolonging disputes.

The people of Jammu, Kashmir, and Ladakh are tired of violence and bloodshed. They are craving for peace. We need to apply the salve of brotherhood on the wounded body of Jammu and Kashmir.

That is why, I recently said that India is prepared to apply the balm for Kashmir's agony within the framework of *Insaniyat* (humanity).

The world knows who has derailed the move to end hostilities and to start the peace process. The world knows who has torpedoed these efforts.

On the one hand, Pakistan says it is willing to participate in talks. On the other hand, it continues to be deeply involved in violence, killings, and cross-border terrorism. Activities of the terrorists and proposals for peace talks cannot go together.

India's willingness and ability to deal firmly with violence, terrorism, extremism, and separatism should not be underestimated.

Dear Countrymen, we have to build a magnificent nation. There is no other country in the world, which is so ancient, so big, so populous, and so rich in diversities; that has preserved its democracy, its unity, and its culture; and that is fast emerging as a modern and prosperous nation.

We have achieved success, too, in this endeavour. Every section of our society has contributed to this success.

In the present times, India is called upon to pursue two major imperatives. These are: Security and Development. They are complementary to each other. Without security, there can be no development; without development, our security is incomplete.

Now we have to make determined efforts to meet the economic challenges before the nation. We have to accelerate and broaden our development process, so that no child of Mother India remains hungry, homeless, unemployed, or is without access to medical care.

We have to reduce regional and social disparities.

We have to make our brethren belonging to Scheduled Castes, Scheduled Tribes, Other Backward Classes, and minorities equal partners in our developmental process.

Therefore, let us together resolve to make this decade, the Decade of Development.

To realise this goal, we have decided to achieve the target of doubling India's per capita income in the next ten years.

Dear Countrymen, to achieve this ambitious target, we have to undertake many important reforms in our economy. At the same time, we need to implement necessary reforms in our administration, our judiciary, in education, and in other areas.

Reforms are the need of the hour. For example, the world has changed much in the last fifty years; and so has India. There have been many far-reaching political and economic transformations throughout the globe.

To Reform is to Turn the Inevitability of Change in the Direction of Progress

To Reform is to Improve the Life of Every Citizen

Take for example, the reforms in the power sector that the Centre and various State Governments are presently carrying out. These will reduce the losses of our electricity boards, stop the theft of power, and ensure adequate availability of power for increasing production and employment.

Similarly, the reforms that we are implementing in the telecom sector will enable us to provide cheaper telephones, mobile phones, and Internet services in all parts of the country.

There is no scope for either apprehension or fear about our economic reforms. I remember that some people had expressed similar fears even during the Green Revolution. These fears later proved to be baseless.

The perspective of our economic reforms is based on our own concept. You know that almost all political parties have, at different times, and in different ways at the Centre and in different States, been adopting the economic reforms programme.

I urge our farmers, workers, other producers, industrialists, and our intelligentsia to contribute to building a consensus in favour of the economic reforms.

In this connection, I would like to express my special appreciation to all the central trade unions. I met their leaders three days ago, and we had a very constructive dialogue. They have withdrawn their proposed nation-wide strike. The interests of our workers will be fully taken into account in the economic reform process.

This year, the Government is going to take many big and important steps to accelerate our economic and social development and bring its benefits to the largest number of people.

I wish to congratulate our farmers for ensuring that we have not faced a scarcity of foodgrains despite a rapidly rising population. Today, there is no shortage of food; rather there is a shortage of facilities to store our food stocks.

We have formulated a National Agriculture Policy for the first time since Independence. This Policy aims to increase agricultural production by four per cent every year. Concrete steps would be taken to check the declining investments in the agricultural sector and to facilitate increase in these investments.

For the first time since Independence, the Central Government has devised a well-conceived and time-bound programme for rural roads. This hundred per cent Centrally sponsored scheme, which is called the *Prime Minister's Rural Roads Scheme*, aims to connect, within the next three years, every village that has a population of more than one thousand, through good all-weather roads. In the next seven years, every village with a population of more than five hundred will be similarly connected. For this project, the Central Government is making a provision of Rs. 5,000 crore in its first year. It will be launched on Gandhi Jayanti this year.

The National Highway Development Project is an ambitious one. A four-lane Golden Quadrilateral connecting Delhi, Mumbai, Calcutta, and Chennai will be ready by 2003. The North-South and East-West corridors will be ready by 2007.

Khadi, village industries, and small-scale industries are the backbone of India's economy. We would like the benefits of economic reforms to reach them too. There will be a national convention of small-scale and cottage industries on the 30th of this month, where we shall announce many important decisions.

In a very short time, India has become a strong power in Information Technology. In software exports alone, India is expected to have exports of more than Rs. 2,00,000 crore by 2008. Through this, lakhs of educated persons are likely to get attractive employment opportunities, both in India and abroad.

To reach the benefits of Information Technology to the common people, our Government has taken many important decisions in the last two years, and will take many more in future.

I want to see every school and every village to have access to computers and the Internet in as less time as possible.

We are committed to ensuring that every village and hamlet gets access to clean drinking water in the next four years. This year, the allocation for the scheme has been increased by Rs. 2,000 crore and its implementation will be intensified.

Before the end of this year, the Government will announce an Integrated National Health Policy, the aim of which will be to quickly achieve "Health For All". The policy will also ensure that every citizen is provided with primary health care. Ayurveda, Yoga, Unani, Siddha, and Homeopathy will be given their rightful place.

Recently, the rapidly spreading disease of HIV/AIDS has become a grave challenge to our nation. I appeal to all sections of society to fully participate in building awareness about this epidemic. They should also make necessary changes in their behaviour so that this disease can be controlled.

The most valuable investment that we can make in India's future is to ensure that every child gets education. We have decided that by 2010, every Indian child will get education up to class eight. We have launched *Sarva Shiksha Abhiyan (Education for All campaign)* to achieve this goal. Education upto graduation has been made free for women. All poor families should take advantage of this.

Science and technology have become the main engine of economic growth. We should ensure that every vehicle of economic development is equipped with this engine. Towards this end, the Government is taking concrete steps to remove the gap between academia and industry.

Dear Countrymen, a bright future is knocking at India's door. We can, however, realise this future to the extent that we are able to further strengthen our national unity, secularism, social goodwill, and our democratic system.

India is a land of diversities. We have, in ample measure, geographical diversities; linguistic diversities; religious diversities; and diversities in customs and traditions. Despite these diversities, or perhaps because of them, India has always remained united.

We are one in many, and many in one. The whole world is amazed at how India has successfully sustained this magic not just today, but for many millennia.

This may be magic for the rest of the world; but for Indians, it is life itself.

Religious intolerance and hate have never been part of India's liberal culture. I appeal to the people of all faiths and castes not to create imaginary enemies, and not to resort to the path of using the sword that inflicts wounds on oneself.

Recently, a few unfortunate incidents have spoiled communal peace and goodwill, in some places. The Government will not tolerate the activities of any organisation that spreads communal discord or incites violence.

As Dr. Babasaheb Ambedkar said, our independence is incomplete without social justice. *In the new century, India needs more social justice.* However, that kind of social justice (*Samajik Nyay*) is needed which also promotes social harmony (*Samajik Samarasata*).

The policy of reservations is one of the important guarantors of social justice for Scheduled Castes, Scheduled Tribes, and Other Backward Classes. The problem of backlog in reservations was persisting for some time. Recently, we amended the Constitution and solved this problem.

Women are the backbone of our social system and culture. Our dreams of India's future can only be realised if our women are educated, are made economically prosperous, are empowered politically, and are enabled to play a bigger role in society.

We have promised to provide reservations to women in the Parliament and the State Legislatures. There is now a need to quickly bring about a consensus to implement this revolutionary idea. I have had several opportunities to meet many women who have become members and chairpersons of panchayats and municipalities by winning from reserved seats. They have, through their performance, proved that they are not second to men, either in the democratic process or in administration.

The North-Eastern States have a special place in the nation's life and in India's development. The implementation of developmental projects and programmes has been suffering from many hurdles. Now, a special cell has been created in the Prime Minister's Office to remove these hurdles and speed up the developmental process. This cell will closely monitor the developmental works in the region. There has been an improvement in the situation, thanks to the cooperation of the people and State Governments of this region.

It is sad that the biggest impediment to faster development in the North-East has been the extremist organisations that are fomenting violence and trouble in the region. I appeal to the leaders and followers of these organisations to give up this dangerous and futile path. The Government is presently engaged in talks with some organisations in the region so that peace and development can be restored in the North-East. I am confident that these efforts will bear fruit.

India is a Union of States. Our States have an important role to play in ensuring that the fruits of development reach every Indian home. We are committed to decentralisation of power. We have decided to give our States more financial and administrative powers. We would like our Panchayati Raj institutions to also benefit from decentralization of power, so that their functioning becomes more efficient and effective. We have taken concrete steps in this direction.

In the last two-and-a-half years, we have made continuous efforts to increase dialogue and coordination between the Centre and the State Governments. All States have contributed to this process. This has improved cooperation and concord between the Centre and the States. Consequently, there has been an increasing convergence in our viewpoints and goals. For this, I thank all the State Governments and their Chief Ministers.

We shall intensify our campaign against corruption in high places. Our country cannot make expected progress in development without probity in administration and in public life.

One of the big failings in our national life has been that people expect the Government to solve even those problems, which they could easily resolve through their collective efforts. The Government, after all, has limited resources. In addition, experience has shown us that, those programmes which are implemented without people's participation, rarely yield the expected results.

Let me illustrate. Be it population stabilisation or dealing with natural calamities, conserving water and electricity, or keeping our public places clean and beautiful—all these initiatives can succeed only when our citizens participate enthusiastically and in an organised manner.

Dear Countrymen, on the first Independence Day of the 21st century, let us draw inspiration from all the good and glorious aspects of our past. However, let us not become obsessed with the past.

I have been emphasising repeatedly that India should turn its attention to the challenges and opportunities of the future. We should not be stuck in the contentious issues of the past.

Come, let us look to the future. We have to create a prosperous, self-reliant, and self-confident India. Indeed, we have already embarked along this path. We will march further in this direction. We are being counted among the ranks of successful nations.

We must not stop. Rather, we must step up the speed of our journey.

I call upon our farmers, workers, artisans, employees, youth, and, indeed, all our citizens, to make their contribution to a happy and prosperous India.

I ask our entrepreneurs to hoist the flag of their capabilities and prowess and demonstrate to the rest of the world that Indian industrialists are second to none in any competition.

I appeal to the Non-Resident Indians to contribute their fullest to this momentous task.

I exhort our scientists and engineers that they scale new heights of knowledge and science to earn a bright name for themselves and their country.

I appeal to India's sportspersons that they take our tricolour to triumphant positions in the arena of international sports.

The entire nation sends its best wishes to our sports contingent that is taking part in next month's Olympic Games at Sydney.

Come, let all of us contribute our mite to the creation of a *Parishrami Bharat* (industrious India), *Parakrami Bharat* (achieving India), and a *Vijayi Bharat* (winning India).

Our motto for all ages has been:

सम् गच्छद्म्
सम् वदद्वम्
सम् वो मनासी जानताम्
Let us walk together
Let us speak in one voice
Let our hearts beat together

In other words, let us march forward united —all of us together, and taking everybody together.

Let us make the 21st Century, India's Century.

This is our resolve. This is our aspiration.

Thank you.

Jai Hind!

Address to the Nation on the occasion of Independence Day

Red Fort, New Delhi

August 15, 2002

Dear countrymen,

My hearty Independence Day greetings to all of you.

My felicitations,

To the brave soldiers of the three Armed Forces and to all our security forces.

To our hard-working kisans and diligent workers.

I greet our scientists, teachers, and our sisters and mothers whose awakening has unleashed India's Woman Power.

And, dear children, you are the future of our Nation. Lots of love to you, and my blessings.

Members of India's Diaspora, living in distant lands of the world, my good wishes to all of you. You may be far away from India, but you are always close to our hearts.

I wish to congratulate all our sportspersons, who did India proud in the recent Commonwealth Games. In particular, our women who have shown that they are in no way behind men. I am confident that Indian sportspersons will earn similar success in the Olympic Games.

Sisters and Brothers,

It is fifty-five years since we became independent. Today, we pay our homage to all the martyrs of the Freedom Struggle. We bow our heads before Mahatma Gandhi, Netaji Subhas Chandra Bose, and all other great leaders.

We salute our soldiers, jawans of paramilitary forces, and police personnel who laid down their lives in combating terrorism. Our tributes also to the martyrs who foiled the terrorist attack on our Parliament on December 13.

Terrorism has become a festering wound. It is an enemy of humanity. Our neighbour claims to oppose terrorism at the international level, but adopts double standards in the context of our region. After facing defeat in wars, it has resorted to cross-border terrorism for grabbing Kashmir. We wish to state once again that Jammu and Kashmir is an integral part of India. It will remain so.

The world cannot accept that the cruel massacre of the Amarnath pilgrims, or the carnage of innocent women and children at Kaluchak and Kasim Nagar are a part of any "Freedom Struggle"

For us, Kashmir is not a piece of land; it is a test-case of *Sarva Dharma Samabhava* — secularism. India has always stood the test of a secular nation. Jammu and Kashmir is a living example of this. And this itself is Kashmiriyat.

We shall defeat cross-border terrorism in Jammu and Kashmir. This is our resolve. We wish to have good neighbourly relations with Pakistan. The Lahore Journey and the Agra Summit are a testimony to this. India wants all issues to be resolved peacefully and through negotiations. We are prepared to take some more steps in this direction. However, for this, it is necessary to create a conducive environment.

Infiltration into Jammu and Kashmir continues even today. Those who call the forthcoming elections in the State farcical should not give us lectures on democracy. Let them take a look at their own track record.

How can attempts to flagrantly provoke the people of Jammu and Kashmir to boycott elections create an atmosphere for any meaningful talks. Instead of resolving problems, this will only exacerbate them.

Sisters and Brothers,

I am deeply saddened when I compare South Asia with other parts of the world. When Japan, which was devastated in the Second World War, today stands as one of the front-ranking nations; when the whole of Europe has united, forgetting all the old enmities; why can't we resolve all our contentious issues through talks?

We can. We will.

Why can't we unite and fight against our real enemy, the poverty?

This is a challenge. No one is going to come from outside and meet it for us.

The process of peace and democracy has now arrived at a decisive turn in Jammu and Kashmir, which has been grappling with terrorism.

Elections are going to take place in the State. The dates have already been announced.

I am confident that these elections will be fully free and fair. No one need have any doubts on this score.

I appeal to the people of Jammu, Kashmir, and Ladakh, as also to their representatives to participate actively and in large numbers in the elections and thereby demolish the motivated propaganda being conducted from across the border.

No one will be allowed to create disturbances in the elections in

Jammu and Kashmir. All the designs to create an atmosphere of fear will be frustrated.

The people of Jammu and Kashmir want to live in peace. For many many years they have seen and suffered violence and bloodshed. They want to create a future for their children.

My brothers and sisters in Jammu and Kashmir, today is an opportunity when we can together heal these wounds. Together, we can participate in the creation of a happy Jammu and Kashmir.

I would like that no citizen of the State feels alone and helpless. The entire Nation is with them.

I am confident that all the displaced people, including Kashmiri Pandits, will be able to go back to their homes with respect, in the new situation that will be created after the elections.

I wish to assure the people of Jammu and Kashmir that if any mistakes have occurred, we shall make amends. For this, we shall talk to the elected representatives and organizations. Discussions will also take place on the demand for more powers to the State.

The desire for peace is growing in India's North-Eastern States too. The demand for faster economic development is intensifying. People are realizing the fact that the gun can snatch away life, but it cannot make people's lives better. Our efforts for permanent peace in Nagaland are progressing towards success. We invite all those who have taken to the path of violence in other North-Eastern States for peace talks.

Sisters and Brothers,

In addition to external difficulties, we also have had to grapple with nature. A large part of the country is reeling under a severe drought. In some places, floods have shown their wrath.

Standing crops are wilting, sown seeds have gone bad. Kisans are concerned. We share their concern.

The Government has taken every possible step to deal effectively with the drought. Our godowns are brimming with foodgrains. We will not let anyone die of hunger.

Relief is being reached to the weaker sections of society by extending the scope of the Antyodaya Anna Yojana. Under the Rs. 10,000-crore Sampoorna Grameen Rozgar Yojana, drought relief programmes are being speedily implemented. Five thousand crore rupees have been given to States to undertake various "Food-for-Work" activities.

Prices of essential goods are under control. But all these are temporary measures. The Government is now preparing an effective, long-term strategy to protect the country from the curse of drought and floods. We will make concerted efforts to save every drop of water. We will have to adopt watershed management, rainwater harvesting, and all such techniques.

We will shortly unveil a new initiative, which will be called Pradhan Mantri Grameen Jal Samvardhan Yojana.

We shall soon start three important programmes:

One lakh hand-pumps will be installed in water-scarce areas;

One lakh primary schools in rural areas will be provided with drinking water facilities; and,

One lakh traditional sources of drinking water will be revived.

Dear Countrymen,

With your trust, affection, and support, I am in front of you for the fifth consecutive year on the ramparts of Red Fort.

There is stability in the country today. People want the experiment of coalition governance to succeed.

Democracy has become stronger. Its roots have reached every village and town. After Independence, thirteen elections to the Lok Sabha have taken place. Governments have been formed and changed, but always without any bloodshed and violence.

My Government is committed to carrying out electoral reforms. It is our firm resolve to keep criminal elements away from power.

Dear Countrymen,

Today, India stands proudly on the world stage — tall, self-reliant, and full of self-confidence. Our prestige is on the rise internationally.

It is necessary that we do not overlook our achievements. Undoubtedly, our progress in certain areas has been tardy. We have to honestly introspect on this. For, we have the potential to achieve much more than what we have achieved so far.

Sometimes, we tend to talk about our shortcomings much more than is necessary. This gives rise to disappointment. The Nation's energy dissipates.

On the other hand, the feeling of national pride inspires us to work to achieve more.

We are proud of our kisans. Until a few years ago, we had had to import foodgrains from abroad. Last year, we exported foodgrains worth Rs. 6,400 crore.

We are proud of our scientists and engineers. They successfully launched into space not only Indian satellites, but also satellites of other countries.

We are proud of our entrepreneurs in the computer industry. Could anyone have even imagined that one day, India would earn Rs. 40,000 crore in computer software exports? But it has happened.

Behind these achievements, is the talent, the hard work, and the determination of us Indians. The credit for this goes especially to the youth of our country. Come, let us congratulate our younger generation for this.

Sisters and Brothers,

We have a multi-party system. The race for power is natural in this system. However, this race has to remain within the limits of the "Nation First" principle.

We will have to draw a *Lakshman Rekha* in our political conduct. This must never be crossed for temporary gains.

Today, there is consensus among political parties on issues of national security. Then, why can't we create a similar consensus on certain pressing issues of social and economic development?

We can create this consensus. We must create this consensus.

Take for example, the problems in the power sector. The scarcity of electricity has assumed crisis proportions in many States.

I appeal to all political parties to arrive at a consensus on the minimum agenda for power sector reforms.

However, it is not enough to change the mindset of political parties. It is also necessary to bring about a change in the mindset of the people.

Just think of the extensive theft of power, and of the Rs. 25,000 crore that is lost through it every year. How can this be tolerated?

Today, kisans want quality power; they are willing to pay more if the power supply is uninterrupted. But there should be no interruptions and cuts and no impediments in its transmission to the desired destinations.

Countrymen,

The economic reforms that have been implemented in the past few years are in front of you. An economy of scarcity has been transformed into an economy of surplus.

Today, there are no crowds in front of ration shops.

There are no lines for gas and telephone connections

The queues for kerosene have become shorter.

Prices of vegetables may have risen in rainy season, but we have strived to keep onion prices in check!

Telecom and Internet services are available to more and more people. Their rates too are continuously falling.

Our chief objective of economic reforms has been to remove poverty speedily. We are moving rapidly in this direction. The living standards of the common man are rising. Today, a fan, a TV, a refrigerator, or a scooter can be seen even in poor localities.

My dream is to see that every family has its own house. In the past four years, we have initiated the process of construction of nearly sixty lakh new houses. Of these, 35 lakh houses are in rural areas and eighty per cent are for poor families.

I dream of an India in which both the Government and Society are sensitive. Our policies and programmes have been formulated with this end in mind.

Brothers and Sisters,

Faster development of the infrastructure in our country is the need of the hour. We are fully determined to ensure that this happens.

A network of world-class highways is being laid across the country. The National Highways Development Project is being implemented rapidly. Rs. 55,000 crore will be spent on it. This is the biggest and most ambitious road project to be implemented in India after Sher Shah Suri's Grand Trunk Road. Similarly, the Pradhan Mantri Gram Sadak Yojana, costing Rs. 60,000 crore, will link every village with an all-weather road in five years. These two road projects are generating jobs for lakhs of people.

Dear Countrymen,

Our aim is to free India from the curse of poverty and unemployment. It is to make India a Developed Nation by 2020.

When this country of one billion people works with a common resolve, then no goal is impossible to achieve.

The Tenth Plan has set the target of eight per cent yearly growth in GDP.

We are taking some important new measures for economic and social development. These will be announced separately today.

Sisters and Brothers,

I appeal to you to display the same emotional unity on the issue of National Development as you always do on the issue of National Security.

Come, let us make Development a powerful People's Movement.

For this, it is necessary that everyone rises above casteism and communalism. We will have to leave behind all those things that divide us.

The horrific explosion of communal violence in Gujarat was one unfortunate example of this. There can be no place for such violence in a civilized society.

We must maintain peace, communal amity, national unity and integrity even in the most serious and provocative circumstances.

It is the responsibility of the Government and society alike to provide security and equal opportunities for the minorities.

Countrymen,

Come, let us as a nation look ahead, look to the future.

Someone has rightly said:

"*Beeti Tahi Bisar De, Aage Ki Sudh Le*"

(Forget what happened in the past, look forward to the future.)

Rather than getting bogged down in the issues and disputes of the past, let us create a new future for ourselves.

All our programmes will succeed and all our dreams for progress will come true only when we strictly adhere to probity and morality in public life.

We will not compromise with corruption at any level. Those who are in high offices should remember that people expect equally high conduct from them.

While on the one hand, there is a need for those in politics and administration to change their behaviour, equally, our citizens need to change their attitude.

Do not talk only of your rights. Remember also your own duties and responsibilities.

The mindset of depending on the Government for every work has to change.

I call upon all citizens and voluntary organizations to come forward for social work.

It is our collective responsibility to ensure that Dalits, oppressed, and people belonging to backward classes enjoy social justice and equality. We do not do them any favour by doing this.

My Government has extended the period of reservations for scheduled castes and scheduled tribes in government service for another ten years. Their opportunities for promotion in government service have also been properly ensured.

These reservations are not a dole, rather they are an instrument for bringing about social equality.

My dear countrymen,

This fifty-fifth anniversary of Independence conveys one more message to us. And that message is that all of us strive to our utmost for the realization of the dream of making India a Developed Nation.

May our goal be the limitless heights of the sky.

May our feet be on the ground.

May our minds be full of unyielding determination.

May our hands be clasped together.

May our resolve be to march together.

If we do this, our victory is certain.

Come, let all of us unitedly affirm this resolve with the victorious salutation of Jai Hind.

Join me in saying thrice:

"Jai Hind! Jai Hind!! Jai Hind!!!

6
National Commission on Population

Speech at Inaugural Meeting of National Commission on Population
July 22, 2000, New Delhi

My colleagues, Deputy Chairman of Planning Commission, Shri K.C. Pant, Minister of Health, Dr. C.P. Thakur, Chief Ministers, Members of the National Commission on Population,

Ladies and Gentlemen:

I am happy to be with you at the first meeting of the National Commission on Population. Many of you have taken time off from your busy schedules to be here. This reflects emerging universal concern over the problem of runaway population growth.

The solution to this problem lies in stabilising our population at a sustainable level. Achieving this stabilisation is a challenge. But once we overcome the challenge, we can truly develop our national human resource into a formidable force that will propel India towards all-round prosperity.

It is expected of the state to look after the basic minimum needs of its people. But, as I had pointed out the day we crossed the one billion mark, it is virtually impossible for any state to meet the legitimate requirements of its people if its population continues to gallop from one high to another. As a result, with the best of intentions, the state fails in its primary task: Ensuring a better quality of life for the largest possible number of its people.

It is, therefore, the state's responsibility to prevent its population from exploding to unmanageable limits.

This was realised by India much before any other developing country faced with a similar problem. Indeed, we were the first country to formulate and adopt a National Family Planning Programme way back in 1952. The objective of that programme was to "reduce birth rate to the extent necessary to stabilise the population at a level consistent with requirement of national economy".

Nobody can fault the intention behind that programme; indeed, it was a courageous step forward, given the cultural, social and traditional realities of Indian society five decades ago.

But, a reality-check on how effective that programme and various policies framed subsequently have been in preventing a runaway population growth, reveals rather disturbing facts. Today, India is the second most populous country in the world. With only 2.5 per cent of global land, it is home to nearly 17 per cent of the world's population.

Every year, more than 15 million children are born here to an unsure future. For, India is among those countries that have a high child mortality rate. As many as 100 of every 1,000 of our children aged under five and more than 200 of every 1,000 of our children aged under 15, risk dying a premature death.

No less disturbing are the facts that more than half our children aged under four are undernourished; 30 per cent of our newborns are underweight; 60 per cent of our women are anaemic. Forty per cent of the world's malnourished children are to be found in our country.

It is indeed paradoxical that this dark reality is in sharp contrast to the progress made by us in food production, disease control and overall socio-economic development. These harsh realities persist in spite of numerous population-related programmes and despite huge sums of money being spent by Government.

Obviously there were flaws in these programmes as well as lapses in their implementation.

If I were to list the reasons why despite elaborate family welfare programmes and huge spending, India's population has shot up to one billion from 240 million in the last hundred years, they would broadly be:

- Lack of universal access to basic healthcare facilities;
- High child mortality rate;
- Low literacy rates, especially among women;
- Persistence of high levels of rural and urban poverty;
- Inadequate awareness of options and unmet needs for contraception services;
- And, of course lack of political as well as popular will to squarely face the problem and overcome the challenge.

Indeed, the success stories of countries like China, Bangladesh, Malaysia and Indonesia show that given the political will, backed by adequate popular response, the apparently impossible task of checking population growth can be achieved.

However, one need not necessarily look for examples outside India. At home we have the examples of Kerala, Goa, Tamil Nadu and Andhra

Pradesh. Each of them has shown exemplary performance in containing the growth of their respective population. The fertility and mortality rates of Kerala and Goa are nearly similar to those of developed countries. These States are reaping the benefits of investing in literacy, especially women's education, healthcare services and awareness campaigns.

At the other end of the spectrum are Bihar, Madhya Pradesh, Orissa, Rajasthan and Uttar Pradesh. These States have very high mortality as well as fertility rates. They also lag behind in providing adequate access to healthcare services, investing in education and empowering women — factors that ultimately play a decisive role in determining family size.

Ironically, there are pockets within these States where investing in health and education, involving voluntary associations and encouraging community participation have yielded good dividends. I would urge these State Governments to take a cue from the success stories of States within the country as well as areas within their own territories.

The Central Government, on its part, is determined to ensure that flaws in programmes are removed and lapses in implementation do not recur. As a first step, the Ninth Plan recognises the need for a strategy to achieve rapid population stabilisation by:

- Reducing infant and maternal mortality;
- Meeting felt needs for contraception.

The Ninth Plan also aims at investing more in the social sector and in synergising health, literacy and women's empowerment programmes. To ensure that these objectives are fulfilled, and to focus attention on the problem of runaway population growth, we took two subsequent decisions.

The first was the adoption of the National Population Policy 2000 that provides the policy framework for improving the quality and coverage, as well as for monitoring the delivery, of family welfare programmes. The policy focuses both on society as a whole as well as the primary building block of society, the family — it targets overall population stabilisation; it aims at encouraging families to achieve sustainable reproductive goals.

Simultaneously, the policy promotes synergy among various social welfare and economic development programmes. It rests on the wisdom that population stabilisation is the *key* to sustainable development which is the *key* to improvement in the quality of life of the masses.

Our second move was to set up the National Commission on Population. This is a broad-based body that includes representatives of both Government and non-government organisations, as well as individuals who can influence society.

Your mandate is to:

- Review, monitor and give directions for the implementation of the National Population Policy so that the goals that we have set for ourselves can be achieved;
- Promote synergy between health, education and related development programmes so that population stabilisation can be achieved by the year 2045;
- Encourage inter-sectoral coordination in both planning and implementing programmes with the help of different sectors and agencies of both the Union and the State Governments; and,
- Build up a people's movement in support of this national effort.

The goals set by the National Population Policy are no doubt difficult, but by no means impossible, to achieve. I am confident that with the help of the National Commission on Population, and through you the people of India, Government will be able to achieve:

- Universal access to quality family planning services so that the two-child norm becomes a reality;
- Total coverage of registration of births, deaths and marriages;
- Full access to information on birth limitation methods and freedom of choice, especially to women, for planning their families;
- Reduction of Infant Mortality Rate to below 30 per thousand live births, incidence of low birth weight and maternal mortality rate;
- Immunisation against preventable diseases;
- Elimination of incidence of girls being married below the age of 18;
- Increase in the percentage of deliveries conducted by trained persons to 100 per cent;
- Contain Sexually Transmitted Diseases, especially AIDS;
- Universalisation of primary education and reduction in the dropout rates at primary and secondary levels to below 20 per cent both for boys and girls.

To facilitate the attainment of these goals by the National Commission on Population, my Government proposes to set up an Empowered Action Group and a National Population Stabilisation Fund.

The Empowered Action Group, attached to the Ministry of Health, will be charged with the responsibility of preparing area-specific programmes, with special emphasis on States that have been lagging behind in containing population growth to manageable limits and will account for nearly half the country's population in the next two decades.

The Group will also concentrate on involving voluntary associations, community organisations and Panchayati Raj Institutions in this national effort. It will explore the possibility of expanding the scope of 'social marketing' of contraceptives in a manner that makes them easily accessible even while raising awareness levels.

The National Population Stabilisation Fund, which will provide a window for canalising monies from national voluntary sources, is being set up to specifically aid projects designed to contribute to population stabilisation. I appeal to the corporate sector, industry, trade organisations and individuals to generously contribute to this fund, and thus contribute to this national effort.

To give it a kick-start, the Planning Commission may consider making a seed contribution from resources available with it. We will associate non-government representatives in the management of the National Population Stabilisation Fund.

Friends, I look forward to the National Commission on Population playing an active role, not only by generating ideas but also helping in their implementation in the coming years.

I began by saying that India's runaway population growth is a challenge that stares the nation in the face. I would like to conclude by saying that together we *can* overcome this challenge.

Thank you.

7
On Kargil Issue

Address to the Nation on Kargil Situation

June 07, 1999, New Delhi

My dear countrymen,

You are well aware of the situation which has developed in Kargil :

- It is a serious situation;
  - It is a situation fraught with danger;
  - It is a situation that has arisen from one simple fact: the decision of Pakistan to cross the Line of Control, to send its men and materials to occupy our territory.

No government can tolerate such an incursion – our Government certainly will not.

Countries the world over have recognised that we have the full right to evict these intruders from our soil. But for me, and for my Government this is not just a matter of our having a right. It is our duty to rid our sacred Motherland of every single intruder.

For this reason, as you have seen, our armed forces have launched a major operation to drive them back. No one should entertain the slightest doubt: they shall not stop till they have completely attained their objective. No one shall stop them till they have done so.

You know well that our relations with Pakistan, as with all our neighbours, were improving rapidly:

- The Prime Ministers and other ministers of the two countries were in regular contact;
- Dialogue among officials of the two countries was proceeding constructively, and satisfactorily;
- Areas of cooperation had been identified, and, at various levels, plans were afoot to work together on each of them;

Most important, people-to-people contacts and exchanges had opened up as never before in fifty years – there had been an outpouring of goodwill on both sides.

In the midst of all this, regulars of the Pakistan Army and infiltrators have been sent across. Fomenting insurgency here was heinous enough. But this time Army regulars have been sent. They have been sent to occupy our territory. And, having occupied it, to choke off our links with other parts of our country – in particular with Siachin and Ladakh.

This step has been taken after a great deal of preparation. It was a preplanned operation.

It is a repudiation of the letter and spirit of the Lahore Declaration. It is a violation not just of one article of the Simla Agreement, but an eightfold violation of that solemn Agreement.

The Simla Agreement binds each side to respect the territorial integrity, sovereignty, and independence of the other. The Clauses repeatedly enjoin that neither side shall use the threat of force or force to affect the territorial integrity of the other.

The Agreement deals specifically with the Line of Control. It lays down that the Line of Control resulting from the cease-fire of December 17, 1971 shall be respected by both sides. Furthermore, that "Neither side shall seek to alter it unilaterally". The Agreement goes a step ahead and specifies, "Both sides further undertake to refrain from the threat or the use of force in violation of this Line."

And yet that is exactly what Pakistan has done: it has used force in an attempt to unilaterally alter the Line of Control.

This having been done, it has now been said that the Line of Control is vague. This is nothing but an ex post artifice to justify aggression. After Agreement in Simla in 1972, the military authorities of the two sides went over the Line of Control – section by microscopic section. The salients, the locations, the coordinates were marked out on detailed maps. The exercise was done thoroughly: five months were expended on delineating the maps so that no ambiguity may remain.

Not just that, at no time in the last 27 years has the Line of Control been called in question – not once, not on a single occasion.

The new assertion, therefore, is just a contrivance to explain away the aggression. It will fool no one. And I do want to make it plain: if the stratagem now is that, the intrusion should be used to alter the Line of Control through talks, the proposed talks will end before they have begun.

India is always open to talks. But the talks must have a definite, specific purpose. In the present instance, the subject is one, and one alone: the intrusion, and how Pakistan proposes to undo it. To discuss this, our doors are always open, and all dates are convenient to us.

India wants peace. We are at peace with all other neighbours of ours. We were taking major steps with Pakistan also – towards undoing the fifty-year history of bitterness. Our people desire it. Our Government is committed to it. We have travelled quite some distance for it.

I remain confident that the people of Pakistan too yearn for peace and harmony. They know the possible costs of hostilities – of how these will push economic gains even further beyond the horizon. They know that in today's world whosoever launches aggression of any kind will get isolated in the international community.

Moreover, both India and Pakistan are nuclear powers. Our responsibilities in this regard are all the greater.

Therefore, I once again urge the Government of Pakistan: undo the armed intrusion.

We must hope, my countrymen, that even now reason will prevail, that those within Pakistan who see the folly of aggression will have their way.

But till that happens, we have a job on our hands.

Our first thought, and our last thought must be for our jawans, for our airmen and our officers who are fighting back the intruders. I want each one of them to know: the entire country stands with you, every Indian is grateful to you. The whole operation has been thrust upon us. To ensure victory, you would not be wanting in your requirements.

Our jawans and officers are laying down their lives. Should we be continuing our petty squabbles at such a time? We should stand by them and avoid unnecessary debates.

Let us use this occasion to learn from our defence forces: let us translate into our own conduct some of the discipline for which they are renowned.

The whole world is watching how our brave armed forces are defending the Motherland in inhospitable hilly terrain and at grave risks to their lives. In this hour of crisis, we must maintain an equanimity and act with confidence.

- We should not be disheartened by some momentary mishap. We must realise the gravity of the situation and emulate the fortitude with which our fighting men take such events in their stride;
- Have confidence in the ability of our armed forces.

The armed forces shall accomplish this task and ensure that no one dares to indulge in this kind of misadventure in future.

Jai Hind.

Statement

June 13, 1999

By sending mercenaries and its own armed personnel across the Line of Control in the Kargil Sector, Pakistan has once again committed aggression against India. Our Armed Forces are coping with this aggression with their customary bravery and efficiency. I have come here first and foremost to register my support and admiration for our soldiers who are discharging their sacred duty in very difficult conditions. They have the entire nation behind them and we shall not rest until the job is complete.

The State of Jammu & Kashmir is an integral part of India. As everybody is aware, there is a Parliamentary Resolution calling for the return of Pakistan Occupied Kashmir to India. Under the Shimla Agreement, India and Pakistan have undertaken not to violate the Line of Control and we have adhered unfailingly to this obligation. Unfortunately, Pakistan is seeking to cloud the issue of its violation of this solemn understanding by suggesting that there are differences of interpretation of the Line of Control. Nothing could be further from the truth. Both India and Pakistan have agreed on the map where the Line of Control runs and Pakistan knows the alignment of the Line of Control up to Point NJ 9842 and north to the glaciers beyond. We will not tolerate any intrusions across this Line of Control and will evict any intruder who violates the Line.

I have been deeply moved by the plight of the people who have been forced to leave their homes in Kargil and other areas close to the Line of Control. The continuous shelling of these villages for the last several years has been particularly heightened in recent months. This tells us the nature of the adversary whom we are confronting. My Government is determined to ensure the return of the displaced persons of their homes, whether in the areas adjacent to the Line of Control or other parts of J&K and we will spare neither effort nor expense in ensuring the safe return and normal living conditions of the displaced persons.

India is for the continuation of the Lahore process which includes a commitment to the Shimla Agreement. For that process to be fruitful it is absolutely necessary for the status quo ante to be restored on the Line of Control. That is the only way to defuse the situation and avoid a costly escalation of the conflict.

8
Address to the Nation

Well, my countrymen, you sent your representatives to the Lok Sabha for five years. They are coming back to you in just 14 months.

You know the reason for this as well I do—for the entire drama has been enacted on the open stage.

There was no issue, whatsoever, for bringing down the Government. During the debate in the Lok Sabha, as well as outside, my colleagues and I asked repeatedly: what is the issue on which the Government is guilty of such misconduct that it should be brought down, that the country should be pushed into an abyss? I listened diligently to the debate—as you would have for hours and hours. Not one new fact was brought out, not one issue of any gravity was raised to warrant what was being done.

It was not an issue that propelled those who acted. It was calculation. A calculation that boomeranged. The Government was working well,

- It was taking steps from which earlier Governments had shied away for years—steps to make India strong.
- Even as the worst ever crisis struck economies of the South East Asian countries, the Government took steps to insulate, to save our economy.
- Having saved it from that typhoon, it took steps to make India prosperous.
- The country was at peace.
- Terrorism was thwarted.

I sometimes wonder: as there was no issue, was the fact that we were doing everything possible to make India strong and prosperous the reason the Government was brought down?

When the debate began I asked, "What is the alternative you have in mind? Who is going to lead the new Government? Of whom shall that Government consist?" My questions were scoffed away. We will provide the alternative in five minutes, it was said. In one minute, it was said. Seven days went by, and you saw what happened.

We will tell the President what the alternative is, it was said, we will not tell you. The President held meetings after meetings. And they could not specify an alternative.

In any case, was this the right way to go about a matter of such grave importance? As you know, the Government has to handle matters of utmost importance for the life and security of the country. It has to handle matters of the utmost secrecy. There are matters so secret that they are known only to the Prime Minister of our country. It is his duty, when he hands charge to his successor, to inform the latter of these matters. Can it be that in a parliamentary democracy, the House should be asked to vote out a Government and a Prime Minister without knowing in whose hands it will be placing matters of such extreme secrecy and importance? Matters that spell life or death for India?

But that is what was done

Friends, democracy rests on one belief. And that is: when the leaders of a country cannot solve their problems, the people will. That is why the President, after having assessed all possibilities, decided, and the Cabinet concurred, that there was no solution to the current impasse except to come back to you.

Such episodes are ruinous for the country. The new election, as our Chief Election Commissioner has told us, will impose a burden of 1000 crores of Rupees on our people. In one week of instability small investors lost Rupees fifty thousand crores. And now, till elections are held, no policy decisions can be taken - even though issues of great urgency are coming up every other week: our negotiations with other countries, our negotiations with international organisations, what we should be doing in regard to international treaties, decisions relating to the security of the country, decisions that directly affect your welfare.

The world is leaping ahead of us: it is not going to pause, and wait for us to settle our internal problems. Our own problems—the enormous growth of population, uncontrolled urbanisation, your getting jobs—are not going to slow down just because we do not have a Government in place.

This is what you must ponder: is this the way the country should be trifled with?

There is only one way to prevent such episodes from recurring in the future: that is, to REMEMBER. Ever so often in the press of day-to-day difficulties, ever so often because peripheral issue are deliberately stoked up to divert us, we forget. The old pattern recurs, the entire ruinous sequence is repeated again. And before we know it, another generation is lost.

So my first request to you is: REMEMBER

Second, our jurists and public men should reflect on the changes, which ought to be made in our system to insulate our country from such buffeting. I will give you an example. You have just seen that a Government was removed without the sponsors of that move having worked out any alternative. Under the German Constitution, to remove a Chancellor, the House has to vote confidence in another person. In the very act of removing one Chancellor, therefore, his successor is installed. This would be a small change in our system. But even such a small change would have prevented what the country is being put through. There are many such small things that can be done and should be done, and I would appeal to our public men: examine such changes, and place them before the people.

Third, while it is true that in the end the Government was done out by the manoeuvers you have seen the basic problem lies further back. Because of the divisive turn which politics has been given over the last 20 years, our electorate has been fractured. This resulted in a fractured Lok Sabha. And that in turn resulted in a situation, in which, whichever Government would have been put in place, it would have been vulnerable to the push and pulls of twos and threes. This is the central problem that confronts us today. And the solution to that lies in your hands alone.

That is my appeal to you:

- Rise above caste.
- Rise above sectarianism.
- Rise above parochialism.
- Rise above the advantage to your immediate group.
- When elections come, DO VOTE.

And vote with only one consideration in mind: THE INTEREST OF OUR BELOVED COUNTRY.

Jai Hind.

Statement on "Bilateral Talks with United States"

December 15, 1998

Sir,

Since the May 11 and 13 tests, the Government has, from time to time, taken the House into confidence and sought views of the Hon'ble Members This was done through statements and discussions in the House on 27-29 May, 8 June and on 3-4 August. Nevertheless, I wish to reemphasise some salience of our policy.

I take this opportunity to reiterate that India's commitment to global nuclear disarmament remains undiluted. As Hon'ble Members are no doubt aware, India has consistently maintained that a nuclear-weapon-free-world would enhance not only our security but the security of all nations. That is why numerous initiatives in this direction were taken during the last fifty years; such steps as would encourage decisive and irreversible measures for the attainment of this objective. Regrettably, the international community, particularly countries that have based their security on nuclear weapons or a nuclear umbrella, have been reluctant to embrace this objective. Keeping open our nuclear option, therefore, became a national security imperative three decades ago, an imperative equally valid for India in the post-Cold War period. The option that was exercised in May '98 was thus a continuation of a decision taken near 25 years earlier; during which period India had demonstrated an exemplary nuclear restraint, given the exceptional security related complexities of our region. I wish to place on record that successive governments continued to safeguard this option, demonstrate our capability and take such steps as were necessary to ensure the viability of the option through weaponisation.

Just as our conventional defense capability has been deployed in order to safeguard the territorial integrity and sovereignty of India against any use or threat of use of force, the adoption of our nuclear deterrent posture has also followed the same logic. We have announced our intention to maintain a minimum nuclear deterrent, but one that is credible. Mindful of our global and enhanced responsibility to address concerns of the international community, and in order to re-assure all countries about the defensive nature of our nuclear capability, we have engaged in bilateral discussions with key interlocutors, in international forums like the United Nations, India is the only country possessing nuclear weapons to raise a call for negotiating a gradual and progressive elimination of all nuclear weapons, within a time bound framework.

We also have an established tradition of consultation with friendly countries on all important international issues. Successive governments have pursued an open, positive and constructive approach in our foreign relations. This is in keeping with our national ethos. It is within this framework that India had been engaged, even before May 1998, in a wide ranging and broad-based dialogue with the United States. This included discussions on disarmament and non-proliferation and on larger strategic issues.

Following the May 11 and 13 nuclear tests, apprehensions were expressed in some quarters. It was, therefore, decided to have more focussed and intensive discussions. Accordingly, Shri Jaswant Singh, Deputy Chairman, Planning Commission was designated as our representative to carry forward this dialogue. Similarly, President Clinton designed Deputy Secretary of State, Strobe Talbott, as the US interlocutor.

This dialogue has been conducted on the basis of a set of comprehensive proposals put forward by India, to the international community soon after the May tests. As the House would recollect, these proposals comprise: a voluntary moratorium on underground nuclear test explosions; our willingness to move towards a de-jure formalisation of this commitment, a decision to join negotiations on a treaty for a ban on future production of fissile material for weapons purposes; and, our determination to make more stringent the existing system of export controls over sensitive materials and technology.

Since the 11 June 1998 Washington meet, six rounds of discussions between Shri Jaswant Singh and Mr. Talbott, have been held. Both teams have worked purposefully to narrow gaps of perception and to establish common ground. These exchanges have been marked by a sense of responsibility, candour and a sincere attempt to understand each other's concerns and points of view. The Government is entirely mindful that the issues involved touch upon matters of vital interest to both countries. In these talks, we have firmly put across our security concerns and the imperative of maintaining a minimum, credible, nuclear deterrent. I wish to inform the House that the talks are premised on this basis. Also there now exists some understanding of our security concerns and requirements.

The talks have focussed on issues related to disarmament and non-proliferation. It is agreed that regional issues shall be kept distinctly apart. As Hon'ble Members are well aware, India's concerns in these matters go beyond the South Asian region, and involve a wider perspective.

After six rounds, talks have narrowed and are now focussed on the following four issues :

India remains committed to converting our voluntary moratorium into a de-jure obligation. In response to the desire of the international community, as expressed to us in our bilateral and multilateral interactions, that the Treaty should come into effect in September 1999, in my address to the United Nations General Assembly on 24 September, I reiterated broadly what I had said in Parliament, that: "India is now engaged in discussions with our key interlocutors on a range of issues, including the CTBT. We are prepared to bring these discussions to a successful conclusion, so that the entry into force of the CTBT is not delayed beyond

September 1999. We expect that other countries, as indicated in Article XIV of the CTBT, will adhere to this Treaty without conditions".

That remains our position. For the successful conclusion of the talks, creation of a positive environment by our interlocutors is a necessary ingredient.

The House will be reassured that in the assessment of our scientists, this stand does not come in the way of our taking such steps as may be found necessary in future to safeguard our national security. It also does not constrain us from continuing with our R&D programmes, nor does it jeopardise in any manner the safety and effectiveness of our nuclear deterrent in the years to come.

FMCT

We have expressed our willingness to join the FMCT negotiations in the Conference on Disarmament at Geneva. It is our understanding, as that of many other countries, who have confirmed this to us, that the objective of these negotiations is to arrive at a non-discriminatory treaty, that will end, the future production of fissile material for weapons purposes, in accordance with the 1993 consensus resolution of the UN General Assembly. We are willing to work for the early conclusion of such a treaty.

It was suggested to us that we might examine announcing a moratorium on fissile material production. We have conveyed that it is not possible to take such steps at this stage. We will, of course, pay serious attention to any negotiated multilateral initiatives in the course of the FMCT negotiations.

Export Controls : Discussions in this area have registered progress. An expert level meeting of officials from both sides was held in New Delhi on 9-10 November. In light of our additional capabilities, as a responsible state possessing nuclear weapons, and as earlier announced, we are taking steps to make more stringent our laws in this regard. We have also conveyed that India should be provided better access to dual-use and high technologies in view of India's impeccable record of effective control over sensitive technologies. The expert-level meeting was categorised as helpful by both, India and the US, to the prospects of continuing cooperation in this area.

Defence Posture : As Hon'ble Members are, no doubt, aware, matters relating to defence postures are sovereign functions, not subjects for negotiations. In fact, our talks are based on the fundamental premise that India will define its own requirements, for its nuclear deterrent, on its own assessment of the security environment. The US and other interlocutors, are interested in understanding our positions and our policies better.

We have formally announced a policy of no-first-use and non-use against non-nuclear weapons states. As Hon'ble Members are aware, a policy of no-first-use with a minimum nuclear deterrent, implies deployment of assets in a manner that ensures survivability and capability of an adequate response. We are also not going to enter into an arms race with any country. Ours will be a minimum credible deterrent, which will safeguard India's security, the security of one-sixth of humanity, now and into the future. The National Security Council, with the assistance of its subsidiary bodies, the establishment of which has been announced, will make important contributions to elaborating these concepts.

We have expressed our reservations about provisions of certain export control regimes that ostensibly seek to promote non-proliferation objectives, but are discriminatory in application. India's missile development programme is an indigenous programme, that was launched almost 15 years ago. This programme is regularly reviewed, taking into account our security environment, particularly missile acquisitions and deployments in our region, We have announced that a new version of the Agni, with an extended range is under development. Flight-testing of such an enhanced range Agni will be conducted fully in accordance with established international practice. While our decision is to maintain the deployment of a deterrent which is both minimum but credible, I would like to re-affirm to this House that the Government will not accept any restraints on the development of India's R&D capabilities. Such activity is an integral part of any country's defense preparedness and essential for coping with new threat perceptions that may emerge in the years ahead. This government remains unequivocally opposed to any suggestions that seek to place India at a technological disadvantage through intrusive or sovereignty violative measures.

At the same time continue to take initiatives in the international forums towards fulfilling the objective of complete elimination of all nuclear weapons. At this year's UN General Assembly, we had taken the initiative for, what could be an important first step, through a resolution on 'Reducing Nuclear Danger'. This initiative was intended to urge countries to move back from the nuclear hair-trigger response postures of the Cold War. If such initiatives are multilaterally accepted by other nuclear weapon states, they will, of course, be accordingly reflected in our own positions, too.

In the course of these discussions with the United States and other countries, I have kept in touch with leaders of various political parties.

We have issued statements from time to time on pronouncements and declarations by various countries. This corpus of Statements in Parliament and through Official Spokesman conveys our position and is well known to Hon'ble Members. These issues have also been discussed, at considerable length, in meetings of the Standing Committee and the Consultative Committee of Parliament. The viewpoints expressed by Hon'ble Members in these discussions, have provided us valuable guidance in conducting discussions with the United States and other countries.

The dialogue with the United States will be continued at the next meeting scheduled to be held in the second half of January, in New Delhi.

While there is no time-frame for the conclusion of these talks, it is the intention of both countries, that a stable understanding should be reached on the remaining issues at an early date. This would provide a further momentum to bilateral relations, which is desired by both countries.

In addition to the talks between Shri Jaswant Singh and Mr. Strobe Talbott, we have had detailed exchanges with France and Russia. Discussions have also taken place with UK and China at the level of Shri Jaswant Singh and at official level with Germany and Japan as well as with other non-nuclear weapon states. I have been in regular correspondence with President Clinton. Our correspondence has touched not only upon issues under discussion between our Representatives but also on larger aspects of Indo-US relations. It is my view that the future of Indo-US relations is much larger than the four issues under consideration. President Clinton has also expressed to me, his desire for a broad-based relationship with India that befits the two largest democracies of the world. I have fully reciprocated these sentiments. Indeed, our ongoing dialogue with the United States is geared towards that end. I am confident this House will want to wish it all success.

Prime Minister's Message to the Nation on Martyr's Day— 'Maintain and Strengthen Peace and Harmony'

January 30, 1999

My Dear Countrymen,

Today—the anniversary of Mahatma Gandhi's martyrdom—is a solemn day of rememberance for us. We remember him and other great patriots who gave the best years of their lives, many of them their very lives, for our beloved Motherland.

It is a day for introspection, for resolve and for rededication This year we observe this solemn day against an unhappy backdrop of sectarian violence—terrorism that continues to claim innocent lives, the assault on nuns in Madhya Pradesh, the attacks on religious places in Gujarat,the ghastly killings of Graham Stein and his two sons in Orissa, and the brutal massacre of Dalits in Bihar.

The Nation cannot but be sad; we cannot but grieve.

Such violence violates our tradition and culture of tolerance. It goes against everything that Gandhiji and our savants have taught us. Even in the dark days of foreign rule this tradition was an article of faith with us. It goes against the very spirit of *Sarva Panth Samabhav*, the cornerstone of the Republic of India.

In expressing anguish over these incidents, the President has spoken for the entire nation. I have felt, and have said publicly that these incidents are an aberration; a blot on our collective conscience.

There can be, and there are, differences of opinion in a rich and diverse democracy such as ours, However, violence is not the instrument to express differences. Dialogue is.

As you all know, Gandhiji was intensely religious. For him questions of faith, of dharma, were matters of life and death. He had delved deeply into the scriptures of all religious. He used to have regular discussions with preachers of different faiths. They often disagreed with each other, without affecting their personal relations. The point of view of the other was heard respectfully, questions were asked, and clarifications given.

The point to remember on this sacred day is the Mahatma's message of truth and love, and the method he employed.

Not violence on one side and spurning on the other.

But through debate and public discourse.

This is the only civilized way of resolving differences.

Our Constitution guarantees security for all. My Government is committed to this guarantee. We are here to protect all sections of the people, irrespective of their gender, caste, or faith.

Let no one be under any illusion: the laws of our land are clear, and they will be enforced—without exception, and to the fullest degree—to punish those who violate this sacred guarantee. Suspects have already been rounded up in Madhya Pradesh, and culprits taken into custody in Gujarat. The situation in Bihar will be firmly dealt with.

We shall bring the criminals to book.

This is our duty. It is my pledge. My government will go to any length to keep this pledge.

I believe that in such cases, we must ensure trial of the accused on a day-to-day basis.

Therefore, there are two immediate tasks—to shun violence and to bring the criminals swifty to book.

Justice cannot and shall not be delayed.

There is a large reservoir of goodwill, understanding, and amity among the followers of different religions.

We must resolve to enlarge and deepen this precious reservoir. This cannot be done by the Government alone. Maintaining and further strengthening peace and harmony is also the responsibility of citizens. I urge all of you, my dear sisters and brothers, to discharge this responsibility unfailingly—in your own neighbourhood, workplace, village, town and city.

As a mark of my own resolve to carry out my responsibility as a citizen and as the First Servant of the Nation, I have undertaken a day's fast today. I know that I have been joined by millions of my countrymen in this act of atonement and introspection. Gandhiji used to say, "My life is my message". By cleansing our body and soul as a homage to the Mahatma on his *puniya tithi*, let us rededicate ourselves to build the India of his dreams.

Jai Hind

Address to the Nation Launching of Agni-II

April 11, 1999, New Delhi

Dear countrymen,

I am happy to inform you that the advanced version of Agni, India's Intermediate Range Ballistic Missile (IRBM), was test-fired this morning. The test was successful on every count.

On behalf of all of you, I congratulate and express our deep appreciation to the team of Indian scientists, technicians, jawans and other defence personnel for this historic achievement. With today's success, they have once again shown that they are second to none in the world.

Agni is a tribute to their dedication and teamwork. It is also a vindication of our steadfast commitment to self-reliance. In a rapidly changing security environment, India cannot depend on others to defend her. We have to develop our own indigenous capabilities. Agni is a symbol of that resurgent India which is able to say: "Yes, we will stand on our own feet."

As was the case with the nuclear tests at Pokhran in May last year, the test firing of Agni missile is also a purely defensive step. It is not meant for aggression against any nation. Rather, Agni is proof of our determination to strengthen our national security so comprehensively that we can defend ourselves. I have said earlier, and I reiterate, that India remains committed to minimum deterrence, to no-first-use of nuclear weapons, and never to use them against non-nuclear weapon states.

In a statement I made on 15 December 1998, I had informed Parliament that an advanced version of Agni was under development. I had also announced that its flight testing would be conducted fully in accordance with established international practices. Today's test is part of this announced programme of integrated missile development.

In order to reinforce the climate of confidence in the world about India's defensive security programme, my Government had in advance informed the Government of Pakistan, along with major powers, on the 9th of this month of our decision to test-launch Agni II.

India wants peace in her neighbourhood and peace in the world. And we shall continue to strive for this noble goal. My recent bus journey to Pakistan is an earnest attempt to open a new chapter of peace and cooperation in the history of the Indian subcontinent.

Dear Countrymen, ever since you elected my Government in March last year, I have been working with one single aim, with one single purpose: to make India strong and self-confident in every sphere of development and defence. We have worked with sincerity and determination. Against all the odds created by global recession and sanctions imposed by some countries after Pokhran, we have put the Indian economy back on the growth path.

Our kisans have produced record output of foodgrains last year. For the first time since Independence, it has crossed the 200 million tonnes mark. We have given a major impetus to the implementation of programmes for rural development and poverty alleviation.

Industrial production is also picking up owing to the dedicated work of our mazdoors, managers and entrepreneurs. Bottlenecks in the rapid development of infrastructure are being removed, even as we have launched new and ambitious projects with high employment potential.

India is making impressive strides in new areas of science and technology. The recent launch of INSAT 2E satellite has taken India into a new orbit of world-class satellite communication. Our success stories in Information Technology have put the country on the path to becoming a Software Superpower.

India is on the move. And no one can hinder our progress if we remain unwavering and determined. The need of the hour is: Unity and Stability.

As we approach Baisakhi, and celebrate the 300th anniversary of the

Khalsa, let us take into our hearts, the prayer of the great Guru Govind Singhji Maharaj.

Dehi Shiva har mohe ihe
Shubh karman ke kabhun na taron.
Na daron ari son jab jai laron,
Nischey kar apni geet karon.
O God, bless me.
That nothing deters me from doing good deeds.
And when I'm obliged to fight, I fight for sure to win.
Let us make this prayer our resolve.
Come let us together make the 21st Century, India's Century.
Jai Hind.

Address to the Nation by Prime Minister Atal Bihari Vajpayee

October 16, 1999

My dear countrymen,

I address you today to perform a very pleasant duty: to thank all of you for your positive and clear mandate to the National Democratic Alliance and its friendly parties in this election.

The NDA represents the aspirations of every region of our great nation and every section of our vibrant society. The NDA, in fact, reflects the spirit of India in all its diversity. It also mirrors the fundamental unity in this diversity.

We may have been sent to Parliament under the banners of different parties. But we all have a common commitment: To give India a stable and good Government.

We are all guided by the lofty principles of Secularism, Social Justice, Social Harmony and Women's Empowerment. Ours is a Government wedded to a common ideal: To create a kinder, gentler and more tolerant society, free from all discrimination, fear and insecurity.

Free and fair elections are the life-blood of a democracy. It is a matter of great pride for all of us that our nation has once again demonstrated its unshakable commitment to democracy.

Our nation continues to march on the path she adopted when she became a republic in 1950. With the successful completion of the last election of this century, India stands taller in the eyes of all democracy-loving people of the world.

It has been a long campaign. A lot of heat and dust were generated during this general election.

But now that the election is over, we should put the acrimony and bitterness of the last couple of months behind us. And get down to the task of nation-building. There is not a moment to lose.

The Opposition's role in a democracy is no less important than that of the Government. It is a role mandated by the people and comes with a lot of responsibility.

Constructive criticism is an essential input for good policies and programmes. Consensus on national issues is necessary for effective action.

I look forward to both constructive criticism and consensus on national issues.

My countrymen, the world rushes ahead— whether or not we look up from our narrow concerns.

Neither do the tasks that confront us abate. The number of young women and men jobs must be provided continues to increase. Children still go to bed hungry. A sense of insecurity prevails.

The soul of India rebels against this reality.

Starting today, our Government has set itself the task of implementing our Agenda for a proud, prosperous India. It is my solemn pledge to all of you that nothing shall prevent us from the task of good governance.

We talk of the 21st century. In just ten weeks from today, India along with the rest of the world, will enter a new era of challenges and opportunities.

We are pledged to the emergence of a 'new' India in the new century.

We can redeem this pledge through collective effort, by resolutely meeting the challenges and seizing the opportunities of the 21st century. We may have sent to Parliament under the banners of different parties. But we have all been sent for a common task: to make India a strong, vigorous, prosperous and caring country.

To meet the challenges, we have to act now. In the coming days, our Government proposes to:

- Speed up economic reforms and focus attention on infrastructure development. The new century demands a new mindset.
- Introduce new laws for financial sector reforms so that India can keep pace with the rest of the world.
- Evolve a programme for achieving fiscal rectitude by improved expenditure management, deep tax reforms and a new mechanism for speedier restructuring and disinvestment of Public Sector Units.
- Promote investment, including foreign direct investment, by adoption of suitable measures and removing bottlenecks that lead to costly delays.
- Re-arrange priorities of development by re-deploying resources and strengthening institutions for providing to all:
- Safe drinking water

- Primary health services
- Primary education
- Rural roads
- Housing to rural homeless

In this task, we seek the participation of the private sector.

My countrymen, all these tasks can be completed if we work together.

Let us proceed, as the Gita counsels us,

Bodhyanta parasparam—imparting wisdom to each other.

The opportunities are unlimited. We can use each one of them to our national advantage if we stand united—both in prosperity and in the face of adversity. India's greatest asset is her unity, and my Government is determined to maintain this unity at all cost.

One of our immediate tasks will be to firmly put down terrorism, which has come to cast its cruel shadow on innocent people. Our message is loud and clear: The life of every Indian citizen under our dispensation is precious. In our fight against terrorism, we will be guided by the principle of 'Zero Tolerance'.

The same principle of 'Zero Tolerance' will apply while dealing with corruption that has bred contempt for the law. One of the first legislations we will take up is the Lokpal Bill so that the rot can be checked from the top.

A broad consensus already exists on electoral reforms to weed out muscle and money power. We propose to soon introduce in Parliament a comprehensive Electoral Reform Bill.

We often talk of the future belonging to our youth. But, for decades their problems, especially that of unemployment, have remain unattended. We believe that our young women and men will be the architects of the 'new' India of the 21st century.

I am confident that a buoyant national economy will create tremendous employment opportunities. I am equally confident that our focus on education and health will prepare today's youth for tomorrow's challenges.

The Government of free India had set itself the noble task of wiping every tear from every eye, of ending centuries-old discriminations and social inequities. Somewhere along the journey from freedom to the eve of this century, Government lost track of that task.

Illiteracy is a curse and a denial of human dignity. As is gender discrimination or, for that matter, lack of something as basic and essential as drinking water and primary healthcare.

My dear countrymen,

- India today needs a Government that cares;

- India needs a Government that will reach out to the last person in the last row.

Our Government pledges itself to narrowing the gap between our performance and your expectation.

The Mandate of 1999 is a bond of trust between people and Government.

We shall not betray this trust.

With the help of a billion people proud of being Indian,

- There is nothing that we cannot achieve;
- No problem we cannot tackle;
- No challenge we cannot face; and,
- No opportunity we cannot seize.

Jai Hind!

We shall Triumph over Terrorism - Prime Minister Vajpayee's Address to the Nation on the eve of New Year

New Delhi, December 31, 2001

My dear fellow countrymen, joyous New Year greetings to all of you. To our brave jawans, security forces, and policemen guarding our borders and vital installations; to our hard working kisans who have ensured our food security; to our workers and managers who, with their toil, are making India an economic power; to our talented software professionals who have burnished India's image abroad; to our children and youth, who are the future of our nation; indeed, to every Indian who in his or her own way is contributing to nation-building, I wish happiness and prosperity in the New Year.

I also send my felicitations to all Non-Resident Indians and Persons of Indian Origin, who, despite the distance in space and time that separates them from us, have maintained unbreakable social, cultural, spiritual, and emotional ties with India.

We leave an eventful year behind us, a year of many trials and tribulations—amongst them the earthquake in Gujarat at the beginning of the year and the terrorist attack on our Parliament at the end of the year. We faced all of them with courage and self-confidence. As we begin our journey in 2002, it is time for all of us together to resolve that we shall grow further in fortitude; that our belief in ourselves shall be further steeled to take on even stiffer challenges that may confront us in the New Year.

Today, let us pledge that our Motherland shall emerge stronger—in national security, which is of supreme importance, and in development that betters the life of those of our brethren who continue to be victims of poverty and neglect.

It is said that Time's ways are inscrutable. This may be true in the life of individuals, not in a nation's life. True, we cannot predict what may happen to our individual destinies but, in my mind, there is no uncertainty whatsoever about India's destiny.

India is marching towards a bright future. We have our share of problems. But these cannot hide the brightness on the horizon. It will be a future free of poverty and all other vestiges of underdevelopment. Indeed, the level of poverty is coming down; and the day is not far when every region, every community, and every citizen in our country shall enjoy the fruits of India's prosperity and progress. If we want, and if we act unitedly to get what we want, then this energizing goal can be achieved within the span of a generation.

The vision: But the future I see is not only one of a prosperous India, free of fear and free of want. In recent years, the world has come to look at India with renewed respect, recognizing a strong and prosperous global power in the making. I have no doubt that India in the foreseeable future will begin to play a decisive role in global affairs, not to advance any partisan agenda at the expense of others but to protect and promote mankind's most cherished universal ideals. It is also a future when the fabled richness of India's culture, arts, intellectual exploration, and spiritual pursuit will begin to show its full radiance, bringing much succour to the troubled spirit of the modern man.

Is this a dream? Yes. Is it an impossible dream? No, it is not. Nations achieve greatness when their people learn to dream lofty dreams and to strive hard—and make sacrifices, when necessary—to realize those dreams, without getting disheartened by the difficulties along the way and without ever letting their faith in their nation's destiny falter.

I am reminded here of the inspiring vision of Maharshi Aurobindo, which he set out in his historic radio broadcast for August 15, 1947.

"I have always held and said that India was arising, not to serve her own material interests only, to achieve expansion, greatness, power, and prosperity—though these too she must not neglect,—and certainly not like others to acquire domination of other peoples, but to live also for God and the world as a helper and leader of the whole human race".

This, I believe, is the quintessence of India's work, now and in the future. Different leaders of modern India have presented the same vision in different words. In the five and a half decades since Independence, we have made definite progress in realizing a part of this vision, although there is a need to introspect on why our achievement has not been greater, faster, and more egalitarian. But let us not get bogged down in the issues and debates of yesterday. Now we must hasten our march forward, correcting the mistakes of the past but always keeping our eyes fixed firmly on where we want India to be in the future.

Pakistan's designs: It often happens that the road to the future is rendered difficult by roadblocks placed by the past. One such roadblock for us, indeed the biggest, is Pakistan's consistent and continuing anti-India policy, beginning with its refusal to accept the constitutionally validated and democratically endorsed accession of Jammu & Kashmir to India.

For a long time, the rulers in Islamabad relied on military confrontation, as exemplified by the wars they waged in 1948, 1965, and 1971, to settle this issue in their favour. After failing abjectly in their endeavor, the anti-India forces in Pakistan decided to foment terrorism and religious extremism as the principal means to instigate separatism in our country. I must say that they are nursing a dangerous delusion. What they could not achieve through open military aggression, they never will achieve through cross-border terrorism.

They failed miserably in their evil designs in Punjab. Terrorism bled Punjab; but, in the end, it fled Punjab. It could not dent Hindu-Sikh unity. Similarly, the terrorists and their mentors are doomed to fail in Jammu and Kashmir, too.

However, the very certainty of failure is driving them, in desperation, to embrace a more dangerous agenda. The terrorist attack on our Parliament on December 13 has shown beyond a shadow of doubt that the anti-India forces in Pakistan are prepared to wreak any havoc on our soil. It was an attack on our sovereignty, on our national self-respect, and it was a challenge to our democratic system. Although India has been a victim of cross-border terrorism for the past nearly two decades and has lost tens of thousands of innocent men and women and security forces personnels the outrage of December 13 has breached the limit of the nation's endurance.

That the terrorists who stormed the precincts of Parliament failed in their core objective, thanks to the exemplary alertness and bravery of our security forces, some of whom laid down their lives in the call of their duty, cannot diminish the diabolical nature of the conspiracy hatched by their mentors across the border. It is useful to presume that more such terrorist strikes can take place. The only way to defend ourselves against such attacks is by forcing Pakistan to stop cross-border terrorism. And this precisely is the objective we have set ourselves in our current multi-pronged strategy.

The many political and diplomatic steps we have taken after December 13 are a part of this strategy. As I have said earlier, India does not want war. India has never been an aggressor in her long history. But we have a sovereign right to defend ourselves against cross-border terrorism, which is a proxy war that is already thrust on us. Pakistan will be solely responsible for the consequences of encouraging terrorism against India and, when expedient, turning a blind eye to terrorist groups with trans-national linkages operating from its soil.

Options before Pakistan: Today I also wish to share a thought with the people of Pakistan and, indeed, with all the right-thinking persons in its ruling establishment.

It is unfortunate that anti-India forces in Pakistan have been allowed to play with fire, apparently with no thought given to what this fire can do to Pakistan itself. I have heard and read many perceptive Pakistanis express serious concern over their government's appeasement of terrorism fuelled by religious extremism. They have voiced alarm over how Pakistan's social fabric and its institutions have been grievously affected by its government's policy of creating and systematically promoting the Taliban, ostensibly to gain strategic depth in Afghanistan and a force multiplier for its anti-India campaign in Jammu & Kashmir. The fate of the first gameplan has already been sealed. The fate of the second will be no different.

Taliban and Al-Qaeda are not merely the names of organizations. They stand for an aberrant mental outlook and a highly regressive socio-political agenda, which rejects the ideals of pluralism, secularism, freedom, and democracy and has no respect even for national boundaries. For the pursuit of its goal to establish global hegemony, it considers the use of terrorism domestically as well as its aggressive export to countries near and far entirely legitimate.

Like you, I too often wonder: Why do some people choose the path of terrorism? Why do they kill, and are ready to be killed? How are they able to create a religious frenzy in support of terrorism, when no religion sanctions terrorism? One can understand if some persons, dissatisfied with the prevailing state of affairs or angered by a sense of injustice or deprivation, want to establish a different social order that they consider is more just and would benefit more people. There is nothing wrong with such striving. Indeed, humanity has progressed through the struggles of such idealists.

But where the path of the terrorist diverges sharply from that of the idealist and the revolutionary is in the choice of the means he employs. Because of his murderous ways, his intolerance, and his extremism, he expels himself from the pale of humanity and descends to barbarism. To allow such barbarians to succeed even partially, even in a single corner of the world, is to invite danger for the whole civilized humanity.

Which is why India stood firmly behind the international coalition's support to the United States' war on terror in Afghanistan following the horrendous terrorist attacks of September 11 in New York and Washington.

The leadership of Pakistan took a commendable decision to join the international coalition against terrorism in Afghanistan, although it meant a drastic U-turn in their policy of support to the Taliban regime. But what was their real intention? If it was the same as that of the international community—namely, to root out terrorism and extremism—then I extend my hand of alliance to them. I wish to tell them: Shed your anti-India mentality and take effective steps to stop cross-border terrorism, and you will find India willing to walk more than half the distance to work closely with Pakistan to resolve, through dialogue, any issue, including the contentious issue of Jammu & Kashmir.

In my Musings from Kumara-kom last year, I had affirmed:

"In our search for a lasting solution to the Kashmir problem, both in its external and internal dimensions, we shall not traverse solely on the beaten track of the past. Rather, we shall be bold and innovative designers of a future architecture of peace and prosperity for the entire South Asian region."

I continue to remain wedded to this commitment. My bus journey to Lahore earlier in February 1999, my invitation to President Pervez Musharraf to come to Agra in July for summit talks, and our oft-extended "ceasefire" in Jammu & Kashmir are a testimony to India's sincere, bold, and innovative search for peace. This search continued even after the betrayal in Kargil. Our efforts will be further intensified, if Pakistan demonstrates its matching sincerity to have peace with India.

Together, let us leave the past of futile hostilities behind us and embrace a future free of tension and full of mutually beneficial possibilities. The common enemy that both our countries face is poverty, illiteracy, disease, and unemployment. Terrorism and extremism cannot solve any of these problems. They can only further delay their solution. Therefore, let us join hands to fight this enemy and, along with other countries in South Asia, make our region a land of peace, plenty, and all-round progress. This is the challenge of the New Year and of the New Century. Let us accept it in a spirit of cooperation.

However, if the intention of Pakistan's leadership is to continue to promote, or condone, cross-border terrorism in Jammu & Kashmir as a matter of state policy, while maintaining that they are one with the world in rooting out terrorism in Afghanistan, then the international community will judge this position to be opportunistic. It will conclude that Pakistan, far from being a part of the solution, will remain a part of the problem itself.

It is for Pakistan to make the right choice.

We shall overcome: After what happened on December 13, we have made certain legitimate demands of the government of Pakistan. Its sincerity to fight terrorism will be determined by its positive response to these demands. We also hope that our friends in the international community will bring requisite pressure on Pakistan to give up its double standards on terrorism.

Dear fellow countrymen, the situation we are facing is unprecedented. I would like you to be prepared for any eventuality. I would also like you to realize that the battle against terrorism will necessarily be a long one. One should neither expect a quick and painless victory nor despair if more terrorist strikes take place.

Today my heart goes out to our jawans, security forces, and police personnel who are doing their duty in difficult conditions, so that all of us can sleep soundly and go about our normal lives. But let us also recognize that, in some ways, every citizen is a soldier in this war against terrorism. Like them, let us be disciplined and ever-vigilant. Like them, let us also be prepared to make sacrifices—sacrifice of our leisure, sacrifice of our comforts, sacrifice of our riches, and, if necessary, sacrifice of our lives.

I am sure that all of us will work harder than before to keep our economy and our civic services fighting fit. I know that, as during the previous wars, our citizens will gladly bear hardships if the government has to take certain temporary measures to support our effort. Our people have shown the fist of unity at the time of every crisis in the past. I am confident that you will do it again, and not allow any other issue to come between us and our goal.

9

India Economic Summit-1998

Address at the India Economic Summit

(Organised by the World Economic Forum and the Confederation of Indian Industry - November 29, 1998)

I am pleased to be here at this conference, in your conference is the inaugural session of the India Economic Summit organised by the World Economic Forum and the Confederation of Indian Industry. It is taking place at an extraordinary moment in India's democratic history. Whatever is happening now is a sign of the vibrancy of Indian democracy. However, I would like to assure you that volatility in Indian politics will have no fundamental impact on the process of economic reforms in the country.

The reform process has become irreversible. Indeed, my Government has depoliticized the economic agenda.

Your summits in the past have fostered constructive interaction between foreign and Indian business and with the Government. They have also facilitated foreign business becoming familiar with India's efforts both to carry out internal liberalization and to integrate itself with the global economy.

Since you met here a year ago a number of new and decisive steps have been taken by my Government to strengthen our economic fundamentals and improve the productive efficiency of our system. In the schedule of your meetings over the next few days you would be interacting with some members of my Cabinet, some distinguished businessmen, economists and senior government functionaries. They would outline for you not only what has been achieved during this period but share their vision of the economic agenda for the coming months.

Over the last nine months my Government has taken important initiatives over a wide gamut of economic issues which cover insurance, capital markets, information technology, housing and infrastructure, to mention a few. The reform process initiated is wider and deeper than any comparable programme earlier. Its multiplier effect would have long-term beneficial impact on the economic and social development of India.

We also take some pride and satisfaction that, given the turmoil in the rest of Asia and many other parts of the world, our macro-economic fundamentals continue to be strong. They create new opportunities for private investment both domestic and foreign. A'GDP growth of well over 5 per cent, inflation below the double digit number, comfortable foreign exchange reserves, positive growth in agriculture, stable exchange rate management coupled with sectoral initiatives, have reaffirmed the Government's commitment to a policy of liberalisation with suitable checks and balances.

I have said so earlier and would reiterate today that there is no panacea or a role model to bring about high rates of economic growth coupled with social development. Each country has to devise a strategy that is appropriate to address its own problems and serve its growth objectives.

Discussions are going on within the Bretton Woods institutions, the United Nations and other forums for a reform of the global economic architecture. We will participate constructively in this dialogue so that the emerging reform process can durably address the malaise that has adversely affected many countries.

Such a reform process should help in the evolution of a new financial architecture based on transparency, symmetry of obligations, equity, effective management in the face of rapid flow of large sums of capital around the world, and orderly development of world trade for the common good of mankind. Poverty alleviation must remain the central objective of international action.

We recognise that globalisation is both a reality and an opportunity. We are convinced that nations cannot prosper in isolation and must forge complementary relationships based on mutuality of interests. India is committed to the continuation of its policy of liberalisation coupled with effective social safety nets. We will also pursue policies to maximise the gains from the opportunities which globalisation offers, while ensuring that credible mechanisms are in place to mitigate the risks that are inherent in this process.

Our aim is to be a strong nation, so as to be able to live in peace, prosperity, and dignity. We recognise, however, that the strength of a nation flows primarily from the strength of its economy.

Whatever we do to strengthen our national economy, we will do it in a manner that will simultaneously strengthen the democratic polity of India; whatever we do to strengthen the democratic polity, we shall simultaneously strengthen the secular unity of India; and whatever we do to strengthen our democratic polity and secular unity, we will bear in mind the need at all times to dramatically reduce poverty in the shortest possible time.

In this endeavour, our approach is the same as that advocated by Prof. Amartya Sen, the great Indian economist who won this year's Nobel Prize for Economics—namely, liberalisation and globalisation yes, but with a credible programme to improve the social sector.

Many of our initiatives in the social sector are aimed at providing nutrition, hygiene, health, and education to those large numbers of our population who continue to be the victims of poverty.

India is a democratic country. Freedom of thought, freedom of action, freedom to live with diverse faiths and customs are fundamental to our culture. It is our greatest strength. I believe that these are essential components of liberalisation and globalisation.

We have another great strength. We have an unbroken record of honouring all our financial obligations to foreign investors and lenders. We have a sound legal system that incorporates many of the canons of Anglo-Saxon jurisprudence.

In a vast country like ours, with a population of a billion, with a middle class nearing the size of Europe, there are unlimited opportunities for foreign investment and management.

I hope your meeting will comprehensively take these strengths into account and discuss India's legitimate claims on international investments. It will not be out of place for your summit to discuss, in terms of figures and specific sectors and projects, what amounts of foreign investment should flow into India over the next fifteen years or so, and how such investments could be mutually beneficial.

We believe that domestic savings need to be augmented and supplemented by external resources to achieve high rates of economic growth. Access to high technology dramatically improves the productivity and efficiency of investment. Foreign investment has an important contribution to make in this process.

My Government has created a new and growing opportunity for investments in infrastructure, especially in power, ports, airports, roads, telecom, information technology, in the services sector, and in insurance. The Foreign Investment Promotion Board has been functioning ever more actively and has approved a large number of FDI proposals. We would like to make India an attractive destination for foreign investment—both foreign direct investment and foreign institutional investment.

We recognise that given the global shortage of capital, nations must compete in creating a milieu that attracts foreign investment. India would be second to none in establishing a transparent framework in which such investment can flourish.

Friends, for us in India, right from the early nineties, when excessive Government controls on business and industry began to be eased, liberalisation has meant a steady but sure approach, consistent with our concern to preserve social stability and democratic polity. I agree with you that the pace of change needs to be—and can be—faster. I assure you that my Government will act a lot faster, and firmer, on our economic agenda in the coming months.

Let me now outline my Government's medium-term economic agenda. In preparing India to face the challenges of full liberalisation and globalisation, my Government will create policies that will:

(1) Achieve an annual GDP growth rate of 7-8 per cent through a strategy that ensures low inflation and high employment generation.
(2) Strengthen the financial and banking sectors by introducing transparency, accountability, and non-interference by the Government.

10
Speech at FICCI Forum

October 24, 1998, New Delhi

President of FICCI Shri K.K. Modi, president-elect Shri Sudhir Jalan, Vice President Shri G.P. Goenka, Patron Shri Charat Ram, Secretary-General Dr. Amit Mitra, distinguished businessmen, ladies, and gentlemen,

As I stand here to inaugurate the 71st annual session of the Federation of Indian Chambers of Commerce and Industry, I am struck by the awareness that we are indeed at a turning point in world history.

There are difficult times for Indian and global business. A massive churning process is taking place in the world economy. The name of this *Samudra Manthan* in the modern era is Globalization. Globalization has brought in unprecedented turbulence, but trapped in that turbulence is also the hope of *amrit* (nectar). It is a moment when the promise of a new phase of long-term prosperity and progress lies in the womb of short-term uncertainty. Today, the process of churning has brought the rhetoric and realities of globalization face to face. Some of these realities are indeed harsh and painful. The international financial markets find themselves in a crisis whose threatening waves have rapidly travelled from local to regional to global waters. There is a distinct downtrend in global trade. Many national economies around the world have shrunk some even registering a negative growth. For the first time in post-World War Two history, even rich nations have begun to worry that the comforting certainties of their continued prosperity are not foolproof. Does this mean that globalization itself is a flawed idea, fit only for a quick burial? I know that there are people, both within India and outside, who say so—and I also know that they represent a minority opinion. Globalization is a historical reality. And, nations cannot prosper in isolation. Forging mutually beneficial and cooperative relations is necessary for growth and prosperity for all. Even Professor Amartya Sen, the winner of this year's Nobel Prize for Economics—and who, as we all know, is one of the sharpest critics of the failures of globalization—has forthrightly argued that globalization can also be a boon for humanity, if coupled with credible social-sector safety nets.

At the same time, history itself is teaching both business and political leaders in the world what Indian philosophy has explained ages ago: namely, there is no single exclusive path of reaching the Truth. Similarly, there can be no single model or solution to the problems of economic development. Each nation has to pave its own path, based on its own concrete national realities and priorities. This is what Swadeshi means. Globalization and Swadeshi are, thus, complementary and not contradictory to each other. Friends, India's strategic response to the reality of globalization has to be two-fold: external and internal, both designed to achieve a common goal—namely, to strengthen the global economy and the Indian economy. Externally, we advocate, with even greater vigor and conviction than in the past, our case for changing the present iniquitous and unsound architecture of the world economy. The World Bank and the International Monetary Fund were set up in the pre-globalization era and at a time when most countries in the world were either not free or had just won their independence. India seeks an innovative restructuring of the Bretton Woods twins, to reflect the needs of today's interdependent world and also to better achieve the goal in their founding charger—namely, "The Achievement of Sustainable Economic Development and Reducing Poverty". We similarly seek a radical change in the approach and functioning of other institutions such as rating agencies and global commercial banks.

The UN is contemplating a major international conference two years from now to suggest a new policy framework for the global financial system. India will make an important contribution to the deliberations at this conference and in discussions which will take place in other fora.

Towards this end, the Government is formulating a six-point conceptual framework for the innovative design of a new global financial architecture.

The six pillars of the new architecture will reflect the need for:

(1) Managing large capital flows without excessive volatility;
(2) Speedy decision-making and timely corrective action in the face of instantaneous electronic fund transfers across the globe;
(3) Transparency among all the players—public and private, government and quasi-government, in developed and developing countries;

(4) Achievement of equity in an inherently unequal world economic order;
(5) Timely preventive steps against the "contagion effect"; and,
(6) An ability to introduce adaptation and innovation in a fast-changing financial system.

We shall soon present this for a national debate, in which the views of the opposition parties and all sections of business, industry, and labour will be invited. We shall also engage constructively with other countries in an effort to promote an international consensus for restructuring of the financial system.

Friends, it is not just the global financial system that is demanding radical restructuring. Our own economy is in urgent need of deeper, broader, and faster reforms. My Government is fully committed to this objective.

Our commitment is not in words, but action.

I can say with considerable satisfaction that our record in taking initiatives in the economic sphere is superior to that of any other government in recent memory, for a comparable initial period of six months in office. In this period, we have demonstrated our resolve to put the Indian economy onto a higher growth path and dispelled all doubts as to our commitment to the philosophy and policies of liberalization. My Government has not gone back on any of the reform initiatives of the earlier governments, but has added a new momentum to the reform process. Delicensing, decontrol and debureaucratization have been my personal belief long before I came to the present office. My Government has delicensed sugar, petroleum, and coal/lignite from the purview of the IDR Act. With this, virtually the entire Indian industry, barring those in strategic areas, has been freed from the regime of industrial licensing.

Technology inputs are being virtually freed from Government approval processes to facilitate free inflows. Intellectual Property Rights are a critical need in the emerging knowledge-based economy. My Government's commitment to the protection of IPR has been demonstrated by acceding to the Paris Convention for the Protection of Intellectual Property on September 7, 1998. We have also declared our resolve to meet the obligations on TRIPs under the World Trade Organization.

Information Technology is revolutionizing every facet of life including, most dramatically, the national and global economy. It has been an area of high priority for the Government. The IT Action Plan prepared by the National Task Force on Information Technology and Software Development, with 108 recommendations to make India an IT superpower, has been accepted by the Government. Many of these recommendations have already been implemented. Others, such as giving a major boost to hardware manufacturing in India, are in the process of being finalized as specific action plans. Recognizing the importance of infrastructure in our development process, the allocation for such projects has been substantially augmented by over 35 per cent—from Rs. 452.52 billion to Rs. 611.46 billion. In the project sanctions of the All-India Financial Institutions, the share of infrastructure projects has gone up by 217 per cent in the current year. Infrastructure projects now account for one-third of the sanctions of Rs. 750 billion. We have also taken other steps to strengthen infrastructure financing. The Infrastructure Development Finance Company Ltd. (IDFC) has been set up with a capital base of Rs. 16.5 billion a unique public and private sector partnership to channel private capital into viable infrastructure projects.

Tax incentives for infrastructure projects have been further liberalized during this period. New initiatives were taken to catalyze the interest of Non-Resident Indians in our developmental process. The success of the Resurgent India Bonds is a demonstration of their willingness to participate in our nation-building mission.

Distinguished friends from industry and business, the point, briefly, is:

If you have a viable infrastructure project of national importance, I assure you that neither finance nor governmental clearances will be a constraint. Regulatory bodies, which can foster a competitive environment, coupled with autonomy and transparency, have been strengthened during this period in order to boost investor confidence. This process will continue.

Friends, I have listed these actions not to claim that what the Government has done so far is sufficient. I am as aware as all of you are that Indian industry and business are passing through difficult times. Confidence is low and expectations from the Government is high. There are valid concerns about the capital market, imbalances in sectoral growth, sluggish pace of infrastructure development, and the slow spread of the spirit of reforms within various levels of the Central and State governments. The present downtrend in the global economy is only a part of the reason for the difficulties faced by Indian business and industry. An equally crucial reason arises from internal factors—and they are not confined merely to the policies and performance of successive governments. It is time for Indian industrialists and businessmen to look within and introspect deeply. Has business and industry lived up to the expectations of the

Indian people and the Government? Let me cite a few issues. What is the main cause of the present depressed state of the stock market? Is it not, at least partially, created by a large number of public offerings by unscrupulous promoters who exploited the market in its boom phase, and later betrayed their commitment to their investors, mostly small investors? Can we allow such predatory promoters to go unpunished? I have instructed the concerned agencies in the Ministry of Finance to promptly look into this malaise and take suitable punitive action within the next three months. I urge organizations like FICCI to cooperate with the Government in taking these firm but necessary measures to restore investor confidence. A reform process without proper checks and balances is neither good for you in business nor for us in government.

Take the matter of good corporate governance. How many Indian companies have adopted its imperatives and improved their own efficiency, transparency, customer-focus, and competitiveness? The time has come when this matter cannot be left to the promoters alone. The Government would like the Financial Institutions, on the strength of the significant stakes they hold in companies, to demand better performance and adherence to sound corporate practices. I must also share my disappointment about a section of your fraternity which continues to base its investment decisions on short-term sentiments, and not on the long-term opportunities that our country offers.

Let me cite the example of the FDI proposals approved by the successive governments since 1991. The approvals amount to US$ 52.67 billion. As against this, the total FDI inflow has been only US$ 13.41 billion—that is only 25 per cent of the approvals. I accept that policy issues and clearance problems are partly the reason for this dichotomy. However, it is also known that short-term vision has delayed investment plans of many project promoters.

I, therefore, urge FICCI and other business associations to make vigorous efforts to create an atmosphere that focuses domestic and foreign investors' attention on the Big Indian Opportunity waiting to be reaped once the cycle of recovery and high growth sets in. The Big Indian Opportunity can be realized only if business, industry, and the Government work with one mind and for one purpose—strengthen the economy at the earliest. As far as the Government is concerned, I have already said that we assert our commitment to this goal not through words, but speedy action. Friends, you will see an accelerated and firm pace of action in the economic sphere in the coming months. I am, indeed, happy to announce some of them today. Restoration of vibrancy to our capital market is an important component of Government's strategy to reinvigorate the economy.

Towards this objective, we shall initiate the following measures that should improve sentiments significantly.

(1) We propose to permit companies to Buy Back shares within the prudential guidelines set by SEBI in order to enhance the value to investors.

(2) The Government proposes to abolish the existing provision requiring its prior approval for inter-corporate investments by one Indian Company in another Indian Company.

(3) Companies will be permitted to enhance acquisition limits in accordance with the recommendations of the Justice Bhagwati Committee on take-over regulations.

(4) Structural improvements will be undertaken for accelerating demat trading and settlements. This would bring great efficiency, transparency, and lower cost and thus serve the interest of small investors.

(5) Restructuring of PSUs and a credible disinvestment programme is critical for improving the productivity of our economy. It is also a centre piece of our fiscal management strategy. Past efforts in this direction have not yielded desired results. We propose to revise this process and set up a more transparent mechanism, so that the pace of restructuring and disinvestment is commensurate with the urgency of the problem. The action to achieve these objectives will be in place within thirty days.

(6) The Government has already initiated measures to open the insurance business to the Indian private sector. This is a major step in mobilizing long-term resources for funding long-gestation infrastructure projects. The Government is presently examining the proposal to permit an appropriate level of majority foreign equity in the insurance sector.

(7) Steps will be taken to speed up the passage of a new Companies Act and FEMA. Views of trade and industry will be invited before finalizing the Money Laundering Act.

(8) I know that developments relating to UTI's US-64 scheme have caused understandable concern among unit holders and the financial community. I wish to assure them that the Government will support the UTI fully in honouring its obligations.

The Government is alive to the need to further strengthen the financial sector with a view to making it more resilient to shocks. Although, we have succeeded in immunizing our economy against the South East Asian crisis, we cannot be complacent to the "contagion effect". This crisis began by serious weaknesses and over-extension by the banks and financial institutions. Steps to improve the portfolio of Financial Institutions, deal with the problem of Non-Performing Assets, and to improve the efficiency of Financial Institutions for making finance available at affordable costs is a high priority for my Government.

I am confident that these and other measures will improve market sentiments significantly, especially since the fundamentals of the Indian economy are strong. There is a valid concern widely shared in political and business circles that Government spending in infrastructure sectors has significantly come down after the start of economic reforms. My Government will remove this damaging imbalance. The Government will start, within this year and from twenty different places across the country, work on a major 7,000-kilometre road project. It envisages a six-lane North-South corridor connecting Kashmir to Kanyakumari and a similar East-West corridor connecting Silchar to Saurashtra. The project, which is expected to cost Rs. 280 billion, will have the scope for maximum private sector and foreign participation. This project also has the potential to create as many as thirty million of years of employment, which will be a major contribution to the realization of the national goal of "Berozgari Hatao".

Cement concrete pavement will be the preferred technology in this, as well as other ongoing projects for four-laning of our national highways. We expect the move to give a big boost to our cement industry, which is facing the problem of excess capacity, and, also, to the construction industry.

Telecommunications is a critical infrastructure for every area of the economy. There are a number of knotty problems in this sector, which are a difficult legacy that we are carrying from the past. However difficult, we have the political will to untie all the knots in the most transparent and consultative manner. A new Telecom Policy will be formulated within the next three months to provide a state-of-the-art nationwide telecommunication network, speed up rural telephone services, and to meet the new challenges of the convergence of telecom, IT, media, and consumer electronics.

In addition, within the next fifteen days, the following actions will be taken:

All the outstanding issues between the Department of Telecommunications and the TRAI will be resolved to strengthen the latter's regulatory role. A suitable out-of-court settlement will be found for the pending legal dispute. Hereafter, we will ensure that two wings of the Executive do not go to court, for this amounts to an abdication of political responsibility.

- The new Internet policy will be announced and licenses issued to private Internet Service Providers.
- The Iridium project for global satellite telephone service will be launched, as scheduled, on November 1. The necessary approval for grant of license for this project was given by the Department of Telecommunications yesterday.
- I have mandated the National Task Force on Information Technology under the chairmanship of Shri Jaswant Singh to prepare a report suggesting a resolution of the outstanding issues in the telecommunications sector, including the license fee structure for basic and cellular telephone operators. The Task Force will submit its recommendations before November 30, and the Government will take appropriate action before the end of the year.

In the oil exploration sector, the Government will offer deep acres with high potential for bidding and bids will be invited within the next two months.

The Government will identify five cities for the construction of world-class international airports with a maximum of 100 per cent foreign equity investment. Housing is a priority for my Government. The National Agenda for Governance has set the ambitious target of construction of 2 million additional housing units each year. Besides giving a fillip to many industries, this will also generate large-scale employment. In order to accelerate activity in the housing sector, the Government has taken initial steps towards the repeal of the Urban Land Ceiling Act.

The Ministry of Environment will prepare a list of all industrial and developmental projects above Rs. 250 million, in which environmental clearance is pending for over six months. Consistent with our commitment to harmony between development and environmental protection, these will be duly examined and all deserving projects will be cleared by the Ministry within the next three to six months.

Friends, these are difficult times for trade and industry. These are also trying times for the Government. Yet, aware as I am of the ingenuity of Indian business to always emerge stronger from crises, I look forward to a more active partnership with you to achieve faster and sustained economic growth. When the going gets tough, India must get going with greater determination and self-confidence. The challenge is yours in industry and business, for you have to refocus and restructure quickly. However, the challenge is also ours in Government, for we too have to redouble our efforts to speed up action—real, visible, creative action. Together, let us confidently meet this challenge—and meet for the occasion next year with more smiles on our faces and more contentment in our hearts.

Thank you.

11
Concern on Brain Drain : Indian Science Congress, 90th Session at Bangalore

The following is the text of the Prime Minister, Shri Atal Bihari Vajpayee's inaugural address at the 90th Session of the Indian Science Congress at Bangalore.

"I am delighted to be here with this distinguished gathering for the 90th Session of the Indian Science Congress. At the outset, I wish all of you a very Happy New Year.

My special greetings to all the distinguished scientists from abroad, who have travelled a long way to participate in this prestigious event. I am as pleased as all of you to know that our respected Rashtrapatiji, Dr. Abdul Kalam, will be coming here tomorrow to grace this occasion. It is a tribute to Indian science that a renowned scientist-patriot has become India's President.

I am happy that this Science Congress is being held in the excellent academic backdrop of Bangalore University. Bangalore has become the IT, Bio-tech and Space Technology hub of India.

Traditionally, this Garden City is known for its beautiful sprawling parks. However, now it is also known for parks of another kind – Technology Parks. I can tell you that India is earning handsomely from the export of the unique floriculture – "software floriculture" — from these parks. My special word of appreciation for Dr. Kasturirangan, the General President of this year's Science Congress. Whenever I see him, I feel reassured by his self-confident and determined approach, which, I am sure, is not his alone, but represents the ethos of all his colleagues at ISRO. The Nation is proud of the achievements of our Space Programme and of your leadership to it, Dr. Kasturirangan.

Today I am delighted to launch the new Science and Technology Policy 2003. The Scientific Policy Resolution of 1958 had inspired India's scientific endeavours in earlier decades.

This was updated in 1983 with the adoption of the Technology Policy Statement of 1983. Exactly after twenty years, we are launching STP 2003. This shows that we can respond to the breathtaking changes that have taken place in the world of science and technology in the closing decades of the last century, and also to the challenges and opportunities before us in the new century.

I congratulate Dr. Murli Manohar Joshi and all the eminent scientists who have worked hard for preparing a forward-looking policy.

Since ancient times India has had an illustrious tradition of scientific inquiry. Numerous fundamental scientific and mathematical concepts are attributed to ancient Indian scientists. They also developed applied knowledge in medicine, metallurgy, chemistry, agriculture, textiles and other fields. But far more important than these specific contributions of ancient Indian scientists and philosophers is their integral approach to Knowledge and Life. They explored all areas of *Jnan* and *Vijnan* in a holistic way, emphasizing that that man's material and spiritual development should be pursued in a balanced manner, without ignoring one at the expense of the other. I believe that our world needs this approach as much in the new century as it did in all the previous ones.

Today I applaud the impressive contributions of our scientists and technologists to India's national development and national security since Independence. In several frontiers areas, our achievements rank among the best in the world.

India's chain of national and regional laboratories, scientific departments in universities, IITs and other academic establishments, can justly claim to comprise the scientific infrastructure of an advanced nation.

My vision is to embrace science and technology, in all its true spirit, to realize our dream of making India a Developed Nation. As you are well aware, the Government is fully committed to supporting you in this endeavour. The Tenth Plan has recognized that productivity-led growth is the path India has to take in order to attain the ambitious target of 8 per cent GDP growth rate. Appropriate S&T inputs at all levels and in all sectors of the economy are needed to pave this path. Some of the thrust areas for Indian science now and in the coming years are obvious.

We have to further consolidate the gains we have made in agricultural science and achieve higher productivity in the production of pulses, oil seeds and vegetables, animal husbandry, dairying, fisheries, horticulture, cultivation of medicinal and energy plants, and agro-processing industries. Application of new scientific and technological capabilities generated through Biotechnology, IT and Space Technologies should be extensively pursued. Minimizing wastage in farm produce continues to be neglected tasks in most parts of the country. All these efforts are essential to increase rural incomes and generate new employment opportunities in the rural economy, which is our first developmental priority.

India is also facing critical challenges in meeting the basic healthcare needs of all our citizens, land and water conservation, energy security, and environmental protection. All these call for greater contributions from Indian science. I would like to make a special mention of the large quantum of energy that would be necessary to raise the living standards of our people. For this, it is inevitable that we develop advanced energy technologies capable of making use of domestic energy resources and satisfying modern environmental norms. Further developments in nuclear energy systems, non-conventional and renewable energy options and technologies for cleaner use of fossil fuels should receive our urgent attention. Technological developments for achieving greater efficiency in the conversion, transport and use of energy should also be our focus.

Disaster prevention and management has become another pressing challenge before the Nation. Although disasters know no boundaries, when they strike, it is the vulnerable sections of society that suffer the most.

The Tenth Plan has placed great emphasis on this task, and called for vital inputs from science and technology. While trying to maximize our work on all these developmental fronts, we should simultaneously intensify our activity in frontier areas of science and technology.

Our space programme has earned India global recognition. About a year ago, it demonstrated India's capability to launch a satellite into geostationary orbit with our own launch vehicles. I am confident that it will soar higher in 2003 and in the years ahead. Like space, oceans are another frontier beckoning India. I am happy to learn about the significant progress made by the Department of Ocean Development in improving ocean observation capabilities. We should firm up our future plans for assessing, exploring and harnessing the vast energy resources in the ocean. This is the most appropriate time, when the international order in respect of the ocean system is evolving and taking final shape, that our scientists and scientific institutions tune themselves to build up a reservoir of human resources and technological infrastructure.

The 21st century is poised to witness exciting breakthroughs in biotechnology. India, too, is poised to be in the vanguard of these developments, thanks to the efforts of the Department of Biotechnology and many enterprising Indian biotech companies. Generation of new vaccines, accurate and low cost diagnostic kits, genetically superior plant material, many recombinant products and technologies – all these would surely help in poverty alleviation, combating malnutrition, protection from dangerous infections, and benefit our society in many other ways.

Distinguished Indian scientists, if your contributions to India's socio-economic growth, as also to the world's body of knowledge, are to increase further, we need to candidly recognize and address several problems. I wish to share my observations with you on some of them.

Disconnect between science and policy: We live in an age when policy problems, whether in the economic, national security, environmental, or social development areas, are characterized by immense complexity. Such issues are incompletely grasped by the concepts and methods of any one discipline. They call for a multidisciplinary approach. I appeal to our scientists and technologists to be pro-active in throwing light on policy concerns. At the same time, I also appeal to our policy makers in the Government, whether at the political or bureaucratic levels, to pro-actively seek such inputs.

Insufficient linkages between R&D Establishments and the broader economy: Till recently, the economic impact of Indian science and technology was far less than its true potential. Economic actors and scientists did not recognize each other sufficiently. On the one hand, during the era of the license-permit-quota raj, industry had little incentive to upgrade its processes or products. On the other, many of our scientists viewed applied research and its commercialization as an inferior occupation.

I am glad to note that, especially in the CSIR, there are clear winds of change. I understand that last month CSIR was granted its 100th US patent during the calendar year 2002, an event that is unparalleled in Indian science.

We need such initiatives in all our publicly funded institutions. Here I would like to repeat my earlier appeal to industries in the private sector. They should invest more in indigenous R&D, in partnership with our S&T institutions, IITs and universities, so that their products and services become globally competitive.

Since R&D has today become a global enterprise, with top corporations spending hundreds of billions of dollars, this partnership should also boldly tap the huge new opportunities that have opened up in this field. Promotion of traditional technologies: Diversity is as much a part of India's technological landscape as it is of our economic landscape.

There is a need to produce useful R&D inputs to enrich all the three kinds of technologies that operate in India – modern, conventional and traditional. In this context, we cannot neglect the immense scientific talent that exists outside the formal S&T establishment. I am told that the National Innovation Foundation, which was set up two and a half years ago, has started championing the cause of grassroots innovators, be they slum dwellers, artisans, school dropouts, illiterate farmers, and so on.

We need to encourage conversion of these innovations into profitable enterprises with appropriate measures.

Bureaucratization of the R&D Establishments: We have to ensure that our scientific institutions do not become afflicted with the culture of our governmental agencies.

Ordinarily, seniority should not displace merit. Talent should not be suppressed and individualism should not replace teamwork. Inadequate attention to these aspects sometimes results in our talented younger scientists getting frustrated.

Internal brain-drain: Closely linked to the bureaucratic culture in many of our S&T establishments is the disturbing phenomenon of internal brain-drain. Apart from the migration of significant numbers of our talented scientists and technologists abroad, we also face a problem of diversion of talent away from R&D careers to non-scientific careers in both Government and the private sector. We need to examine why a career in science is not considered worthwhile by so many of our talented younger scientists. Whatever the reasons, we must face this issue squarely, by taking visible, concrete steps to give promising scientists and technologists the necessary opportunities, recognition, standing, and adequate material compensation.

Attracting the Indian Scientific Diaspora: Another related issue is the need – and the opportunity – to attract our large and accomplished scientific Diaspora. They are more than willing to contribute to our national development. We can use their expertise in critical R&D areas. Wherever necessary, we should devise pragmatic and flexible schemes to enable them to come and work in our S&T institutions.

Scientific education: Lastly, I wish to briefly touch upon a disturbing trend. While we have several exceptional scientific and technological institutions, some others turn out graduates and post-graduates, even doctorates, of indifferent quality.

We need to reflect on this and take corrective action.

Friends, I am full of optimism about the future of Indian science. If your Today is brighter than your Yesterday, your Tomorrow will be brighter still. What is needed is pursuit of excellence with single-minded determination and dedication — not just individual excellence but institutional excellence — and making it a sustainable hallmark of the entire S&T establishment. Like in sports, achievements in science and technology are a source of national pride.

Therefore, the Nation expects you to aim higher, be ambitious and achieve big things. I am sure that our scientists and technologists will serve role models to all other participants in building a self-confident India.

Before I conclude I have to make an announcement. Dr. Joshi has made a very good suggestion that we institute an Indian Science Award of Rs.25 lakhs to be given each year. I agree to this suggestion. The selection committee will comprise eminent scientists from India and the world.

With these words, I am pleased to inaugurate the 90th Session of the Indian Science Congress.

Thank you.

12
Address to NRIs

Title: Assimilation and integration comes naturally to Indians
Author: Mr. A.B. Vajpayee, Prime Minister of India
Publication: *Organiser*
Date: December 20, 1998

I EXTEND a hearty welcome, on behalf of India, to all the Parliamentarians of Indian Origin who are participating in this conference. It is a happy day for all of us in India. And it is not a coincidence that you Parliamentarians of Indian Origin are holding your conference in the Annexe of Indian Parliament. It signifies our shared commitment to the ideals of democracy.

Democracy for us is not merely a political system. It is an integral part of India's civilisation and ethos. Not only is India a mature and vibrant democracy today, but People of Indian Origin, too,- have been promoting it in whichever part of the world they happen to live. Your conference is a proof of this fact.

For me personally, welcoming you is a matter of added satisfaction. I am also a parliamentarian like you. I have served in Indian Parliament for more than four decades. I have interacted closely with my brothers and sisters of Indian origin who have been living and working in foreign lands. This interaction has always made me marvel at their achievements in business, academics, research and other walks of life.

But today I am interacting with a very special set of people those Indians who have made a mark in the parliamentary system of their respective countries. You are very special to us because you show that India's children, who are living outside India, are now winning the trust of their fellow citizens. Friends, I am truly proud of you.

Who would have imagined that the sons and daughters, grandsons and great-grandsons of our forefathers who had left India's shores to work so hard in lands that were across the seven seas, are now legislators? Who would have imagined that in many countries, that are so very different from each other. Persons of Indian Origin could some day contest and win elections?

You imagined this, and then you did it. You have worked hard to become legislators. Your constituents are from different nationalities and cultures and religions. Yet, they have chosen to elect you, because they think that you are the best person to represent their interests.

Truly, this is a success story without parallel. Many other nations have a Diaspora. However, it is only the Indian Diaspora that has: first, settled in almost every country on this planet; second, taken up almost every profession there; third, succeeded spectacularly in everything that they have done. Finally, in spite of these achievements, they have still retained their emotional, cultural and spiritual links with Bharat, our common motherland.

Why has a person from India done well wherever he is and whatever he is doing? That is because, assimilation and integration comes naturally to Indians. Our scriptures have taught us : *Vasudhaiva Kutumbakam*—The entire world is one family. This means that we are not rootless when we settle abroad and we can accept and work with people of other cultures and religions.

Our culture and our scriptures emphasize the pursuit of knowledge. Which is why, Indian are doing so well in every knowledge-based industry. In computers, in the sciences, in management, in law, in medicine, and in all other professions. People of Indian Origin have earned a name of themselves and for India.

Our culture emphasizes the pursuit of commerce and industry. The Indus Valley civilisation was the cradle of trade. Hence, those persons of Indian origin who originally came from a part of India that had a strong commercial culture have prospered as entrepreneurs all across the world. Our culture also emphasizes the acquisition of skills. India's skilled—builders, mechanics, carpenters and technicians are valued in many parts of the world. They have established their dominance especially in the Gulf countries. The biggest source of foreign exchange for India is, indeed, the remittances of these Indians working abroad.

Be it in knowledge-based professions, trade and commerce, skilled jobs or in legislatures, what is the secret of your success? It is hard work. Every one of you has gotten where you are because you have worked much harder than others.

Indians have become known as the smartest in their profession, the cunniest business persons, and the hardest working immigrants. Today, however, the world should acknowledge that India's children are also becoming leaders in politics and community life.

The figures speak for themselves. There are two hundred legislators in nineteen countries, sixty-eight of whom are ministers, four of whom are speakers in their national legislative assemblies, and two are Prime Ministers. Dr. Chhedi Jagan in Guyana, S. Ramgoolam and Dr. Anirood Jugnauth in Mauritius, Noor Mohamed Hassanali in Trinidad reached the highest officer because of their leadership qualities.

There are many local reasons for the increasing number of Indian parliamentarians. However, being originally from India would be your most powerful reason. The values of seeking a consensus, accommodating and harmonising divergent views and lastly not seeking a hegemony over others, come naturally to persons from India. Whatever success that I have achieved in fifty years in public life, has been because of the same values.

Dear brothers and sisters, you live in different countries. As parliamentarians, you are also influential opinion makers in your respective countries. On this occasion, I would like you to know some important truths about what is happening in India and carry them to your constituents.

My Government is committed to deepening, broadening and speeding up economic reforms. We have managed our economy fairly well, in spite of many odds and constraints. At a time when many countries in Asia and elsewhere are facing the effects of financial turmoil, India has shown stability and resilience in her economic system.

The present slowdown in the economy is a passing phase. India offers excellent opportunities for investment and business—both for foreigners and, even more so for people of Indian origin.

In this context, I should gratefully acknowledge the excellent response from the people of Indian origin to the recent issue of Resurgent India Bonds. We could raise more than 4 billion dollars through these bonds. I am confident that you will respond equally positively when we decide to create similar investment opportunities in future for Indians abroad.

At the same time, I would like you to create awareness among investors and businessman in your respective countries about opportunities in India. I wish to touch upon another important issue. On May 11, India conducted nuclear tests and became a nuclear weapons nation. We took this step to strengthen our national security and also to contribute to the cause if global nuclear disarmament from a position of strength.

We are as committed to the ideal of world peace as ever. We have declared that our nuclear weapons are meant exclusively for self-defence. We will never make first-use of them, nor will we ever use them against a non-nuclear nation.

Some countries criticised our action and even imposed economic sanctions. India has shown that we will not buckle under any threat or sanctions. With the passage of time, even those who criticised us earlier have gained a better understanding of our action and our overall philosophy about disarmament.

Nevertheless, there is still a great need to educate people in foreign countries—especially politicians, businessmen, media and the intelligentsia about India's stand on the nuclear issue. I would urge you to participate in this exercise of communication and education.

I should also mention here India's contribution to peacemaking and consensus-building around the world. From Korea and Vietnam in the 1950s to Cambodia and Iraq in the 1990s, Indians have helped bring peace. In Bosnia and Somalia, Indian peacekeepers have served with distinction. The United Nations has often asked Indians to lead sensitive posts. The first commander-in-chief of the multinational peacekeeping force in Bosnia and Herzegovina was an Indian. An Indian representing the United Nations in Iraq has made an important contribution to easing of tensions there.

This strengthens my point that Indians everywhere have it in them to succeed as leaders of people who belong to different backgrounds. Friends, we are all Bharat Mata's children. I acknowledge and applaud your achievements in your respective countries. I only hope that you will, by doing better at your work, bring greater glory for yourself, your home country, and for Bharat Mata. The more you succeed, the better ambassadors of goodwill for India you become.

New Delhi

January 06, 2001

"It gives me great pleasure to join you for, the inauguration of this International Convention of Global Organisation of People of Indian Origin. Many of you have travelled great distances to attend this conference. In a sense, this is also a homecoming for you.

Today, there are nearly 20 million people of Indian origin living in almost every corner of the world. Rare is the country where you will not come across people of Indian origin. They have adopted foreign shores as their own. But neither the passage of time nor the distance between their ancestral land and their new homes has "been able to sever the umbilical cord between Mother India and her children abroad.

You are as much the inheritors of India's rich civilisational heritage as your brothers and sisters back home in India. And, we are proud that you have kept alive your distinct cultural identity even while making a place for yourselves in a foreign social and cultural milieu.

We are equally proud of the fact that people of Indian origin, wherever they may be living, have greatly enriched the society, economy and culture of their adopted countries. The success stories of Indian entrepreneurs abroad are legendary. From hi-tech chip laboratories to curry restaurants, from renowned hospitals to famous educational institutions, from well-known research centres to leading think-tanks—everywhere you will find an Indian who has overcome all odds to establish himself through skill, dedication and hard work.

Your adopted countries have benefited from your unique contributions to their social and economic transformation. You have also contributed towards enhancing awareness about India's past history, present reality and future potential.

Indeed, from the sweat and tears of indentured Indian labour toiling on colonial sugar and tea plantations in the 19th century to the intellectual achievements of the Indian software community in the Silicon Valley of the 21st century, the odyssey of the Indian community at large is a reflection of the potential of our people and the magnitude of their contribution towards global prosperity.

The Indian diaspora's contributions are not merely confined to the culture and economy of their adopted countries. Despite their numerical disadvantage, the Indian communities living abroad have made deep impressions on the political processes of their adopted countries.

The active participation of people from India in the nationalist movement in Africa as early as the beginning of the 20th century is well documented. Mahatma Gandhi's baptism in mass politics was in South Africa. His joining the struggle against racial injustice and discrimination was an event that proved to be a turning point in history — not only in South Africa but also in India.

India's struggle for independence was greatly strengthened by the substantial support of Indian communities. The India League in the UK and the Gadar Party in the USA played an important role in mobilising support for our struggle for independence. Netaji Subhash Chandra Bose and his INA received the unstinting support of Indians living in South-East Asian countries.

Between then and now, the Indian community living abroad has come to play a determining role in the politics of their adopted countries, not only as leaders of the Indian diaspora, but also as leaders in the truest sense of the term. I recall that the Commonwealth Heads of Government Summit at Durban in 1999 was attended by as many as five heads of state or heads of Government who are of Indian origin.

However, in this impressive success story, a blemish has recently crept in. We have watched with distress the overthrow of a democratically elected Government in Fiji and a series of subsequent actions that have hit at the people of Indian origin in that country and more particularly the poorer among them. The Indian diaspora abroad has an important role in mobilising public concern the world over at the events in Fiji and in seeking nothing less than a restoration in that country of due constitutional processes as enshrined in the 1997 Constitution.

Friends, I have often come across people of Indian origin who are eager to participate in India's nation-building efforts—as a tribute to the country of their origin, as a means of strengthening the bonds of love and affection that exists between them and India. The cooperation and valuable support extended by people of Indian origin and non-resident Indians during the last decade of economic liberalisation and structural reforms have greatly encouraged us and contributed to the birth of resurgent India.

Today, India stands on the threshold of a technological revolution in many areas that define the 'New Economy' of the 21st century; information technology, biotechnology, agriculture, space and energy. The Indian diaspora, has made seminal contributions to the development of many of these sectors in their adopted countries. They can now play a vital role by making a similar contribution to India in these sectors. Let me give an example: We aspire to make India a knowledge superpower by the year 2010: you can help us fulfill this aspiration.

Many of you owe your current success to the quality education which you have received in Government-run institutions, be they Indian Institutes of Technology or medical colleges. You now owe it to your motherland to associate yourself with India's search for rapid and enduring social change and economic progress.

I would like to emphasise that we do not merely seek investment and asset transfer. What we seek is a broader relationship—in fact, a partnership among all children of Mother India so that our country can emerge as a major global player. We value the role of people of Indian origin as unofficial ambassadors providing a link between India, and the rest of the world.

My Government's policy is to assist the—overseas Indian community in maintaining its cultural identity and strengthening the emotional, cultural and spiritual bonds that bind them to the country of their origin. We will provide all help to the overseas Indians in maintaining their cultural identity even while encouraging their political commitment to their adopted countries.

With this objective in mind, we have constituted a high level committee on the Indian diaspora, headed by Shri L. M. Singhvi. This Committee has been tasked to study the expectations of overseas Indians from India. It will study the role that people of Indian origin and non-resident Indians can play in the economic, social and technological progress of India. It will examine the current regime that governs your travel and stay in India as well as your investment in the Indian economy. It will recommend measures to resolve the problems faced by you.

More fundamentally, the Committee has been asked to review the status of people of Indian origin and non-resident Indians in the context of the constitutional provisions, laws and rules applicable to them both in India and the countries of their residence.

These will go a long way in developing a strong, and mutually beneficial relationship between India and the Indian diaspora.

Friends, the underpinnings of our civilisational history and cultural heritage have been the tradition of tolerance, openness to new ideas, respect for ancient wisdom, intellectual pursuit and abhorrence of violence. The people of Indian origin and non-resident Indians are a living testimony to the noble tradition of blending the old with the new.

With these words, I am pleased to inaugurate this International Convention of the Global Organisation of People of Indian Origin.

13
Conference with Chief Ministers

Speech at the Chief Minister's Conference
July 07, 1999
New Delhi

This meeting has been called in order to discuss the situation arising out of the Pakistani aggression in Kargil. Also the internal security situation as a result of hostile operations by foreign agencies and mercenaries. The consensus within the country, on the need to defeat Pakistan's plans, is heartening. I am sure our discussions today will further strengthen the national resolve. I shall brief this meeting on the military and diplomatic situation first, and then would like to hear from the assembled Chief Ministers about the internal security situation in their States.

We have seen terrorist operations master-minded by Pakistan since the early 1980's. The initial target was Punjab and we all know the consequences of that. The people of Punjab stood up to the challenge unitedly and we were able to defeat the plans of the enemy. I pay tribute also to the police in Punjab which tackled the situation with grit and determination.

After Punjab, the target has been the State of Jammu & Kashmir. Starting from 1989, extremist groups such as the JKLF, Lashkar-e-Taiba or the Harkat-ul-Ansar have been infiltrating into the State from Pakistan and committing terrorist acts against innocent people. Our Armed Forces and the Para-military had succeeded in containing this challenge also by the mid-1990's. J&K had returned to normalcy, economic activity was picking up, tourism was flourishing. In desperation, Pakistan turned to actions such as the large-scale massacre of innocent civilians. About this, too, you are familiar.

Yet again, in desperation Pakistan raised the ante. This time in Kargil. But the current action in Kargil sector represents a qualitatively new move by Pakistan. This time, the numbers are higher, they intruded to hold territory rather than simply to infiltrate. This is also the first time that Pakistan is holding out a military challenge to try and alter the LOC. Pakistan clearly miscalculated, and we have made explicit that we shall not countenance any alteration of the LOC. We categorically reject any attempt to question the validity of LOC.

This new escalation represented a challenge to our national resolve since it called into question the sanctity of the Shimla Agreement. The Services Chiefs are present and you will be briefed in detail on the conduct of operations and the readiness of our Armed Forces. I am sure you will all join me in paying a tribute to the Armed Forces for their gallant performance.

The military threat of interdiction of the Srinagar-Leh highway has been eliminated. The capture of important mountain features such as Tololing Top and Tiger Hill demonstrate the bravery and skill of our soldiers. These were extremely difficult operations and I take this opportunity of saluting the brave men who gave their lives for the protection of our security. All too often, unfortunately, our gratitude is short-lived and the sacrifices are forgotten after the campaign. Instances have been reported where promises made in the past to the soldiers or their families have not been kept. I know that several States have announced that they will provide such schemes for the families of those soldiers who have died in this campaign. This is welcome. I appeal to all the Chief Ministers to ensure that there are no delays in implementing these schemes nor should they be allowed to be forgotten.

Our military operations will continue until the last of the intruders has been driven back. There will be no stopping or scaling back until this objective has been achieved. At the same time, we are willing to give diplomacy a chance if that will enable us to achieve our objectives. For this reason, we have had some contacts with Pakistan in recent weeks. The objective is one and only one. It is the complete and unconditional withdrawal of the intruders from our side of the Line of Control. There is no other objective and no other subject that we are discussing.

We have also been in close touch with the international community. This is not an internationalisation of the Kashmir question, since they all recognise that this is a bilateral matter to be settled between India and Pakistan. We have ourselves made it clear that there is no room for third-party involvement, however well-intentioned. Nevertheless, it was important for us to explain our position.

We have had success in this regard. Russia has shown understanding and has expressed support for the action that we are taking. The United

States has clearly named Pakistan as the country responsible in the incursion. They have actively engaged Pakistan in trying to persuade that country to withdraw the intruders. In pursuit of this, the Commander-in-Chief of the Central Command of the USA, General Zinni visited Pakistan for talks with their military and civilian leaders. More recently, Mr. Nawaz Sharif has been to Washington. We are informed that Pakistan has agreed to withdraw. We will watch for results on the ground. In the meantime our operations shall continue unabated.

A little earlier, the G-8 countries had clearly recognised that the intrusion across the LoC was an irresponsible act and had called for the withdrawal of the intruders, all this points to the success of our diplomacy and the correctness of our decision to engage the outside world more actively.

However, I wish to stress that no outsider owes it to us to reverse the present incursion. We alone are responsible for safeguarding our security and protecting our interests. While we are grateful for the support and understanding of the international community, there will be no compromise on our military operations. We have therefore to continue to rely on our Armed Forces to deal with this and other challenges that are bound to come up. This obliges us to look to our defence preparedness in the future. In the 1980's, our defence spending was of the order of 3.5 per cent of our GDP. This fell below 2.5 per cent in the 1990's, which is among the lowest in the world. My Government raised the Defence Budget last year shortly after taking over. We must be realistic and recognise that our security requirements need to be met and that we are confronting an enemy who is resolute and unwilling to see reason. We have to be clear that if we will the end, we must also will the means. I believe the national consensus is changing in the light of our current experience and I hope we can tap the national mood in order to ensure that such situations do not recur in future.

Similarly, we need to guard against internal threats. Our foe is bent upon sowing terrorism and disaffection throughout the country. We are an open democratic society, and are determined to preserve our freedoms. However, the system does permit unscrupulous elements to exploit it, and to spread terror through killing innocent people. We must, therefore, increase our counter-terrorism capabilities and our vigilance. This is a long-term challenge and we have lived with it for close to two decades already. It is time to take resolute measures and to deal firmly with a situation which is threatening to escalate. I have been moved by the plight of the families of the innocent victims who have been massacred by cowardly night-attack or bombs that have been set off in various cities.

Our states must cooperate more closely in order to deal with this threat. This applies with special force to states that lie along the international border. Attempts are being made by the enemy and will continue to be made to aggravate the communal situation. We must be on our guard against this. While this requires efficient and impartial administration in the short-term, the long-term remedy is to bring to all sections of society the benefits of development without any discrimination. I look forward to hearing from the Chief Ministers their views and proposals for improving our internal security arrangements.

Some concern has been expressed in the country that the Government will accept mediation or internationalisation. I tell you categorically that this will not happen. If in our interaction with the international community we are told that Pakistan has violated the Line of Control, that it must withdraw the armed intruders from the Indian side of the LOC, that the sanctity of the LOC must be restored, that the Lahore process must be reinitiated, and we express our satisfaction with this objective reaction of the international community, it does not mean that we are seeking mediation or agreeing to internationalisation. All it means is that while our Armed Forces are doing everything to throw out the armed intruders, we are also engaged diplomatically to achieve the same purpose.

I will now request the Services Chiefs to brief this meeting on the current situation in the Kargil sector. After they have finished their briefings, they will take leave of you and we shall continue our discussions. In that I request the Hon'ble Chief Ministers to limit their intervention to not more than 10 minutes each.

Prime Minister's Concluding Remarks at the Chief Ministers' Conference

July 07, 1999
New Delhi

We have had a very focussed and fruitful discussion on the Kargil situation. Also on some of the issues relating to internal security in our country.

As many as 28 Chief Ministers, Administrators and representatives from three Union Territories, took part in the meeting. I have profited greatly from it and would like to thank all of you for sparing the time to come here and share your perspectives with us.

It is clear from our discussions that the country stands united on the need to repulse the enemy across the Line of Control. Today, we have spoken in one voice.

In spite of the many political differences, the participants in today's conference have once again upheld the principle of giving primacy to national security over everything else. Today only one determination dwells in the hundred crore hearts in India—the determination to beat back the enemy's armed aggression.

This unity is our strength. The conference of the Chief Ministers has reflected our unity and hence our strength. It boosts the morale and the fighting spirit of our jawans on the borders like nothing else does.

I, therefore, congratulate the Chief Ministers and Governments of all the States for heir unflinching support to the Armed Forces and to the Union Government in this hour of trial.

I have also been reassured by the consensus, which has been reflected in the discussions today, on the need for us to do everything possible for the families of the soldiers and airmen who have lost their lives in the current operation.

I have been touched by the spontaneous expressions of support that I have seen throughout the country from all sections of society, all of them wanting to do their bit for the brave men who are fighting to safeguard our nation's security. I am sure this must have been your experience, too.

Soon after the Kargil action started, voluntary contributions to the National Defence Fund and other funds operated by the Defence Headquarters have started pouring in—both from the country and from abroad. A meeting of the Executive Committee of the National Defence Fund was held yesterday. Several major decisions were taken at the meeting.

A very good suggestion has been made in today's conference on constituting a committee to evolve a National Policy on welfare of our jawans and ex-servicemen on a permanent and institutionalised basis. I am happy to announce the constitution of such a committee comprising the following members :

- Shri George Fernandes, Minister of Defence
- Shri Yashwant Sinha, Minister of Finance
- Shri Jyoti Basu, Chief Minister of West Bengal
- Shri N. Chandrababu Naidu, Chief Minister of Andhra Pradesh
- Shrimati Shiela Dixit, Chief Minister of Delhi
- Dr. Farooq Abdullah, Chief Minister of Jammu & Kashmir
- Shri Prakash Singh Badal, Chief Minister of Punjab
- Prof. Premkumar Dhumal, Chief Minister of Himachal Pradesh

Another welcome suggestion has been made for the erection of a fitting national martyrs memorial to all the soldiers who have laid down their lives in defence of the Motherland in all the wars since 1947. Your acclaim implies its acceptance. The Government, in consultation with all the political parties and State Governments, will soon take appropriate action in the matter.

I have also noted the support that has been expressed today for our diplomatic efforts. These are not intended in any way to blunt the cutting edge of our military, but are a supplement to those efforts. Today's conference has demonstrated the complete consensus amongst us that there shall be no internationalisation of the Kashmir question.

Some participants have referred to the joint statement issued by the US President Mr. Bill Clinton and the Pakistani Prime Minister Mr. Nawaz Sharif. This is a welcome development. I would, however, like to assure you that it does not create any scope for third-party mediation in the Kashmir issue. India is firmly committed to the principle of bilateralism in resolving this issue and there will be no deviation whatsoever from it. Indeed, the United States itself has stated that the issue should be resolved in a bilateral framework.

At today's conference we have also discussed in fairly concrete terms the internal security situation. We all recognise the need to raise our vigilance in this matter and I am sure that the Home Ministry and the various security agencies will be equal to the challenge. Corruption at the ground level is the root of many of our troubles in this regard and we must combat this particular evil with greater resoluteness than we have done so far.

Some members have made the suggestion for a Rajya Sabha session to discuss Kargil, and also the presentation of a White Paper on the subject. This suggestion was also made at the recent All-Party meeting. At both meetings, the discussions have revealed a sharp division of opinion. I shall, however, continue to evolve a consensus on the matter by examining the proposal afresh. We have already had two All-Party meetings. We will convene more meetings of the leaders of all political parties as and when necessary. Another meeting of the Chief Minister can be called.

Once again I thank you all for sparing your time and for sharing your views and analysis with me.

Thank you.

Ladies and gentlemen,

The Minister for Power has just recently announced wide-ranging initiatives on the power front. My Government will take firm decisions — and also support firm decisions of State Governments — to bring financial viability to the power sector.

The State Electricity Boards are bankrupt and need restructuring. The drain on internally raised resources has to stop. In this regard, the country should take note of the bold but painful steps the Andhra Pradesh Chief Minister, Shri Chandrababu Naidu, has taken to guard and raise the viability of power generation and distribution in his State. We also support, in this regard, the initiatives of the Orissa Government.

Towards this end, the Prime Minister's Office will directly monitor all projects capitalized at more than Rs. One hundred crores each in the areas of power, roads and bridges, dams and irrigation, telecommunication, oil and energy, railways, ports and airports. My office will seek a monthly progress report on all such projects and ensure that they are completed and commissioned on due dates.

Agriculture is the very heart of our economy and culture. Farm production has to reach a growth rate of at least 5 per cent. Otherwise our goals of overall economic growth and employment generation, as also our promise to build a Hunger-Free India by the year 2010 will remain unfulfilled. Food security on a long-term basis is our urgent and immediate concern.

The Government plans to earmark substantial Plan funds for public investment in agriculture, rural development, irrigation, horticulture, afforestation, wasteland development and related rural infrastructure. We will also pay special attention to the modernization of the agro-processing industry. It has immense potential for employment generation.

Agro-processing industry provides a critical link between the agriculturist and the urban consumer. We will strengthen this link, among other things, by encouraging collaboration between the cooperative agriculture sector and the corporate sector. Opportunities in exports of food products will be vigorously pursued.

We intend to give vastly higher policy attention to the small-scale industry and the Bhagidari sector, as these are important sources of self-employment.

This sector makes the highest contribution to the country's GDP. My Government will welcome suggestions from the CII and other Industry organizations as how to provide to this sector critical developmental inputs such as easy, adequate and timely credit; marketing infrastructure; and appropriate technology

Housing and construction are the greatest generators of productive employment, next only to agriculture and services. The National Agenda for Governance has pledged to facilitate construction of two million new housing units each year, with priority for low and middle-income family needs.

Within the next 60 days, my Government will unveil a National Housing

Policy. All impediments in the realization of our stated goals in the Policy will be removed forthwith. The Urban Land Ceiling Act will be suitably amended to facilitate realization of housing goals and to boost construction.

Information technology is an area of special importance. It has already revolutionized the world. No country can hope to develop global competitiveness if it ignores information technology.

This is one area where India can quickly establish global dominance. India can be fully competitive in this area with tremendous pay-offs in terms of income generation and creation of high quality jobs. This area also provides an alternative, attainable opportunity to Indian business and industry to become software czars. Just three Indian companies, not exactly household names, have today a market capitalization of Rupees Thirteen thousand crores. And all are also aggressively exporting. In this connection, I invite specific suggestions from trade and industry for removing any bottlenecks in the way of faster growth of the Infotech industry.

In the National Agenda, we have pledged to make India a software superpower. Within the next 30 days, we will set up a National Information Technology Task Force, which will formulate a draft National Informatics Policy.

The Government will initiate immediate steps to effect reforms in the Public Sector. These will embrace the whole gamut of imaginative restructuring, including transparent disinvestment and reducing PSU losses

Indian industry must improve its global competitiveness and strengthen its export muscle. We cannot succeed in Swadeshi development if we do not export. The new Exim Policy seeks to provide special support to our exporters.

There is a social dimension to making Indian Industry competitive. Capital-intensive structural adjustments in industrialized countries have given them a competitive edge in global markets. But they have also entailed massive lay-offs. Many of these countries have welfare schemes to cushion unemployment. India does not. Unemployment in India is more than a statistic. It means hardship and ruin for the unemployed person and his family. Sometimes even suicides. Let us keep this dimension in mind when we formulate growth strategies. In view of the rigorous time table of the World Trade Organization (WTO), I suggest that Industry and the Government sit together and draw up a schedule upto the year 2005. We should then work backwards to closely monitor our forward movement in export promotion.

Let me also say a few words on our policy towards foreign investment. Swadeshi does not mean that we do not value foreign investment. It only means that the bulk of the resources needed for our development must be mobilized by ourselves.

This is why we propose to take necessary steps to raise the rate of savings from 26 per cent of GDP at present to about 30 per cent. However, these domestic resources can, and need to be supplemented by foreign resources also. We welcome foreign investment in areas of our special priority such as infrastructure development, hi-tech, transfer of better management practices, upgradation of product quality to help export capability, and critical global marketing linkages.

I would also like to state categorically that no investor who has been given permission hitherto to operate will find the permission withdrawn or narrowed in scope. Government is a continuing entity. Towards this end, my Government will soon formulate transparent, non-discriminatory and non-discretionary policies governing Foreign Direct Investments. The Foreign Investment Promotion Board (FIPB) will be required and also empowered to give a firm "Yes" or "No" answer to every proposal involving FDI within a deadline of 60 days.

The importance of education in achieving our national objectives in growth and employment can hardly be overstated.

Enriched Human Resources are a critical input in any economic activity. In the knowledge-driven economy of today, they have become the most precious forms of capital. We need to improve quality and standards at all levels of the Education Pyramid. My Government is fully committed to promoting the cause of Total Literacy through elementary education, informal education and adult literacy.

I urge the CII and other Industry organizations to take a lead in giving an impetus to employment-oriented technical education on a massive scale. This will help the country develop much-needed primary and intermediate industry skills to improve the productivity of industry and services in cities, towns and semi-urban areas throughout the country.

Ladies and Gentlemen, as a nation, let all of us Think Big. I would particularly urge Indian Industry to —

- Draw up big plans. When the big become bigger, the small and medium players would grow up to occupy their places;
- Set up manufacturing, marketing and finance units of global size and eventually global presence;
- Develop brands and products that will rule the world;
- And, through all this, plant the proud flag of India on the map of

global business and industry in the early years of the 21st Century.

My Government is more than ready to be your partner in the realization of your dreams. Will you be a partner in the realization of my Government's agenda?

I seek the active participation of one and all in this endeavor, confident that I'll have it in full measure.

Thank you.

Speech at the Meeting with Chief Ministers on the Issue of Control and Prevention of HIV/AIDS

New Delhi,
May 22, 2001

I thank you for attending this meeting on the important issue of control and prevention of HIV/AIDS.

It has been estimated that 3.86 million people are infected with HIV in India. Recent surveys conducted by the National AIDS Control Organization have shown a high prevalence of over one per cent in the general population in the six States of Maharashtra, Andhra Pradesh, Karnataka, Tamil Nadu, Manipur, and Nagaland. The prevalence level among the STD clinic attendees is even higher. This is truly a cause of serious concern.

Experience in several African countries has shown that if the spread of the infection is not controlled at a level of one to two per cent of the general population, it leads to a geographical increase in the prevalence level. Thereafter, the situation could go out of control. The African experience has also demonstrated that the gains of development, achieved painstakingly over many years, can be nullified by a widespread AIDS epidemic. The economic and social costs of care, support, and prevention, when the HIV prevalence exceeds the level of one per cent can be more than the health budgets of developing countries.

In India, therefore, we still have an opportunity to prevent the AIDS epidemic from becoming as widespread and devastating as we see in Africa today. However, this necessitates urgent and concerted action by both the Government and the civil society.

The Government of India has earmarked substantial funds under the National AIDS Control Programme to undertake preventive measures and care and support of those already infected. A decentralized administrative mechanism has been established through the State AIDS Control Societies. These have autonomy and flexibility to implement a multi-sectoral programme. However, your leadership and support is critical and absolutely necessary to make the programme effective and to secure people's participation.

The six States that you represent are already in an advanced stage of the epidemic. These States today carry the burden of almost 75 per cent of the total estimated HIV infections in the country.

In Andhra Pradesh, seven districts have high prevalence. During the past year the State AIDS Society has initiated a number of NGO projects. It has also stepped up its awareness campaign. However, there continues to be a great deal of stigma and discrimination against those infected and their families. It is important to intensify the awareness drive based on community participation. The STD treatment facilities in both the Government and private sector need to strengthened. Referral of patients and proper care and treatment is another important challenge in the State.

Maharashtra illustrates how fast the infection can spread. The first case of HIV was detected in 1986. Today twelve districts have high prevalence. Maharashtra attracts a large number of migrant labour from all over the country. Intensive programmes for industrial workers, dock workers, slum population, and truck drivers should be strengthened. At the same time, we must expand the education programmes for youth both in schools and out of schools.

The first AIDS case in India was detected in Tamil Nadu. The latest survey has shown that six districts in the state are high prevalence districts. NGO activities in Tamil Nadu have been one of the most successful interventions undertaken in the country. However, these need to be expanded to ensure that the high-risk groups are fully covered under these programmes. Operational research has started in Tamil Nadu to use Ayurveda and Siddha drugs in clinical care of AIDS infected persons. These studies can provide us important feedback on the values of Indian System of Medicine in fighting the epidemic. These remedies can be a low cost alternative to anti-retroviral drugs.

Karnataka has ten districts that have high prevalence. We need to accelerate and expand the involvement of NGOs in Karnataka to cover all the high-risk groups. In particular, migrant labour from the northern districts of Karnataka needs special attention as many of them go to Maharashtra and Gujarat in search of employment. There are also certain social evils in this region, which contribute to the spread of HIV. These need to be countered through concerted action by social groups.

The HIV epidemic in the North East is different from that in the States, I have just mentioned. In both Manipur and Nagaland, a majority of the infections occur due to sharing of infected syringes and needles by drug users. In both these States we need to coordinate with the drug de-addition programme of the Government of India and the NGOs.

Dear Chief Ministers,

The AIDS epidemic presents a grave challenge. It seriously affects the present as well as the future development of your States. Your six States must, therefore, intensify prevention activities and focus on awareness of young people who are the most vulnerable. These should include programmes for school children, street children, and other young people to help them to adopt a responsible lifestyle. We should also actively involve religious establishments who can have a strong positive influence over large sections of our society.

Just as the world's attention is focussed on India's efforts to counter the AIDS challenge, our country's attention is focussed on your six States and how they are dealing effectively against the looming threat. Our success in these six States will greatly boost both our ability and our confidence in fighting the menace elsewhere in the country.

I wish to reassure you that the Centre will continue to partner with you in every possible way in our joint war against HIV/AIDS.

Thank you.

Speech at the Conference of Chief Ministers on WTO and Agriculture and Food Management

New Delhi,

May 21, 2001

I welcome you all to this important conference. It pertains to a subject, which both the Centre and all the State Governments regard as being central to the future direction of India's agriculture and our national economy.

It is also a subject that has engaged the attention of our kisans, like no other issue has done in the recent past. There are many apprehensions on how the unfolding WTO regime will impact Indian agriculture. Many of these apprehensions and fears are unfounded or exaggerated, as would become clear, I am sure, in the course of our discussions today.

At the same time, some of the concerns expressed by various socio-political organizations are indeed genuine. As a responsible and responsive Government, we felt it to be our duty to both allay the fears as well as deal with the legitimate concerns that all of us share.

It is out of this realization that I felt that a conference of Chief Ministers on this vital subject was urgently necessary. I thank several Chief Ministers, belonging to different parties, who made the same suggestion on their own. Since our intent is the same, and since our purpose is uninfluenced by considerations of party politics, I am confident that we will reach a broad consensus on the necessary course of action at the end of this conference.

The Government's approach to WTO and agriculture is based on our conviction that the emerging world trade regime is both a challenge and an opportunity for India. The challenges arise out of the fact that the WTO bears the birthmarks of a deeply divided world, in which the developed countries have many unfair advantages over the developing countries. India is playing an active role in mobilizing other developing countries for removing these disadvantages and establishing a truly just, equitable, and fair world trading order.

Contrary to the wrong impression being spread by some people, the record of recent years clearly shows that the Government has taken adequate measures to protect the interests of our farmers. Our hands are in no way tied to prevent us from taking further protective and promotional measures.

Since there is so much misinformation on this matter, I would like to elaborate:

- Fears have been voiced that removing Quantitative Restrictions would dramatically increase agricultural imports. There have been allegations that uncontrolled imports are hurting Indian farmers. These fears and charges have been proved unfounded. Recent data released by the Commerce Ministry shows that removing QRs has not affected either our total imports or their composition. Non-oil imports have actually decreased by 14.7 per cent in 2000-01.
- The Government has taken effective action by way of adjustment of tariff, imposition of safeguard duties, anti-dumping duties in a number of cases. We have also established a Standing Group at the Centre to function as a "War Room" for tracking and analyzing imports of three hundred sensitive items including several agricultural products.
- Since the present rates of import duty are less than the maximum possible rates, or what are called the bound rates, we have ample scope to increase our import duty still further if necessary.
- For fifteen sensitive items, whose maximum import duty had been historically set at zero or a low level, India was able to raise the maximum import duty in 1999-2000.
- India has not committed itself to providing minimum market access to other countries.
- The Agreement on Agriculture (AoA), came into force in January 1995. It has not reduced India's domestic policy options in any way. Our Minimum Support Price Scheme and the Public Distribution

Scheme can continue without any hindrance. India does not have to reduce her domestic support and subsidy to agriculture. The present level of support is below the permissible level of ten per cent of the value of agricultural production.

- India can continue to subsidize research, pest control, marketing, and providing various infrastructural support and extension services.
- India has adequate provisions under the Agreement on Agriculture to take effective steps in case of a sudden surge in imports.
- A new round of mandated negotiations on agriculture began on January 1, 2000. These negotiations will continue for two to three years. During these negotiations, we will argue strongly for a complete level playing field in global trade so that domestic producers do not suffer from any disability. The fundamental requirement of the GATT agreement since its inception, and later of the WTO, is that imports should not be subjected to more stringent rules than those applicable to domestic goods. By the same logic, imports cannot have any inherent advantages over domestic goods.

The main point I wish to make is: Let there be no doubt in anybody's mind that our national interests are supreme for our Government — and, indeed, for every other Government.

I say this with confidence because Indian negotiators at the WTO have developed sophisticated skills and sound knowledge of all the complex issues. This is in no small measure due to the intense debate that is taking place within the country on the various contentious issues thrown up by the WTO. Several State Governments have independently taken up in an in-depth study of the impact of WTO agreements on agriculture in their States. I particularly compliment Karnataka for its study, which makes many sound proposals to be implemented at the national, state, and sub-state levels. I urge other States to conduct a similar exercise, fully involving experts and all the social partners.

Dear Chief Ministers,

Liberalization of world trade in agriculture has opened up new vistas of growth. Agriculture is one of the areas in which India has an inherent strength to dominate the global markets. As we move away from an economy of scarcity to an economy of plenty, it is now both possible and necessary for us to fix our sights on the vast opportunities in the export market. At the same time, our country also stands exposed to price fluctuations in the world markets.

We cannot effectively address the issues arising out of WTO's Agreement on Agriculture, without urgently removing the many bottlenecks in food management. The success of this effort depends on the closest possible cooperation between the Centre and the State Governments. I would, therefore, like our Conference to produce a consensus action plan on some of the crucial imperatives.

Productivity Increase: A major challenge before us is to reduce costs and raise the productivity and quality of agricultural produce to global standards. This is necessary both to increase our exports and to ensure affordable food to our households, so that all our one billion people have nutritional security.

The possibilities of expansion of farm area are minimal. Hence, future increases in production have to come essentially through major improvements in productivity. For this, we need to quickly remove the obvious constraints such as scarcity of power, inadequate irrigation facilities, and poor rural infrastructure. This task also calls for a significant increase in science and technology inputs in agriculture, improved extension services, and raising the educational levels of our farmers.

It is highly disturbing that we waste enormous quantities of foodgrains, horticultural produce, vegetables, and the produce of the livestock and fisheries for want of adequate storage, post-harvest, and processing facilities. We can ill-afford to incur such huge losses. I would urge the State Governments to make full use of the many schemes for the construction of cold storages, rural godowns, etc. unveiled by the Centre recently, including the big opportunities in the National Storage Policy.

Falling public investment in agriculture is a matter of serious concern. Both the Centre and the States should use the available limited resources more efficiently, especially for capital formation. In addition, we must devise attractive policies to encourage private investment in agriculture, especially in extension services.

Crop diversification: Our strategy to raise foodgrains production has somehow remained confined to only two crops, namely wheat and rice. The production of coarse cereals has stagnated at about 30 million tonnes since the last thirty years. The production of pulses has in fact declined slightly since 1970. This is alarming. We need to revamp our strategy to attain self-sufficiency in pulses and edible oils.

Another attractive area of diversification is horticulture. The Government has recently approved a Technology Mission for Integrated Development of Horticulture to foster the rapid growth of the North Eastern Region. Similarly, the Eastern States, which have ample groundwater and fertile soil, need to be encouraged to become another national granary.

Procurement, Stocking, and Distribution: Our policy on procurement, movement, and stocking of farm produce originated when India was still suffering from scarcities. Now, although we have moved into an era of plenty, our policies and procedures have not changed suitably.

We have today surplus foodstock in our godowns whose value is estimated to be over Rs. 50,000 crore. The cost of centralized procurement, storage, and distribution is unacceptably high. This has resulted in both higher subsidies and higher issue prices. This has serious administrative and fiscal consequences, both for the Centre and for the States. Therefore, the time has come to look for better alternatives that will help the farmer, the consumer, as well as the Government.

As a first step, we propose to restructure the Food Corporation of India. This year's Budget has unveiled a new system of decentralized, state-level procurement and distribution. Instead of providing subsidized foodgrains, financial assistance will be provided to the State Governments to enable them to procure and distribute foodgrains to BPL families at subsidized rates. Since many State Governments are still unclear about the advantages of this new initiative, I would like the Finance Minister to give an exposition to the Chief Ministers.

The eminent agricultural scientist, Dr. M. S. Swaminathan, has made an interesting suggestion on the setting up of community grain banks to be administered by panchayats. Such ideas also deserve our serious attention.

Restriction of movement and stocking of agricultural produce has prevented farmers from getting the best price. Therefore, we should review the operation of the Essential Commodities Act and remove all restrictions on free inter-state movement of goods. Besides, the various Control Orders that limit the stocking of farm produce also require an urgent re-look.

Asset creation in rural areas: We must find an effective solution to the present anomaly between surplus foodgrains and hungry stomachs. It is both possible and necessary to improve our implementation of "Food for Work" programmes to create durable rural assets. However, this cannot be done without strengthening our district administration and increasing the monitoring role of panchayats. States need to learn from one another's success stories in this as well as in other areas.

A major programme where surplus foodgrains could be used for asset creation is the National Rural Roads Project. This is an ambitious attempt to achieve universal rural connectivity before 2007. It will also mak a big contribution to employment generation and improving farm incomes. I appeal to all of you to extend your full support in this scheme's speedy and effective implementation.

I would like to conclude by restating the obvious: India can avoid the pitfalls and seize the prospects of freer global trade in agriculture only if we treat this as a national mission. This calls for collective and coordinated action by the Central and State Governments, and all those who are associated with agriculture and the food economy, like agricultural universities, Krishi Vigyan Kendras, farmers' cooperatives, credit institutions, and of course our hard working and innovative kisans. Let us fully mobilize the vast pool of our people's traditional knowledge, just as we harness the latest advances in technology. Let us together resolve to make India a leading agricultural power in the world in the 21st century.

Thank you.

14
The Labour Problem

Speech at the Inauguration of the 37th Indian Labour Conference
New Delhi,
May 18, 2001

Friends, I am happy to be with you today to inaugurate the 37th Session of the Indian Labour Conference.

The Agenda prepared for discussion in this session of the ILC clearly spells out the Government's commitment to labour welfare. It also presents our overall perspective on labour reforms and our specific approach to the immediate tasks on hand. I am happy to note that action has been taken on many conclusions arrived at in the last session held a year ago. I urge speedy action on the remaining decisions.

This session of the ILC is taking place at a critical point in the development of our national economy. India has embarked on an ambitious path of nation building to meet the legitimate aspirations of our one billion citizens. The non-fulfillment of even the basic needs of a large section of our population, more than five decades after Independence, is a reality that our people find totally unacceptable. With the passage of time, this unacceptability is breeding impatience, which too is legitimate.

Given that our country is blessed with bountiful natural resources and a large population of talented and hard-working people, there can be no reason:

- why a single Indian should go to bed with a hungry stomach;
- why a single Indian should be without a good roof over their head;
- why any Indian family should be deprived of other basic amenities of life;
- and why any Indian youth should be tormented by the worry of unemployment.

However, if such is still the sad reality for tens of millions of our brethren, it only means that we have failed to build an economy that harnesses the full potential of our natural and human resources. It shows that our economy is forced to function under the heavy weight of many growth-hindering rules, regulations, laws, and systems. These are self-imposed constraints. They are preventing our economy from growing to its full potential and, thus, eradicate poverty and unemployment.

It is out of this realization that our country embraced the principle of economic reforms a decade ago.

This momentous shift in our economic thinking and policies did not mean then — nor does it mean now — that most of what India did in the first four decades of Independence was wrong. Such an interpretation of economic reforms — and I know that some sections of our intelligentsia think so — would be highly erroneous. Indeed, it would be counter-productive.

There can be no denying that India has made significant socio-economic progress since Independence. This is primarily because of the strong and self-reliant base of industry and agriculture that was laid in the initial decades of Free India. Specifically, our impressive achievements in industrialization were due to the dominant role played by our Public Sector Undertakings. Our organized workforce made a valuable contribution to this.

In course of time, however, our economic policies and laws developed rigidities. They failed to respond to the changing needs and opportunities, both nationally and internationally. Our private sector was shackled by many unnecessary restrictions. The worst hit were our small and medium enterprises, which have the highest potential to create employment and wealth.

Many of our government-run undertakings, in which the country had made enormous sums of public investment, started to produce very poor or even negative returns. Similarly, our policies and laws prevented both the public sector and the private sector from effectively responding to the challenges as well as the opportunities of a rapidly integrating and highly competitive global economy. We were also slow in recognizing the revolutionary ways in which new technologies were re-designing the landscape of manufacturing, investment, business management, and trade.

India's decision in the early '90s to effect economic reforms was an inescapable answer to this internal compulsion and external necessity.

Since the early nineties, successive governments at the Centre have carried these reforms forward. Our own Government has been steadily broadening and deepening the scope of reforms. Realizing both the need and benefits of reforms, several State Governments are also moving ahead on the same path. Thus, nearly the entire political spectrum has participated in the promotion of economic reforms, indicating that a broad national consensus on the subject already exists.

To strengthen this consensus, we must constantly review the content of economic reforms in the light of our own positive and negative experiences, as well as the experience of other countries. My Government welcomes such debate both inside and outside Parliament. It helps all of us to gain a clearer understanding of what should be done and how it should be done.

Such healthy debate,

- which is rooted in sound economic logic,
- which is not influenced by any political and sectional considerations,
- and which is guided by the long-term interests of all constituents of the nation, will strengthen both our economy and our democratic system.

At the same time, it will also underscore the necessity and urgency of speeding up reforms.

During my recent visits abroad, I have seen how even countries in the developing world, which are much smaller than India, have progressed far ahead of us. Many of you too have seen or known this. The world is not going to wait for us, if we choose to be slow and half-hearted in our reform march. Delay and dithering in doing what is decidedly in the interest of the nation, is going to harm our people's welfare.

This will also seriously imperil India's capacity to effectively engage the world in security and other matters.

Friends, I am being as candid as is possible on this platform because I am convinced — and I know that many of you are also convinced — that there is a lot at stake in the success of our economic reforms.

Some of you might wonder why I am sketching this larger picture about the need to accelerate the reform process at a session of the Indian Labour Conference. I am doing so deliberately, to drive home my conviction that labour, understood in the broadest sense of the term, can make the greatest contribution to the success of our reforms. I am convinced that workers and the poor will also be the principal beneficiaries of the success of our reforms.

A sea-change is taking place in the economic environment of our country as well as the world, after the advent of the WTO. Businesses are being forced to reorient themselves to face tough competition, both within the country and globally. There is simply no alternative to raising the efficiency of our production units, reducing costs, and improving the quality of our goods and services. Needless to add, such re-orientation is impossible without the ability to restructure labour within individual businesses.

This situation has given rise to divergent responses from employee and employer organizations. Trade unions perceive a threat to employment in economic reforms. Both private entrepreneurs and PSU managements, on the other hand, think that reforms introduced so far are not yielding optimal results because they are not fully complemented by administrative, judicial, and labour reforms.

Similarly, workers have apprehensions that any change in the existing labour laws will place them at the mercy of employers, reducing the many rights and safeguards that they have won through years of struggle. On the other side, it is strongly argued that the present labour laws and institutions provide job security and other safeguards without any linkage to productivity and efficiency.

I feel that there is merit in both perceptions. Recognizing the problem and its ramifications is half the battle won. Thereafter, the challenge before us is how to balance and harmonize these divergent views in the larger interests of achieving faster, multi-sectoral growth. My Government is engaged in precisely this endeavour. I seek the cooperation of trade unions and all other concerned organizations in this national effort.

I urge all of you to view the proposed amendments to the labour laws in the broader perspective of how we can make our economy grow faster — at a sustainable rate of eight to nine per cent. To term these labour reforms as anti-labour, as some people are doing, is misleading. They are pro-labour because they are pro-employment. They seek to protect Indian industries and businesses by enabling them to become more competitive, more profitable, grow faster, and, hence, employ more people both directly and indirectly.

Often some people put the entire blame for industrial sickness and uncompetitiveness of Indian businesses on our inflexible labour laws. This is wrong. Worse, such argument seeks to cover up wilful misuse of funds and mismanagement of enterprises by the employers. The Government will take firm action against those who indulge in such criminal practices that defraud both our workers and our financial institutions.

I would like to reassure our workers that their interests would be fully protected, even as we rationalize some of the outdated labour laws. This assurance is a natural corollary of my Government's commitment to pursue reforms with a human face. Enterprise without empathy, commerce without compassion, and development without dignity of labour have no place in our national ethos.

Which is why, one of the main issues for discussion in this session is, how to further expand the scope of social security for our workers. No economic development can sustain itself without an in-built assurance of social justice. At present, only ten per cent of the work force, most of it in the organized sector, is covered under formal security arrangements. The Government is fully committed to expand the social security coverage to include the vast majority of workers in the unorganized sector.

In this year's Budget, we have announced the launch of the Khetihar Mazdoor Bima Yojana. I would request this assembly of experts to recommend how we can cast the social security net wider, especially to benefit those in the most vulnerable categories, such as rickshaw pullers, roadside vendors, and others in the informal sector, which sustains the livelihood of the largest section of our workforce.

Social dialogue, which is the basis of our labour policy, has acquired a special relevance in the context of our resolve to implement economic reforms speedily. There is a need for continuous consultation among the Government, labour unions, employer organizations, and other social partners. Indeed, none of these dialogue partners is an adversary of the other.

Just as economic reforms demand that the Government and managements reform themselves, they also require the trade unions to reform themselves to better serve the interests of the Indian working class. It is the collective national duty of all of us to think, plan, and work together so that we can evolve a common energizing vision to boost productivity, production, and competitiveness of the Indian economy.

On this occasion, I would like to assure our PSU workers that their interests would be fully protected in our ongoing programme to restructure government-owned enterprises. Training and retraining for redeployment of workers is an important component of this commitment. I agree that the period of transition could be slightly difficult. Ultimately, however, the results will be rewarding for workers, their enterprises, and for the entire country.

I am happy to note that you will also be discussing the impact of globalization on Indian industry and labour. There is a need to study this issue more closely and from various angles. Experience so far shows that globalization has an uneven and iniquitous impact on different countries. Within a country, too, it affects different sectors of the economy differently. Therefore, we need to have a deeper understanding of the cross-currents and complexities of globalization.

Nevertheless, two things are certain. One, no country can ignore multilateral and bilateral obligations in today's world. The need to expand regional cooperation also imposes its own imperatives. Therefore, we have to carefully calibrate the pace and extent of external liberalization to fully protect and promote our national interests. Our Government is doing precisely this.

The other thing that I am certain about is that economic reforms will greatly benefit our country and our people. A well-conceived strategy to gain wider access to export markets, especially in developed countries, could give a big boost to Indian businesses. This will fuel faster growth and create still more employment opportunities.

New technologies also have the potential to create new businesses, which can employ hundreds of thousands of our educated young men and women. The global dominance that our IT sector is gaining, with its promise to bring huge export earnings, is perhaps the best example that India can indeed reap the benefits of globalization.

We are keenly awaiting the report of the Second Labour Commission, which is expected by the end of this year. I am confident that the report would throw useful light on many issues and guide the Government in its progressive evolution of policies and programmes for the welfare of labour.

With these remarks, I declare the 37th session of the Indian Labour Conference open and wish it all success.

Thank you.

Vajpayee and Fernandes at Bokaro Rally

February 9: Atal Bihari Vajpayee accompanied with George Fernandes of the Samata Party, among others, addressed huge rallies at Bokaro and Jamshedpur. He also met with newsmen at the Ranchi airport.

In his address he: promised the creation of a Vananchal State in just a few months after the election is completed and the new Assembly sworn in. He informed the people that the cabinet's proposal has already been sent to the President. As soon as the new Assembly convenes, the president will send the Bill for its consideration and recommendation. He assured the masses that the economic loss that the rest of the State will suffer due to this separation will be compensated by the Centre.

For the prevailing widespread lawlessness in Bihar, he held the Congress and leftist parties responsible, in addition to the RJD. He reminded people that it was to control and improve the situation that his government had imposed President's Rule on the State. But thanks to the collaboration of the Congress and leftist parties, his government was forced to lift up President's Rule.

He held the Congress and the leftists equally responsible for the prevailing condition in Bihar. Hence, he exhorted the people to completely repudiate these parties and the RJD at the polls.

He accused the Laloo-Rabri government to be neck-deep in corruption. He blamed them for siphoning off central funds given to the state for its development.

He challenged the people that only they have to realize how wrong it is for the Laloo-Rabri government to misuse the crores of rupees sent for people's upliftment while 58 per cent of its population lives below the poverty line.

He expressed his confidence that the NDA is bound to come to power in the coming election. He assured the people that there would be no problem for a coalition government to work smothly in Bihar as it is working at the centre. He did not leave the issue of chief-ministership untouched, a topic Laloo keeps harping on. Vajpayee assured the crowd that as in any democracy that will be decided only after the elections are completed, and it will be decided by democratic process by members of the ruling party.

At Jamshedpur on learning that in view of the heightened security arrangements people had to walk on foot for about 2 kms to reach the venue, he expressed his regret and apologized to the crowd. "*Mein pradhanmantri kya bana hoon, meri wajah se aane-jaane ke raaste bund ho jate hain. Suraksha prabandh hone chahiye, per yehan suraksha prabandh zaroorat se jyada hai*", declared the Prime Minister at the very beginning of his address. He went on to add: "*Suraksha aur nagarik suvidha donon saath saath honi chahiye aur agar aisa nahi hota hai to yeh suraksha vyavastha ki khami hai.*"

According to eyewitnesses, the meeting ground looked more like a cantonment than a civic meeting ground with paramilitary forces also present in large number in addition to the local police.

15
Foreign Policy

Speech by Singapore Prime Minister Goh Chok Tong at the State Banquet Hosted by Prime Minister Shri Atal Bihari Vajpayee on,
New Delhi, 8 April, 2003

Your Excellency Prime Minister Shri Vajpayee
Distinguished Guests
Ladies and Gentlemen

I am pleased to be back in India, and among good friends. On behalf of my delegation, I would like to express our deepest appreciation for your generous and warm hospitality. We felt your kindness even before we arrived. I refer to the honour you have bestowed on Singapore, by according us two state visits within three months—President S R Nathan's visit in January, and now, mine.

This is my fourth visit to India as Prime Minister, my first being in 1994. This visit has special significance for our two countries. Both Prime Minister Vajpayee and I have agreed to launch negotiations for a Comprehensive Economic Co-operation Agreement (CECA) between Singapore and India. This heralds a new phase in our bilateral relations.

Your Excellency,

It has been possible for us to do this because of your strong and far-sighted leadership. The Indian people share my confidence in your government. Your National Democratic Alliance government passed the five-year mark just a week ago. As you mentioned on that occasion, this is no mean feat for such a large and diverse coalition. I extend my warmest congratulations to you. The political stability you have achieved has boosted investor interest in India.

Your other achievements are equally impressive. Your government has launched several projects for the modernisation of the Indian economy and the alleviation of poverty. There has been significant liberalisation in the financial and telecommunication sectors. And the world now regards India as a software superpower. If economic and national development may be compared to cricket, then there are certainly many world-class talent batting for India. In your IT professionals, literary talent and scientists, India has demonstrated its ability to compete with the best in the world.

Your Excellency,

Over the past ten years, I have had the privilege of witnessing substantial growth in our bilateral ties. In particular, our economic co-operation has been intensifying. Since your visit to Singapore in April last year, no fewer than six Singapore trade delegations have visited key cities in India to explore business and investment opportunities. The areas of interest are wide-ranging, including highways, ports, special economic zones, tourism and hospitality, healthcare and education. There is this surge of interest among Singapore companies because they are confident of the economic reforms and market liberalisation taking place here. They have found new synergies between Singapore's management capability and India's human resources. Singapore was the 8th largest investor in India in 2001.

Investment activity has not been one-way. There are now over 300 Indian companies in Singapore, using Singapore as a business hub for their operations in the Asia Pacific region. We warmly welcome more Indian companies to set up base in Singapore.

Trade ties between Singapore and India are also strong. In fact, despite the global economic downturn in recent years, bilateral trade has continued to grow. Singapore remains India's largest trading partner in ASEAN, with total trade amounting to almost S$7 billion in 2001.

The CECA between Singapore and India will deepen and broaden our already robust economic relations. It will also enhance our mutual complementarity and competitiveness. Our common goal must be to increase connectivity between India and Singapore, not only for the flow of investment, goods and services but also the movement of talent and ideas. This will strengthen the web of relations between India, Singapore and ASEAN.

Your Excellency,

In this last regard of strengthening India's relations with ASEAN, I am encouraged to know that India and Thailand are also working on a free trade agreement (FTA). Your FTA with Thailand and the CECA with Singapore send a positive signal about India's seriousness in engaging ASEAN.

We should therefore aim to make good progress in the CECA, and the India-Thailand FTA, by the ASEAN-India Summit later this year. They are important building blocks for the ASEAN-India FTA which Prime Minister Vajpayee so boldly proposed at the ASEAN-India Summit last year. All these initiatives will provide a good foundation for a vibrant economic community in Asia.

Indeed, India will play a key role in the stability and progress of Southeast Asia this century. Your country has long, historical links with our region. India's economic success will generate a tremendous amount of spin-offs for all of us. When both China and India do well, these two wings will lift Southeast Asia to higher growth. Excellencies Distinguished Guests Ladies and Gentlemen May I now invite you to join me in a toast: to the good health and success of Prime Minister Vajpayee; to the peace and prosperity of the people of India; and to a lasting friendship between our two countries.

The growing hubris-driven, illiberal, intolerant nationalism in India falsifies and glorifies the country's "Hindu" past. It is viscerally hostile to Pakistan, but servile to the United States.

Have Indians reached such a point of moral degeneration and self-brutalisation that plotting to assassinate Pakistan's leaders becomes the ultimate test of "patriotism" for the country's youth? A terrible story from Shivpuri in Madhya Pradesh, not far from Gwalior, suggests that this may be actually happening. This is the story of two boys, Pinku (10) and Rinku (17), who wanted to become the "heroes of the nation" by avenging the December 13 attack on Parliament House — by assassinating Pervez Musharraf, no less.

Brought up on a daily diet of Bollywood-style "patriotism", and hero-worship of the Knights in Shining Armour who take on the mighty with their macho strength, Pinku and Rinku decided that India must wage war on Pakistan, or else they would become good "patriotic" terrorists, buy arms, smuggle themselves into Pakistan, and go and kill Musharraf.

On January 11, they kidnapped Shanu, the eight-year-old son of a businessman, for ransom, with which to procure the weapons for the Great and Holy Deed of killing Musharraf the Monster. Driven as they were by the role-models offered in films such as Gadar and Indian, and Fiza and Mission Kashmir, they hatched a plot to hold the boy, Shanu, hostage and collect the money they needed to execute their plan.

But once they abducted Shanu, they realised they could not really hide him anywhere. Nor could they invent credible alibis, nor even ways of collecting the ransom. They panicked and strangled him to death with a shoelace. According to *The Telegraph* (January 21), the boys confessed to their crime, but the district authorities believe that their motivation was indeed "patriotic".

It is tempting to discount this gory incident as a mere aberration, a rare case of "juvenile delinquency" coupled with "misguided patriotism", as exposure to "too much Bollywood", and so on. But it warrants serious, sober, reflection on the kind of values we are imparting to a whole generation of young people — through textbooks, through extremely competitive merit-ranking at school, through cinema and television, through accepted but aggressive patterns of behaviour in the street, and more generally, through our general social and political discourse.

These values have long glorified maleness, raw power, violence, aggression and war, and "normalised" or routinised cruelty. For years, India's "popular" cinema and television have shamelessly promoted negative, hate-driven images of heroes as well as vamps and villains. This phenomenon has recently got even more perverse as the hero and the villain have merged, and the vamp has become the quintessential bride-dancer whom wedding parties emulate, especially in northern India. The cynical depiction of violence and aggressive behaviour has kept pace with sex and sleaze in the mass media.

Take education. Many of our schools, cast in the post-colonial "nation-building" tradition, valorise military-style discipline and a stressfully competitive view of "achievement" and excellence. The typical child grows up believing that hubris and pride in India's "inherent" greatness and moral-cultural superiority is a "normal" characteristic of the good citizen. The tone and tenor of school and college debates has become increasingly raucous under the influence of the same kind of aggressive nationalism.

This nationalism is self-aggrandising. It pits itself against reason, logic and truth. It constructs indefinitely continuous communities (for example, "Hindus", from the Vedic period, followed by the rise of Buddhism, through the Brahminical-caste consolidation phase, and the Bhakti movement, to the late medieval period), where none existed. This nationalism validates aggressive and militarist notions of power relations as part of "human nature". Thus, India is "naturally" great. It has always been. Millions of Indians are being drilled and coached into believing 'Mera Bharat Mahan'!

Human Resource Development Minister Murli Manohar Joshi and his people in the National Council for Educational Research and Training, and numerous other institutions, have added a particularly toxic ingredient to this already foul cocktail of values and prejudices by saffronising education and rewriting history. This enterprise, a veritable cultural counter-revolution in itself, has been subjected to so much incisive criticism that it is unnecessary to recall the factual inaccuracies, the lies and half-truths, the indelible ethnic-religious prejudices, and the sophistry and irrationality that suffuse it.

The larger, central, overwhelming, purpose of Joshi and Co's project is to "prove" that India is the greatest civilisation and culture in world history, that virtually everything valuable in the "ancient" world was derived from India. This "ancient" periodisation can be arbitrarily stretched to the 10th or even the 13th century, as in the case of the Konark or Lingaraja temples of Orissa or the Nataraja temple of Chidambaram. Joshi claims that it is now "proved" that the river Saraswati actually existed. The other day he proudly announced the discovery of a 7,500 year-old "civilisation" in the Gulf of Cambay — a strange thing for a Minister to do in the absence of an academic paper, and when the "finds" there are still under interpretation and in need of corroboration.

The concept of nationalism involved here is ethnic—religious and cultural. It conceives of India as a quintessentially traditional society. It cannot accommodate modernist notions of universal values, political identity or citizenship. It demands total, blind, loyalty to the woolly concept of an "Eternal India", which is further mystified and deified as "Bharat Mata".

In this view, respect, or rather reverence, for the nation is based on unquestioning devotion to the abstract notion of India's "inherent" greatness and its unique superiority, its spectacular, unmatched achievements in all fields. These are grossly exaggerated and mystified. (For instance, Rashtriya Swayamsevak Sangh sarsanghchalak K.S. Sudarshan claimed in his last Vijayadashami address that an Indian had built and flown an airplane in Baroda years before the Wright Brothers did so — a ludicrous assertion!)

In this scheme, pride in one's nation is premised upon disdain for, or hatred of, other nations or identities. Islam and Muslims have functioned as the Other longest of all within this ethnic-nationalist demonology. Everything that is "Eastern", but other than Indian, is trivialised, minimised, parodied or reviled. This could be Persian or Chinese, or from Sumer or Sri Lankan. These cultures are considered at best derivative (and unimportant) in relation to India. The "true", essential, authentic, subject of the Nation is one particular community. "Others" can be accommodated on its fringes. But that is because 'We' are tolerant, not because India is plural.

In the contemporary context, this hatred of the Other gets focussed upon Pakistan, which is demonised as a country, society, state and regime which is inherently inimical to India and with which peaceful co-existence is virtually impossible. Pakistan is credited with virtually mystical powers to subvert and destabilise India and create havoc. As in the classical Savarkar formulation, Pakistan is the external manifestation of the eternal "internal" threat embodied by Muslims — just as Indian Muslims represent Pakistan's Fifth Column.

India's sheer size allows the votaries of this nationalism to look at our other neighbours (barring China) as dwarfs, midgets and non-entities compared to the Indian giant. India is unique, India is exceptional, India is unmatched, India is eternal. This is precisely the kind of nationalism that Rabindranath Tagore described as a "great menace". As he put it: "It is the particular thing which for years has been at the bottom of India's troubles".

This toxic, aggressive, exclusive, competitive, belligerent nationalism is the very opposite of a relaxed, self-confident, inclusive view of the nation and the world. It binds and encloses. It does not liberate. In fact, it lacks a progressive character. It is not anti-imperialist. At least no longer. It does not question the skewed distribution of power in the world. It accepts the dominant-dominated duality as the "natural" order, but wants India to be the cock of the walk.

This nationalism kowtows to the powerful, the dominant, the hegemonic. In its present form, it is servile to "the West", in particular to the United States, just as it is arrogant towards "the East" (minus India, of course, which being Aryan, "really" belongs to the West). Nothing illustrates this better than the Indian official reception to Musharraf's landmark address of January 12, and the growing intimacy between the Vajpayee government and President George W. Bush, now leading to dangerous liaisons in intelligence-sharing and even ground-level operations.

Musharraf in his speech set out to do something exceptionally bold: undermine a major part of the foundation of his own state (namely extremist political Islam). This is the sharpest and most comprehensive criticism of ethnic-religious fundamentalism voiced by the head of any South Asian state in the past half-century. Musharraf minced no words in laying out Pakistan's pathology, marked by its mix of Islam and politics, the military and the mullahs, the Taliban and terrorism. He posed the choice for Pakistan clearly: between a "theocratic state" and a modern, moderate, liberal, tolerant society.

Musharraf also told *jehadi* militants not to mess around with other countries, whatever the offence to Islam there. Implicit here is the view that Pakistan has paid dearly by pandering to pan-Islamic ideas. Musharraf has since cracked down on *jehadi* militants, arresting 2,500 of them. He may have started cutting the umbilical cord between the Pakistani state and political Islam, and proceeded to dismantle communal electorates.

Musharraf has launched only "half a revolution". His reform agenda lacks a "perspective from below", one that arises from the struggles of the working people. It has no economic content worth the name. Musharraf's chosen agency for his reform "from above" is none other than the Pakistani state, a thoroughly corrupt, compromised and unreliable entity. He may not succeed. Formidable forces are arrayed against him.

To point this out is one thing, to term his address an exercise in "deception" or "doublespeak" is quite another. This approach ridicules the very possibility of reform in Pakistan by declaring it irredeemable. Indian leaders have at best been grudging and mean-spirited in acknowledging that Musharraf has done something remarkable. Thus, L.K. Advani called the address "path-breaking", but only for its domestic agenda. Vajpayee only saw some "positive elements" in it.

This leaves one wondering if this parsimonious response has something to do with the Bharatiya Janata Party's general fear of secularisation and modernisation—contrasted to its own agenda of turning India into a morass of obscurantism, superstition and communal prejudice.

Contrast this with the Vajpayee government's kowtowing to the US never before has any Indian government so pusillanimously colluded with hegemonic US moves in this region or actively invited American interference in its internal affairs. Vajpayee & Co not only uncritically supported the US "war on terrorism" with all its excesses and its devious manipulation of the United Nations. They did not let out even a squeak of protest or concern at the US' current construction of four military bases in Pakistan.

It allowed an agent of the Federal Bureau of Investigation to visit Kolkata after the recent "terrorist" attack just as it welcomed a whole stream of FBI, Defence Intelligence Agency (DIA), "counter-terrorism" and other officials. According to *The Telegraph* (January 21 and 22), it is about to launch joint operations along with US agencies to stop possible terrorist infiltration and activities in Jammu and Kashmir. The Indo-US Joint Working Group, which met in New Delhi in the third week of January.

has announced a broad range of "cooperative" activities including "political, diplomatic, military, intelligence and financial measures".

India has "welcomed" a US "pilot project" involving equipment and technology to strengthen "border management and surveillance". The two sides reportedly also discussed "forensic cooperation" and added aviation security to their agenda, and placed "special stress" on ways to beef up intelligence and investigative cooperation, including the possibility of access to each other's databases on terrorists.

This goes far beyond "intelligence sharing", even "cooperative monitoring" through agencies such as the Sandia National Laboratories of New Mexico, a well-known US weapons design and production facility. On the cards are "joint operations" on the ground, for which the way may have been paved by the visit of DIA chief Admiral Thomas Wilson to the Kashmir Valley, including to "sensitive" border areas. This spells serious interference in India's affairs and erosion of its sovereignty, with potentially dangerous consequences.

Economy to Grow by over 6 per cent this year, says PM

Prime Minister Atal Bihari Vajpayee today said the economy will grow by over six per cent this financial year. 'This is coupled with modest inflation, comfortable foreign exchange reserves and outward looking policies," he said.

But the government's target for the future is higher. "Our intention is to double per capita income within one decade. This means an annual GDP growth of eight to nine per cent." the Prime Minister added while delivering the inaugural address at the India Economic Summit 2000 organised by the World Economic Forum and the Confederation of Indian Industry.

Vajpayee also disclosed that fresh contracts for over 2,500 km of road construction (under the golden quadrilateral programme) will be awarded by March 2001. "New contracts at this level will continue for several years for enabling us to build a 6,000-km road network by 2003 and another 7,000 km by 2007," he said.

The Prime Minister went on to add that as many as 10 power projects will attain financial closure by end-March 2001. Also, Electricity Bill, 2000 is in the offing.

According to Vajpayee, the government's focus in the last one year has been on improving the quality of the national infrastructure. Highlighting some of the achievements of his government, he made a mention of the total deregulation of the telecom sector which has led to considerable private investment into the sector.

A strategic management group in the Prime Minister's Office is meeting every week to hasten the pace of implementation of government policies, Vajpayee said. "I am receiving support from Chief Ministers many of whom have set up similar monitoring groups for their state governments." The Prime Minister added.

Vajpayee acknowledged that there was evidence of global slow-down. But, he was hopeful that India's business environment will improve steadily and significantly. "This will encompass policy-making, procedures and implementation," he said. Earlier in his address, the Prime Minister outlined nine steps to strengthen industry-government relationship which would allay fears about globalisation. "The privilege of being a global player must be matched with the responsibility of making the process universally acceptable by making it universally beneficial," he said.

AB Vajpayee with Gerhard Schroeder in Berlin. (Reuters)

Berlin, May 29: Singing paeans to the inclusive character of Indian democracy, Prime Minister Atal Bihari Vajpayee urged Germany to "reform old mindsets" and not see India through a restrictive South Asian prism. He argued that "the remnants of Cold War ideologies" which promoted this view should be eliminated.

Germany, Vajpayee suggested, should act on its understanding of "India's global presence" and not see it in a restrictive regional perspective.

Addressing a meeting of MPs of the German lower house of parliament, the Bundestag, Vajpayee appeared hurt that people often did not recognise the enormity of India's achievements.

Vajpayee criticised the West for its two-faced attitude to terrorism. He said India had suffered both from terrorism as well as "from the consequences of the double standard applied by countries to deal with terrorism in different places".

He said correct lessons needed to be learnt from the events of 9/11 or else the fight against terrorism would not succeed.

There were two important lessons of September 11 and its aftermath, he felt. First, the reach of terrorism could be countered comprehensively only through global cooperation. Second, and perhaps more important lesson in Vajpayee's eyes, "we cannot and should not, negotiate with terrorism or differentiate between its various constituent elements".

He argued that "our success against terrorism will depend on how well we have learnt this lesson".

Terrorism, Vajpayee claimed, targeted democratic societies because they "seek peace, protect freedoms, permit dissent and value consensus" and terrorism aims to destroy these attributes. He said that though India continued to suffer from cross-border terrorism, he was seeking peace with Pakistan to inspire action to end the menace and the infrastructure which supports it. He urged all friends of India to use their influence on Pakistan to make this happen.

The Prime Minister claimed that India's achievements in building a vibrant democracy were often not appreciated. India, despite a high illiteracy rate, with no experience of universal adult franchise before Independence and, despite the doubts expressed about its democratic future at that time, had nurtured democracy well.

India, he said, had successfully preserved its multi-cultural, multi-ethnic and multi-religious social fabric within a constitutional, democratic and federal framework. It had institutionalised fundamental freedoms, human rights and the rule of law. The change of governments in India happened through "a peaceful, non-violent expression of popular will".

However, packing a punch against those who did not give India credit for these achievements, Vajpayee said: "As I look around at the functioning of real and sham democracies around the world, I sometimes feel that the enormity of India's achievements in this direction is not fully appreciated."

Although he did not mention the name of any "sham democracies", one could be forgiven for wondering whether this was not a broadside against Pakistan and how being coupled with Pakistan hurts India's global ambitions.

Continuing on the theme of democracy and governance through reconciliation, Vajpayee drew parallels between India and Germany, even though one was a developing country and the other developed. Economic reforms and liberalisation processes, in both India and Germany, he said, had to take into account conflicting interests and demands of labour unions, political parties, Parliament, civil society and the government.

India was trying to move forward by reconciling these differences and in a manner which would lead to both equitable development and social justice.

"It may not be a very rapid process but it does make for greater stability."

This was the process that the European Union was also following, the Prime Minister observed, adding that "my coalition government has nearly as many parties as the number of countries the European Union would have, after its expansion."

He made an impassioned plea to the Parliamentarians for realising the true potential of the economic and strategic partnership that was possible between Germany and India.

India, Turkey set up JWG on Terrorism

Ankara, Sept. 17.

India and Turkey have established a "complete identity of views" on the need to combat global terrorism and they appear to have achieved a convergence of views on the situation in Iraq, including an increased role for the United Nations before either country could examine afresh the question of sending troops to Iraq.

This morning, the Prime Minister, Atal Bihari Vajpayee, and his host, Tayyip Erdogan, had one-to-one talks and then delegation-level discussions.

After the two-hour long talks, the two countries initialled three agreements, including the setting up of a Joint Working Group on terrorism.

The Turkish Prime Minister, Mr. Erdogan, described the Joint Working Group as "an example of new approach to the problem" of tackling international terrorism.

Mr. Vajpayee said the group was being set up to "enhance our cooperation against this grave threat to democratic societies. Both India and Turkey have suffered greatly from terrorism".

The Indian side exuded a sense of satisfaction over the talks. One senior participant even said that "we found an echo" on the Turkish side on the issue of terrorism. Also, it was enthused by the "chemistry between the two Prime Ministers".

The Indian delegation, indeed, had good reason to be pleased.

The Turkish Prime Minister said all that India wanted to hear on the issue of terrorism. Talking to reporters after the official talks, Mr. Erdogan disapproved of a selective approach to terrorism. "Terrorism is terrorism". Terrorism is not confined to any religion, any race or any nationality. It is a phenomenon by itself." At the same time, he cautioned against creating " artificial terror, artificial terrorists and artificial terrorism".

At the delegation-level talks, the two countries reiterated that they could put in place a "durable partnership" based on a positive affinity of democracy and secularism as well as on a perceived need to counter fundamentalism and terrorism. The Indian side appeared to be particularly pleased that Turkey did not display any kind of proactivism in wanting to sort out India-Pakistan relationship.

There was no mention of Pakistan or Kashmir: this, it was pointed out, stood in sharp contrast to the mood in June 2002, when the Turkish Parliament passed a resolution urging the Government to "play a role" in the India-Pakistan standoff.

It was a resolution that India "did not like"; and, now, the Turkish side chose not to raise Kashmir or Pakistan.

Mr. Erdogan told reporters that if at all Turkish troops were sent to Iraq, the decision would be based not on account of concern with one ethnic group (the Kurds) but what was best in the interests of the Iraqi people.

Mr. Vajpayee also noted that "there was no clarity as yet" on what the new Security Council resolution was all about and that "when the Security Council does take action, we will take a decision, keeping all aspects in mind, including our internal security situation".

There was a convergence of views on what needs to be done in Iraq. India and Turkey agree that the territorial integrity of Iraq must be maintained, that all possible help to the Iraqi people be made available, that the political process must begin in Iraq so that sovereignty can be transferred back to the people of Iraq, and that eventually the control of economic resources devolves on to Iraq.

Mr. Vajpayee was asked by Turkish reporters about the situation in the Middle East. He said he had made it clear to the Israeli Prime Minister, Ariel Sharon, during his recent visit to India that the "cycle of violence" would not achieve anything.

Mr. Vajpayee also put on record that India would not support the removal of Yasser Arafat, who was an elected leader of the Palestinians. On Afghanistan, India shared with Turkey "our concern on regrouping of the Taliban". On the bilateral front, the two agreed to energise the political ties. It was decided that the Foreign Ministers meet at least once a year, and the Commerce, Defence and Tourism Ministers would keep in active touch. Efforts should be made to increase the trade between the two countries to one billion dollar from $650 million.

The Prime Minister has a busy day today. Beginning with the ceremonial laying of a wreath at the Mousoleum of Kamal Ataturk, he led the official talks, and later attended a luncheon hosted by Mr. Erdogan.

PM Identifies Six Mutual Themes with Turkey

Ankara, Sept. 17. The Prime Minister, Atal Bihari Vajpayee, today identified six areas of "obvious convergences of interests and objectives" between India and Turkey which would become the basis of building up "a comprehensive dialogue architecture" between the two nations.

Speaking before a select gathering at a Turkish think-tank, the Centre for Strategic Research, Mr. Vajpayee noted that while history provided enough evidence and inspiration for ties between India and Turkey, he wanted to talk about "contemporary relevance, which sustains and strengthens international relationships in today's globalised world." Besides commonalities of democracy, supremacy of parliamentary institutions, secularism and vibrant media, he thought that new "convergences" needed to be underlined.

Of these, terrorism topped Mr. Vajpayee's list. He said that the two countries agree "there can be no double standards in identifying or fighting terrorism. We do not accept the dangerous logic of 'root causes' as excuse for inaction against terrorism."

Second, beyond terrorism, he identified "our common stake in the development of a just and equitable international order." Referring to the reduced role of the United Nations, he observed: "Multilateral institutions have recently come under considerable criticism and strain. Many of them have become ineffective, while others have been paralysed. Most importantly, the functioning of the United Nations and its various agencies has been less than optimal."

Third, Mr. Vajpayee referred to a common approach between India and Turkey on "seeing a more equitable spread in the benefits from free trade in goods and services."

He said that both countries were "particularly interested in removing distortions and inequities in the regime for exports of agricultural commodities. The failure of the Cancun WTO Ministerial Meeting Summit illustrates that those who lecture us on immediate sacrifices for long-term gains are not willing to follow their own prescriptions."

Fourth, economic development could become the spark for cooperation between the two nations; in particular, India would want to learn from Turkey's "state-of-theart expertise in infrastructure construction and development". Areas like power, telecom, tourism, health and education offered immense scope for cooperation.

Fifth, science and technology could be catalysts of economic cooperation. India's experience in information technology, biotechnology, space sciences and civilian nuclear power could be shared with Turkey.

And, sixth, an interest in regional peace and stability. The two countries, according to Mr. Vajpayee, had interests in Central Asia, West Asia and the Gulf. He noted that "while our interests overlap in this area, nowhere do they clash." He added that "Indian and Turkish companies are collaborating on the construction of an oil pipeline in Central Asia and in the prospecting for oil in North Africa."

Mr. Vajpayee's address this evening to the Centre for Strategic Research was being billed as part of a larger exercise, aimed at reaching out to the Turkish intellectual community.

Three Accords Signed

Ankara, Sept. 17. India and Turkey today signed an agreement to set up a Joint Working Group on Combating Terrorism.

This and two other agreements were signed on India's behalf by the Minister of State for Commerce and Industry, Satyabrata Mookherjee, and on Turkey's behalf by the Minister for Transport, Binali Yildirim. The signing ceremony took place in the presence of the Prime Ministers of India and Turkey. The JWG's mandate is to share experience and exchange information in combating terrorism, organised crime and illicit trafficking of narcotic drugs.

The second agreement is on cooperation in the field of science and technology. It is intended to promote joint research and development projects, exchange of scientists and scholars as also of scientific and technical information. Besides, there was a protocol signed on cooperation in the field of Information Technology and Computer Software.

Turkey Lauds PM's Peace Initiative

Vajpayee unveils bust of Rabindranath Tagore

Istanbul, September 18

Prime Minister Atal Bihari Vajpayee today held discussions with Turkish President Ahmet Nacdat Sezer on the growing menace of terrorism, latest developments in West Asia and the Iraq crisis.

During the 40-minute meeting at the Presidential Palace, where Mr. Vajpayee drove straight from the airport after his arrival from Ankara, both the leaders discussed bilateral issues of regional and international concerns.

An official spokesman said though Pakistan did not come up for discussion, the Turkish President appreciated Mr. Vajpayee's peace initiative towards the neighbouring country.

Mr. Sezer said he supported the Indian Prime Minister's views on issues like terrorism and Palestinian President Yasser Arafat.

"Mr. Sezer shared views that removing Mr. Arafat would not help matters as he was an elected representative of the Palestinian people," the spokesman said.

On Iraq, the Turkish President said like India he was also for the early restoration of the democratic rights of the people of that country. Later, Mr. Vajpayee visited an Indian exhibition.

Meanwhile, Tukish Airlines today resumed its services to Delhi after a nine-year gap, with a flight carrying 250 passengers including 170 invitees on board.

The regular operation will begin from September 29, with flights from here on Mondays, Thursdays and Saturdays, an official in the state-owned

Turkish carrier said:

Mr. Vajpayee, had announced the resumption of the Istanbul-Delhi flight yesterday. The invitees would stay in India for three days, the official said.

Ankara: Symbolising growing ties with India, Turkey on Thursday named an avenue in capital Ankara after Gurudev Rabindranath Tagore.

Mr. Vajpayee, on the third day of his visit, inaugurated the 'Rabindranath Tagore Avenue' and also unveiled the Nobel laureate's bust at a ceremony here.

By naming the avenue after Tagore, he said, Turkey had honoured "one of India's greatest poets, philosophers; and we celebrate another valuable stand of Indo-Turkish connection".—

Visit Significant for Indian Expatriates

Ankara, September 18

In all likelihood every Indian in Tukey could get to see Indian Prime Minister Atal Bihari Vajpayee simply because there are just 200 or so of them here. Most are based in Istanbul where Mr. Vajpayee will meet them at a reception, but here in Ankara, for the 25 odd families, it is a significant visit, as they have little contact with India.

In Ankara, there are no temples nor any stores selling Indian wares. There is no India Street or Mahatma Gandhi Avenue. The bust of Rabindranath Tagore to be installed here will be a first.

For Gajanan Thorat, a Hindustani classical singer and tabla player, who came here in 2000, it was quite a disappointment to hear the Prime Minister speaking in English from a prepared speech.

But in his defence, Mr. Vajpayee could not have spoken in Hindi at the Centre for Strategic Research where think-tanks had gathered and the Indian community was invited.

But back to Gajanan. He had met his lady love, a blonde Turk, who was on a holiday in Mumbai. He maried her and came to Ankara. Funda Thorat fell in love when she saw him perform at a classical music concert in Mumbai. It took three years for Gajanan to visit her here and secure a visa to reside in Turkey.

For Rathi Shankar, a housewife, life revolves around her home and her Turkish friends and planning her annual visit to India. Married to Vijay Shankar, a senior manager at Mitsubishi in Ankara, she has lived as an expatriate in Kuwait as well.

Pak Using Terrorism as 'a Tool of Blackmail': PM

New York, Sept. 25

As expected, the Prime Minister, Atal Bihari Vajpayee, used the United

Nations General Assembly today to tell Pakistan and the rest of the world that New Delhi would not have any dialogue with Islamabad as long as Pakistan continued to sponsor terrorism in Jammu and Kashmir.

Using the Pakistan President, Pervez Musharraf's words heard 24 hours earlier, to the Pakistani leader's disadvantage, Mr. Vajpayeee said: "Yesterday, the President of Pakistan chose this August assembly to make a public admission for the first time that Pakistan is sponsoring terrorism in Jammu and Kashmir.

After claiming that there is an indigenous struggle in Kashmir, he has offered to encourage a general cessation of violence within Kashmir, in return for 'reciprocal obligations and restraints,"

The Prime Minister said that Pakistan was using terrorism as "a tool of blackmail", and that just as the world had refused to negotiate with the Al-Qaeda or the Taliban, India too would not negotiate with terrorism.

Sparring with Gen. Musharraf over his formulations about what was happening in Jammu and Kashmir, Mr. Vajpayee said the recent elections in the State were "an equivocal expression of both determination and self-determination". After the recent election, there was no question of India negotiating with Pakistan. As Mr. Vajpayee put it : "If we do so, we would be betraying the people of Jammu and Kashmir, who defied a most ferocious campaign of violence and intimidation sponsored from across our borders, and participated in an election, which has been universally hailed as free and fair."

A dialogue would take place between India and Pakistan only when cross-border terrorism stopped or was eradicated by Indian, and then : we can have a dialogue with Pakistan on the other issues between us".

Mr. Vajpayee practically told Gen. Musharraf not to try to play above his league. Reacting to the General's plea yesterday that India should not be allowed to acquire a new conventional defence superiority, he said : "I would like to point out to the President of Pakistan that he should not confuse the legitimate aspiration for equality of nations with outmoded concepts of military parity."

Even when Mr. Vajpayee elaborated India's point of view on global issues such as terrorism, Pakistan seemed to be very much on his mind. Talking of partial success in the global war against terrorism after 9/11, Mr. Vajpayee said : "The global coalition against terrorism has registered successes in Afghanistan, but has not been able to extend this elsewhere. Some of its members are themselves part of the problem. We are sometimes led into semantics about the definition of terrorism. The search for 'root causes' or imaginary 'freedom struggles' provides alibis for the killing of innocent men, women and children."

In his speech on Wednesday, Gen Musharraf had accused India of raking up "cross-border terrorism" to refuse a dialogue and of wanting to "delegitimise the Kashmir freedom struggle".

Pakistan was again on his mind when Mr. Vajpayee stressed the need for pooling of resources, intelligence and information "to prevent terrorists from evading capture, simply by crossing national borders. No state should be allowed to profess partnership with the global coalition against terror, while continuing to aid, abet and sponsor terrorism. To condone such double standards is to contribute to multiplying terrorism".

And, again on Gen. Musharrf's indirect reference of India's demand for a place in an expanded Security Council, Mr. Vajpayee had a gentle rebuke for the General : "Most UN members today recognise the need for an enlarged and restructured Security Council, with more developing countries as permanent and non-permanent members. The permanent members guard their exclusivity. Some states with weak claims want to ensure that others do not enter the Council as permanent members."

Roadmap for Iraq

On Iraq, Mr. Vajpayee demanded a "roadmap of political process for a representative Iraqi government" and a "crucial role" for the UN in the reconstruction.The tone of Mr. Vajpayee's brief reference to Iraq was clearly defiant of the American preferences. On Wednesday, the US President had told India that he intended to stay the course in Iraq, that too on American terms.

Asserting that India would not allow Pakistan to use terrorism as a "tool of blackmail", Prime Minister Atal Bihari Vajpayee today firmly rejected President Pervez Musharraf's call for the resumption of late dialogue until Islamabad completely stopped cross-border terrorism.

"We totally refuse to let terrorism become a tool of blackmail. Just as the world did not negotiate with Al-Qada or the Taliban, we shall not negotiate with terrorism," Mr. Vajpayee said in his address to the 58th session of the United Nations General Assembly.

He said if Indians did so, it would amount to betraying the people of Jammu and Kashmir who defied a most ferocious campaign of violence and intimidation sponsored from across the the border and participated in an election, which had been universally hailed as free and fair.

Speaking in Hindi, Mr. Vajpayee said India could have a dialogue with Pakistan on "the other issues" between the two countries when cross-border terrorism stopped or when India eradicated it.

Lashing out at President Pervez Musharraf for his utterances against India in his UN address yesterday, the Prime Minister said the Pakistan leader had for the first time publicly admitted that his country was sponsoring terrorism in Jammu and Kashmir.

After claiming for a long time that there was an indigenous struggle going on in Kashmir, Gen Musharraf had now offered to encourage a general cessation of violence within Kashmir, in return for "reciprocal obligations and restraints", Mr. Vajpayee noted.

Mr. Vajpayee said he would like to point out to Gen Musharraf that he should not confuse the legitimate aspiration for equality of nations with outmoded concepts of military parity.

Strongly pitching for India's inclusion in the UN Security Council, the Prime Minister said the Iraq crisis had reinforced the need for its enlargement and restructuring with the inclusion of more developing countries as permanent and non-permanent members:—

Power of Truth

Truth is not any less powerful for not being acknowledged. Nor is it any less universally applicable for not being universally applied. If terrorism is an ugly reality that unites civilised nations in their resolve to fight it, the truth of their shared victimisation authomatically follows—the pain of each victim equal to that of all others. What Prime Minister Atal Bihari Vajpayee did in the course of his combative and hard—hitting address to the UN General Assembly was to state nothing but this truth—and force a recognition. He categorically asserted that India could not be asked to barter with terror sponsors. The moral basis of his stand made it unimpeachable by a world that itself claims to be acting upon moral imperatives : "Just as the world did not negotiate with Al Qaeda or the Taliban," he said, "we shall not negotiate with terrorism." Indeed, the argument was as faultless as it was forceful : To hierarchies suffering, by which 9/11 could be seen as any more agonising and reprehensible than the two-decade-long savagery India has faced, would be unworthy of a truly democratic international order.

That Mr. Vajpayee turned the tables on Pakistani President Pervez Musharraf by blowing holes in his peace posturing was, therefore, only a spectacular sideshow, an easy triumph; his real challenge was successfully directed at the global community, calling upon it to unreservedly recognise the fact of India's long-standing, victimisation at the hands of cross-border terrorism, as well as its inalienable right to preserve itself against Pakistan's onslaughts. Just as the comity of nations stood firm in not succumbing to intimidation, India too would not capitulate to terror as "a tool of blackmail". The point did not need labouring. President Musharraf's statement that Pakistan would "encourage a general cessation of violence" in Kashmir as a trade-off for "reciprocal obligations"—a euphemism for dialogue—was itself an unwitting "admission" of its continued export of *jihad.* Using the General's own term against him, Mr. Vajpayee described the Kashmir polls as a symbol of "self-determination". Here too the message was directed at a global community that, by applauding the free and fair elections had recognised the fact Kashmir's mandate was an emphatic rejection of Pakistan-backed bloodletting. That Mr. Vajpayee thus laid to rest all doubts about India's perceived vacillation on dialogue in recent months, and did so at a symbolically charged venue like the UN, deserves applause. India's peace offer, he rightly reminded both Pakistan and the world, was never unconditional. For peace could not be negotiated at gunpoint.

Widening the critique of the anomalies of the global anti-terror combat—including its selective focus—Mr. Vajpayee called upon the UN to give teeth to terrorism-related Security Council Resolutions. If the bottomline was that carnage could not be justified by semantic quibbling, states promoting violence in the name of "root causes" would have to be ejected from pretended membership in the anti-terror camp. His lament over absence of "enlightened multilateralism" was more than just an indictment of the unipolar world's self-serving distortions. So long as there were "limits" to what the UN, by not reflecting the collective will of nations, could achieve, universally accepted norms would continue to be applied unilaterally—or selectively. Iraq was one manifestation. The anti-terror combat's confinement to Afghanistan, courtesy US patronage of Pakistan, was another. Given the tentacular nature of global threats, the interdependence and, therefore, equality of civilised nations were realities the world could ignore only at its own peril. Mr. Vajpayee did some tough talking and, hopefully, the world will be the better for it.

Keep the Process on Track

Pakistan provided the opening and India pounced. That is a brief summary of the debate that unfolded in the United Nations General Assembly over two days. Pakistan's President Pervez Musharraf though he could buck the trend in international public opinion and distinguish between militancy for "legitimate causes" and terrorism pure and simple. He also contradicted himself, just as he did barely a month ago, when he ascribed the violence in Jammu and Kashmir to indigenous causes and yet claimed that he could scale it down if India reciprocated. The military ruler apparently forgot that his country's support for cross-border terrorism has only been temporarily overlooked by the international community. Pakistan's failure to give the required support to anti-terror operations in Afghanistan and its complicity in terrorism directed at India have not gone unnoticed. General Musharraf's effort to portray his support for terrorism in Kashmir as springing from noble causes may yet rebound on him. In the short term, his address offered provocation, and provided an opportunity, to Prime Minister Atal Bihari Vajpayee. Prior to the General Assembly session, Minister for External Affairs Yashwant Sinha signalled that India was ready to break the habit of using international fora for public disputes with Pakistan. Mr. Vajpayee was clearly unable to resist the temptation to take advantage of General Musharraf's miscalculation. While references to Pakistan formed a relatively small part of the Prime Minister's address, the Musharraf-triggered controversy has not helped the prospects for reconciliation in the subcontinent.

The latest exchange of rhetorical fusillades proves the wisdom of the policy India has followed since the Prime Minister initiated the most recent peace effort. The truce between India and Pakistan is too delicate to be subjected to the shock administered by any effort to grandstand. This time India kept to a steady pace and a middle-key approach in its efforts to re-engage with Pakistan. It avoided a hasty rush into exchanges at the Ministerial level even as it took measures to restore normality through the resumption of full diplomatic relations and the revival of people to people contacts. This approach reflected the assessment that creating and strengthening goodwill between the people of the two countries would help create an atmosphere for discussing the substantive and critical issues in a constructive manner. While this effort at normalisation made slow progress, it did proceed in the right direction. An attempt was concurrently made to unravel the different strands of the India-Pakistan entanglement, with minor issues quickly sorted out. In its projection of policy, India also indicated that it would not again resort to aggressive military postures in the manner it did after the terrorist attack on Parliament on December 13, 2001. From the response of the Pakistani Public, it appeared this measured approach has registered some success. The responsibility of both sides, in the wake of the fire exchanged at the UN, is to keep the process initiated five months ago firmly on track.

It will be sensible to clear the track of the fallout and debris from the public dispute before the Prime Minister travels to Pakistan early next year for the SAARC summit. The unspoken accord between India and Pakistan to insulate SAARC, to the maximum extent possible, from their bilateral differences is still fragile. Constituencies in India opposed to the attempted detente will dwell on General Musharraf's short-sighted confrontationist as they press Mr. Vajpayee to hedge on, if not withdraw from, the summit. Pressing on with his current course, the Prime Minister must firmly reject such importunings. The enhancement of people to people contacts, economic cooperation, and cultural and sports exchanges between the two countries is necessary for the restoration of normality.

We'll Fight Terror on our own : Atal

Prime Minister Atal Bihari Vajpayee on Friday sought not to draw any "major conclusions" from the fact that India did not figure in the list of terror victims read out by US President George Bush in his address to the 58th session of the United Nations General Assembly (UNGA).

Asked in the context of Deputy Prime Minister L K Advani's reaction to the omission back home expressing disappointment, Mr. Vajpayee said, "It is not a question of being satisfied. President Bush may not have mentioned it but UN Secretary General Kofi Annan did. So one cannot draw any major conclusions from this. I keep talking to Mr. Bush on this issue."

He, however, admitted that it was disappointing to see the reaction of certain countries to the ongoing terrorism in India. He asserted that no country should adopt any double standards in combating terrorism, that there cannot be two yardsticks for measuring terrorism, depending on a country's individual perception. He said India has been fighting terrorism for a long time now and will continue to do so "on its own strength."

On Pakistan's charge here at the UN that India is the "mother of terrorism," Mr. Vajpayee said, "The level of the ongoing debate is not good. We have always fought terrorism. It is our policy to resolve issues peacefully. I do not know in what context the Pakistani side made that comment. But I have extended my hand of friendship thrice. Now Pakistani leaders are saying all peace efforts must be counted Agra onwards. Lahore did not happen for them. Why do Pakistani leaders want to forget Lahore? This shift is recent." He cited the various steps India has taken after his Srinagar peace initiative, a fact noted by the international community and also discussed during his lunch with Mr. Bush.

Asked whether the Srinagar peace initiative had ended in New York, the Prime Minister said, " We are also disappointed with whatever happened here but I do not think the peace initiative is over, it should continue." On Pakistan reading India's peace efforts as a sign of weakness, the Prime Minister said, "We did not take the peace initiative from a position of weakness. It is because of our hand of friendship that the world understands India wants genuine peace. No one is willing to believe Pakistan's complaints." In this regard, he cited a White House spokesperson's statement about continuing cross-border terrorism in India and the fact that it is increasing. As compared to Pakistan's routine anti-India posturing at the United Nations, Mr. Vajpayee said India adheres to certain limits. The verbal duel in New York meanwhile has sent India and Pakistan further away from the dialogue table. "Right now neither is there any proposal for dialogue nor a conducive atmosphere. Talks at this juncture would be unproductive," the Prime Minister said.

He admitted that the Americans keep asking India and Pakistan to talk but underlined the fact that they do acknowledge that cross-border terrorism is continuing and increasing. Instead of Pakistan proving its commitment to dismantle the terror infrastructure within its territory, there is daily news about more and more young men being recruited in their training camps, indicating otherwise.

Mr. Vajpayee also touched upon issues of international concern, primarily Iraq and a new UN Security Council Resolution, a subject that figured during his bilateral meetings with Mr. Bush and Russian President Vladimer Putin. On the hotly debated issue of Indian troops for Iraq, Mr. Vajpayee said, India in the past has sent peace-keeping forces abroad. "But this time it is not the issue of peace-keeping but peace-enforcement. The question is about establishing peace in Iraq and then carrying on reconstruction efforts. Who will do this? India has apprised world leaders of India's concerns. We have said there are questions of internal security involved. Terrorism has increased... We want the reins of Iraq's Government in the hands of the Iraqi people. India is willing to help in the reconstruction efforts."

In the context of a world post-Iraq, Mr. Vajpayee once again reiterated the urgent need of reforms in the UN's existing structure. After attending this year's UNGA, the Prime Minister said, "I feel the largest issue right now is UN reforms. Even the Secretary General spoke about it. The kind of situation that prevailed in Iraq and the manner in which this world organisation proved ineffective is an indication that the UN needs some serious changes." He wondered how the UN would act if a situation similar to Iraq develops in some other part of the world. The world needs to debate this question urgently and seriously.

On India's claim to a permanent membership of the UNSC, Mr. Vajpayee said the question is no longer one of membership but reforms. "Will the UN continue to operate like this?" he wondered, adding that the UN must learn to cope with the new challenges faced by the world today.

Peace Process not Dead, says PM

New York, Sep. 26. The Prime Minister, Atal Bihari Vajpayee, today expressed the view that the peace process with Pakistan was not over, notwithstanding the unpleasant exchange of words between the two countries in the United Nations General Assembly here. At the same time, he ruled the possibility of any dialogue with Pakistan during the next SAARC summit, due to be held in Pakistan early next year.

However, Mr. Vajpayee regretted that the level of debate had come to this pass. At the same time, he asserted that India had replied tit for tat, though with becoming dignity. He was interacting with the media at the end of his visit.

Mr. Vajpayee did not agree with a suggestion that the good work that began with the Srinagar initiative had collapsed here in New York. "The peace efforts should continue."

The Prime Minister also rejected Pakistan's charge that "India was the mother of all terror" as well as the suggestion that India had rejected the Pakistan President, Pervez Musharraf's peace offer.

He said India had always opposed terrorism and it was he who had thrice extended the hand of friendship to Pakistan. Mr. Vajpayee wondered why Pakistani's present rulers were keen to suggest that the search for peace began at Agra, and why they were eager to delegitimise the Lahore effort. However, he did concede that the United States President, George W.Bush, had asked India (as also Pakistan) to engage in a dialogue. But he hastened to add that this had been Washington's consistent policy.

He told a reporter that any kind of bilateral dialogue with Gen. Musharraf during the coming SAARC summit was not possible. "The atmosphere is not conducive; it won't be productive." Nonetheless, Mr. Vajpayee took considerable satisfaction from the fact that the US had agreed—during the course of a luncheon meeting two days ago—that cross-border terrorism was on the rise.

Asked how this assertion of rise in cross-border terrorism could be reconciled with his continued search for peace, and whether Pakistan would not be tempted to infer this as a sign of weakness, Mr. Vajpayee said, "I do not think so. We offer peace not from a point of weakness. India is not weak. Pakistan should know this, particularly after Kargil."

The Prime Minister was challenged to justify why troops were deployed and then re-deployed without the decisive battle (*aar-paar ki ladhai)* he had promised to the nation when P arliament was attacked on December 13, 2001. Mr. Vajpayee defended the deployment/and redeployment decision (s) as having "achieved their limited purpose."

"Iraq discussed"

He said that he had discussed the Iraq situation with both Mr. Bush and the Russian President, Vladimir Putin. He noted that it was not a simple question of traditional peace-keeping in Iraq, rather it was now a matter of "peace-enforcement."

There was also the question of who should have the responsibility for reconstruction in Iraq. He repeated his U.N. General Assembly formulation that sovereignty should revert back to the Iraqis at the earliest. India, according to him, would be ready to help with reconstruction once the Security Council came up with a new resolution ; but, he hastened to add, in his view a new resolution was not going to come about in a hurry.

Onthe question of sending Indian trooops to Iraq, Mr. Vajpayee said that he had told the American interlocutors New Delhi would have to keep in mind its internal security situation. And, this internal security situation hinged very much on the intensity of cross-border terrorism.

The Prime Minsiter was asked about Pakisatn's recognition of the break-away faction of the All-Party Hurriyat Conference (APHC).

He noted that the split in the Hurriyat Conference was of no concern and that the invitation to the APHC to talk to New Delhi's interlocutor "still stands". However, he declared that there would be no special invitation to the APHC.

Mr. Vajpayee refused to be drawn into domestic issues; and pointedly refused a comment on the acquittal of the Deputy Prime Minister, L.K. Advani, in the Ayodhya case.

PM in Favour of Regional Trading Arrangements

Nusadua (Bali), Oct.7. The Prime Minister, Atal Bihari Vajpayee, said today that regional trading arrangements offered immediate advantages, particularly for geographically contiguous regions.

Speaking in the context of the stalemated World Trade Organisation talks in Cancun, Mr. Vajpayee asserted that while a rule-based and fair multilateral trading system remained the goal, regional trading arrangements offered immediate benefits.

"They can provide our domestic industry and agriculture a valuable learning period, before being exposed to the far greater competition of global free trade," he said in an address to the ASEAN Business and Investment Summit.

Pointing out that India had lagged behind China, Japan and South Korea in developing relations with the Association of South East Asian Nations (ASEAN), he said this "situation was changing rapidly."

The Prime Minister was, however, not satisfied with the level of the two-way ASEAN-India trade, which currently stood at $12.5 billion. Trade was growing, but not fast enough.

"We have recognised this fact in the India-ASEAN Framework for Comprehensive Economic Cooperation, which we have been negotiating over the past year. We are working on eliminating trade and investment barriers to facilitate business."

India, he said, was conscious of the concerns of Cambodia, Laos, Myanmar and Vietnam (CLMV) nations — the less developed section of ASEAN— as it negotiated the free trade regime.

"We are offering unilateral tariff concessions on items of export interest to the CLMV countries. We are also seeking to incorporate an Early Harvest scheme to provide the incentive for a long-term engagement. If we procesd along this course, we can target a trade turnover of $30 billion by 2007 and a free trade area within 10 years," he said.

Taking the free trade argument forward, Mr. Vajpayee said that for open economic interaction, there was a need to "improve and harmonise" travel regulations and restrictions, including visa regimes. "We have to upgrade our air, sea, road and rail links in capacity and quality..."

The Prime Minister also addressed concerns about India's investment regime. "It is liberal and transparent... we may occasionally have some problems, because of the difficulties if reconciling competing interests and concerns. This is normal in an open, democratic set-up."

"We are constantly trying to refine our regulations and procedures. At the same time, if you analyse the experience of our foreign investors, returns on investment are generally higher..."

Addressing the ASEAN business community, Mr. Vajpayee pointed out that perceptions about India were often incomplete, or flawed, and went on to point out that spiritual traditions of the country were but one aspect. The India the 21st century was, however, not so well known.

"India is today a country on the move," he said pointing out that the country was undergoing information technology, socio-cultural, demographic and psychological revolutions simultaneously.

"We are experiencing a demographic revolution, where the numbers of young people are increasing. Already, 54 per cent of our population is below 25 years of age. This has created a revolution of expectations..."

"The combined effect of all these has been a psychological revolution, in which a defensive, introverted approach has given way to an outward-looking, self-confident attitude, willing to accept challenges and take risks, rejecting fear and shunning fatalism."

India, he said, was an inherently strong economy driven primarily by indigenous skills and domestic enterprise. As an example of the Indian market, Mr. Vajpayee said it had been absorbing nearly two million mobile telephones every month.

"Import duties are moving towards ASEAN levels, and sectoral caps on foreign investment are rising," he said adding that India had a rich pool of human resources, English-speaking with research and development skills.

Also, India was one of three countries — the other two being the United States and Japan — that had indigenously designed and manufactured supercomputers.

It is one of only six nations that could build and launch satellites.

"Non-Asians view Asia as the principal market of the future. But it will also emerge as a manufacturing hub and a global provider of services.In the next 50 years, as the population of the developed world ages, a younger and better-educated work force will emerge in Asia to fill the breach," the Prime Minister added.

Vajpayee Hardsells, ASEAN buys

Bali: Prime Minister Atal Bihari Vajpayee on Tuesday did a hardselling of India to the Association of South-East Asian Nations (ASEAN), projecting it as "a nation on the move".

True to form, the PM made a strong pitch for Indo-ASEAN partnership, to quickly make up for the lost time and to target a tripling of trade in four years to $30 billion.

The PM also referred to the blue-print agreement for setting up an Indo-ASEAN free trade area (FTA) to be signed on Wednesday and announced that India would offer unilateral tariff concessions on items of export interest to the four less advanced countries of the 10-member ASEAN. He said there would also be an "early harvest scheme" of exchanging import duty concessions to provide the incentive for a long-term free trade engagement.

The PM's address, delivered to the first-ever ASEAN Business and Investment Summit that focussed on the multiple strength of a "21st Century India" and the numerous achievements in recent years of a resurgent India, could in fact have gone very well with a domestic audience.

It had all the ingredients that would have made Vajpayee's poll-bound BJP and the NDA proud and would have provided ready fodder for the compaign mill.

It was not as if Vajpayee was exaggerating for effect when he spoke of the multiple "revolutions" being experienced in India simultaneously.

Some of the ASEAN leaders, notably Thai PM Thaksin Shinawatra, speaking from the same podium earlier, had already acknowledged the huge strides India was making. "In Asia, China and India are emerging as economic powerhouses of the region," Shinawatra had noted.

But Vajpayee hammered the point and gave a full list of the "revolutions" under way in India lest it should have passed the outside world or for that matter his domestic constituency.

India Favours Asian Bond Fund

Bali: Flush with foreign exchange reserves of over $85 billion, India has pledged $ 1 billion towards development of an Asian Bond Fund, which will work as a safety net in events of financial turmoil of the kind that swept East Asia in 1997-98.

Winning back investors to ASEAN (Association of South East Asian Nations) and making it again a competitive production base for world markets was the focus of the first ever ASEAN business and investment summit here on Tuesday.

Prime Minister of Thailand Thaksin Shinawatra, who along with other leaders of ASEAN countries as well as Japan, Korea, China and India, addressed business leaders, laid particular emphasis on the development of the Asian Bond Fund as an alternative financial architecture to the International Monetary Fund.

The Asian Bond Fund is expected to play a crucial role in both imparting financial stability as well as in repairing any possible damage in the wake of a crisis.

ASEAN sources said the Asian Bond Fund of $ 1 billion was launched in June by 11 central banks of the Asia-Pacific region. It was given political support by the 18 members of the Asia Cooperation Dialogue (ACD) at its second ministerial meeting in June.

India had since pledged $ 1 billion, taking the corpus of the fund to $ 2 billion. India's role in building a new financial architecture is being considered important because the 1997-98 East Asian currency crisis took a toll of several emerging economies with its contageon effects, but India stood out as one economy that remained unaffected

Prime Minister Vajpayee also alluded to this strength of India's financial sector in his address to the ASEAN business summit. He offered India's cooperation in the field of financial services.

The Asian Bond Fund, according to officials, will play the role of lead investor in future development projects in Asia. The Fund and the Asian bond market will create more wealth in Asia from its own resources. An

Asian credit rating agency is also proposed to be set up in due course to make the operation of the Fund effective.

India's strong support to the Asian Bond Fund will be highly complementary with the economic integration New Delhi is seeking with the economies in South East Asia as part of its "look east" policy, diplomats said.

India and ASEAN—Shared Perspectives

Address to the Institute of Diplomatic and Foreign Relations Kuala Lumpur,
May 16, 2001

I am very happy to be here in this prestigious institution to share some thoughts with you on the future of the India-ASEAN partnership. It is entirely appropriate that I do so on the soil of one of ASEAN's most dynamic members, which also happens to be the country coordinator within ASEAN for its relations with India.

The theme of shared perspectives between India and ASEAN should be self-evident. History, geography, and economics have provided compelling logic for unity of purpose and action between us. Yet, roughly 50 years after India and the ASEAN countries attained their independence, we are discussing a subject, which should now have been accepted wisdom.

The most basic historical factor, which unites us is a civilisational bond formed from the strands of spiritualism, culture and commerce. The cross-fertilization of our human experiences was not through conquest or domination, but through a meeting of minds. Evidence of this confluence between India and South-East Asia abounds in the art, architecture, language and culture of every ASEAN country.

We are conscious that in the first few decades after our independence, we did not attain the full promise of our relationship. Our cultural and civilizational bonds remained firm. But, the full scope of our partnership was constrained by divergences in economic ideology, political outlook and security assumptions, which the Cold War imposed on us.

Today, we can say with great satisfaction that these artificial wrinkles have been ironed out. We also have a number of additional objective factors, which assure us that the complementarities between us today are both stronger and more enduring.

The Cold War moulds have been broken, and this has enabled us to strengthen our links without ideological barriers. India became a sectoral dialogue partner of ASEAN in 1992, full dialogue partner in 1995, and member of the ASEAN Regional Forum in 1996.

Over the last few years, we in India have consciously focussed on rejuvenation of our ties with the countries of ASEAN. This came to be known as our "Look East" policy. But, even as we looked east, ASEAN moved west. The admission of new countries brought ASEAN literally to India's doors. From a maritime neighbour, ASEAN became our close neighbour with a land border of nearly 1,600 kilometres. This has added a new dimension to India-ASEAN relations.

Asian countries are today at the forefront of developing and introducing cutting edge technologies into their economies. We are in the very epicentre of the Knowledge Revolution. This provides us with a major opportunity to overcome our historical disabilities and to compress the time gap between successive levels of development. Each of our countries has achieved expertise and even dominance in certain areas of technology. It is crucial that we should cooperate in exploiting the synergies between us, rather than duplicating capacities or undercutting each other. A link up between some of India's software sectors with hardware capabilities of South-East Asian countries is only one example. There should be many other possibilities, which we need to explore.

India is now launching the second generation of its economic reforms, seeking to reach the benefits of the new technologies and new opportunities of globalisation to its entire population. The immediate requirement for this is infrastructural support in the form of communications, roads, ports and power. These are areas of strength and expertise in the ASEAN countries and we look forward to their participation in these infrastructure projects in India.

The security of India and that of ASEAN are closely interlinked. We believe that a multi-polar world order would provide the best guarantee of equal security for all states. We respect the status of South-East Asia as a nuclear Weapons Free Zone and, as a nuclear weapon state, we are willing to convert this recognition into a de jure commitment.

For decades after its independence, India has been campaigning for nuclear disarmament. Instead, much of the world went along with a discriminatory NPT, which preserved the right to nuclear weaponization of a few countries, even while keeping the rest in a permanently disarmed condition. The nuclear weapon states showed no intention of implementing Article VI of the treaty, which committed them to nuclear disarmament in a phased manner.

Unfortunately, non-nuclear states effectively connived with them by subscribing, in 1995, to an indefinite extension of this hopelessly flawed treaty. India had then to draw its own conclusions. Three years ago, we decided to conduct nuclear tests, based on an objective evaluation of our security environment, and to create for India the necessary strategic autonomy and space. In doing so, we did not violate any treaty, agreement or understanding to which we were party.

There is better understanding in the world today of our decision to maintain a minimum credible nuclear deterrent. We have declared a unilateral moratorium on underground explosive tests. We have a declared policy of no first use, and a commitment never to use nuclear weapons against non-nuclear states. We have proved that India is neither a proliferation threat nor an exporter of sensitive nuclear or missile technology. This cannot be said to be true of all parties to the NPT. Our approach is further underpinned by our abiding commitment to the goal of a nuclear weapon-free world.

We are conscious of the striving for a new security structure in the world, moving away from obsolete Cold War constructs. We are engaged in a process of dialogue and consultation with our friends and partners to help shape a new security environment free of confrontation and tension. Our security dialogue with ASEAN can also include this theme.

The nature of the Global Village has made it necessary to tackle even non-military issues of security in a comprehensive manner. Our region lies along side sea lanes of great strategic importance, which need to be protected. Poverty and shortages of food and energy threaten the stability of societies. Population growth and the spread of diseases like AIDS and TB are factors of deep concern. Environmental degradation and cyber crime are relatively newer concerns.

There can be no effective solution to these problems within national boundaries. They have to be tackled through a cooperative approach, holistically and regionally. The security dialogue between India and ASEAN is therefore, of utmost importance.

Threats like religious extremism, drug trafficking, money laundering and terrorism have cast a dark shadow over our region. India has been a victim of state-sponsored and cross-border terrorism seeking to redraw national boundaries. Such violence in the name of holy war is a grave menace especially to pluralistic societies and endangers a peaceful and civilized global order.

India and ASEAN are on the same side of the socio-economic divide in the debate on globalization. Opening up our national economies to global markets cannot become a *mantra* at the cost of equitable development and social justice. The passion for rapid globalization should be tempered by compassion for its unintended victims.

The financial and economic crisis in this region in 1997 vividly demonstrated how volatile capital flows could threaten the very existence of even vibrant economies. The recovery process of various countries has also shown that external prescriptions for economic measures or the pace of reform do not necessarily guarantee economic recovery or political stability.

We need to draw appropriate lessons from these experiences so that developing economies do not remain vulnerable to destabilisation or stagnation from a headlong rush into globalization. During our discussions, Prime Minister Mahathir and I agreed on the urgent need for an early reform of the international financial architecture.

Eight months ago, speaking in the US Congress, I had proposed a global dialogue for development. This call was prompted by our concern that some of the most vital issues of development and poverty alleviation are in danger of getting marginalized in our hurry to introduce new regime in trade, investment and intellectual property. I believe such a dialogue should include in its ambit such impediments to development as the international financial architecture and the imposition of impossibly harsh timetables for globalization.

Our economic engagement with ASEAN will also be based on these perspectives. We seek a dialogue bilaterally and multilaterally with countries of the region to harmonize our positions on key issues of development, trade and investment and environment.

Our outlook is entirely in harmony with the high-resolution road map of development priorities and regional integration, which was drawn up in the Hanoi Plan of Action and its Vision Twenty Twenty (2020). We follow the same logic in exploring the possible linkages between the ASEAN Free Trade Area and India to increase trade and investment flows in directions, which would promote growth and development.

Thus, we have an impressive catalogue of congruences in outlook and platform for joint action.

India already has a fruitful annual dialogue with the European Union at the Summit level. We consider it in the mutual interest of both ASEAN and India that we have a similar institution. If we could intensify our interaction and synchronize our actions in world fora, we can together form a formidable force working for global peace and security, equitable economic development and social justice.

It is an ambitious agenda. But we have the collective strength to implement it. What we need is the political will and highest level commitment to a sincere, frank and comprehensive India-ASEAN dialogue.

This vision must also find a way to be expressed through instruments commensurate with its historic and grand sweep. My government stands ready to work towards the realization of this vision.

Thank You.

Statement on Returning from Visiting Portugal and Italy

New Delhi, June 30, 2000

I visited Lisbon from 27 to 29 June, 2000 to join the leaders of the European Union at the first ever Summit held between India and the European Union. The Summit was attended on the European side by the Prime Minister of Portugal, Mr. Antonio Guterres; the Secretary General / High Representatives for Common Foreign and Security Policy, Mr. Javier Solana and the president of the European Commission, Mr. Romano Prodi. I was assisted by External Affairs Minister, Shri Jaswant Singh; Finance Minister Shri Yashwant Sinha; Commerce and Industry Minister Shri Murasoli Maran and Minister for Information Technology, Shri Pramod Mahajan.

The India-EU Summit was a historic event, which symbolised the goal of India and the European Union to build a new strategic partnership based on common values and aspirations.

I shared with the European leaders our perception that terrorism remained a major threat to international peace and stability.

In this context, I drew the attention of the European leaders the threats faced by India from cross-border terrorism and of the dangers posed by extremists religious groups which were spreading intolerance and violence within our region. The EU extended full support for the Comprehensive Convention on International Terrorism sponsored by India.

We agreed on the importance of sustaining a dialogue between our respective civil societies. An Indo-EU Round Table comprising of eminent non-official personalities on both sides and a network of Think Tanks will be established as a part of this dialogue.

On the economic side, we agreed to elevate our co-operation through the enhancement of trade and investment. The EU agreed to encourage larger flows of Foreign Direct Investment especially in the infrastructure sector.

Following our discussions, the EU announced that an additional textile quota of 3500 tonnes would be released for India under exceptional flexibility. Discussions would continue on prospects of further release of textile quotas under this provision.

An agreement was concluded with the EU for financing infrastructure projects in the field of civil aviation.

We found common ground in our discussions on environment issues and agreed that a Joint Working Group on Environment would be set up.

We agreed on institutional arrangement for carrying forward the India-EU dialogue. The summits will take place hereafter on a regular basis. I invited the European leaders to the next summit which will take place in India next year. Annual dialogues will also be held at the level of the External Affairs Minister and other Ministers, as also the meetings between the senior officials on both sides.

My visit to Lisbon was also utilised for a bilateral dialogue with Portugal. I had detailed discussions with President Sampiao and Prime Minister Guterres, which covered bilateral, regional and global issues of common interest.

With Portugal, we have transcended our colonial past and entered into a new relationship based on mutual respect and appreciation. In the recent past, visits have taken place to Portugal of our President, the Vice President and the External Affairs Minister. During our stay, I and my colleagues experienced the exceptional warmth and the hospitality of the Portuguese leaders and the people.

Portugal has endorsed India's legitimate claim for joining the Security Council as a permanent member. There was equally strong support for India's initiative for a Comprehensive Convention on International Terrorism.

We agreed to strengthen our economic ties. Portugal expressed appreciation of our economic progress in recent years, especially in areas like Information Technology. It was agreed that a Joint Working Group would be set up on Information Technology.

A Bilateral Investment Protection Agreement (BIPA) was signed with Portugal during my visit.

The Portuguese leaders made warm references to India's emergence as a global player. We shared perceptions on multi-polarity and agreed to work closely together for International Peace and Prosperity.

I invited the President and the Prime Minister of Portugal to visit India. It was agreed that the dates of the visits would be decided on the basis of mutual convenience.

I am convinced that my visits to Italy and Portugal have further strengthened the bonds of friendship and co-operation between India and the European Union.

I had an extremely productive discussion with President Ciampi and PM D'Amato on a range of regional and international issues of common interest. Italy appreciated our concerns on cross border terrorism and expressed support for our draft Convention on Inter-national Terrorism. I sensitised the Italian leadership with regard to our security and strategic concerns.

Italy is also appreciative of our economic reforms programme and would like to improve and increase trade with India. An agreement on tourism was signed. Italy is greatly interested in our expertise in IT.

Address at the Asia Society

New York, September 7, 2000

Ladies and Gentlemen,

It is a great pleasure to return to Asia Society. It is a privilege to once again address this distinguished gathering of scholars, thinkers, captains of industry and practitioners of foreign policy.

Two years ago, I had the opportunity to share my thoughts with you on future relations between India and the United States of America. This March, President Bill Clinton and I outlined the vision of a new relationship between the world's two largest democracies in the 21st century.

This vision is anchored in something that is fundamental to both countries. And is best captured in the joint declaration we signed, A Vision for the 21st Century:

"We are nations forged from many traditions and faiths, proving year after year that diversity is our strength. From vastly different origins and experiences, we have come to the same conclusions: that freedom and democracy are the strongest bases for both peace and prosperity, and that they are universal aspirations, constrained neither by culture nor levels of economic development."

As India and the United States work to deepen their ties, these common conclusions are greatly strengthened by institutions such as Asia Society.

You provide a forum to examine the antiquities of Asian civilisations, study current Asian affairs and analyse possible future developments. These interactions have helped us understand how the USA perceives Asia, especially India. I hope they have also helped members of the Asia Society acquire a deeper understanding of India's aspirations and her desired place in the world.

Since I last addressed Asia Society members, there have been several political and economic developments in India.

In the fall of 1999, we had a fresh mid-term general election. By giving a clear and decisive mandate for the National Democratic Alliance, the people of India have once again reposed their faith in our policies and programmes. More importantly, they have wholeheartedly reiterated their unflinching commitment to democracy.

Ironically, even as my Government was being sworn in, an elected Government in our neighbourhood was being dismantled and democracy being snuffed out by that country's military. The irony was even greater because the coup took place in the dying light of the 20th century whose passage into history was supposed to herald a new era free of militarist triumphs over democratic values.

These and other developments in India and her neighbourhood represent, in a larger sense, India's success as a democracy in South Asia, indeed in Asia. The political, economic and social transformation that is taking place in India today embodies the aspirations of a billion people as well as our Government—equality of opportunity, power of participation and freedom to succeed.

We believe that empowering the individual means empowering the nation. And empowerment is best served through rapid economic growth coupled with rapid social change. To keep pace with the fast changing global economy, we have taken several steps to deepen and broaden the process of economic reforms.

It is true that only by opening our doors can we usher in the wind of change. But it is equally true that we need to be cautious so that all we have and value are protected if the wind were to turn into a storm. And because we are a vibrant democracy, we have to be sensitive that the weak and the vulnerable benefit from economic reforms and globalisation.

We will continue to make our markets more conducive to enterprise and initiative. We will continue to make our institutions stronger and more transparent. We will continue to invest in people, who are our greatest resource and strength. In short, the course we have charted hinges on the twin goals of economic growth with social equity.

Impatient investors and eager sellers can often be heard saying that India is slow to change. To them, I have this to say: We are a diverse democracy and we need to carry the people with us. Efforts are being made in this direction and we are confident of success.

India today is a nation on the move. The momentum for progress has started gathering speed. Nowhere is this more pronounced than in industries that will shape global economic relations of the future, industries that also are the prime movers of Indo-US relations—information technology, knowledge intensive industries, entertainment, communications and services.

I would also urge those who tend not to notice this change to heed the fact that we have averaged a stable and consistent growth of over six per cent a year in the last decade. We have laid the foundation for significantly higher long-term growth of seven per cent and beyond. This is something few economies can claim with certitude.

It is, in a fundamental sense, our emphasis on stable political and dynamic economic environments that has helped accelerate growth. Openness and transparency, rule of law and free flow of information that characterise democracy are also the institutions on which durable and stable market economies are founded.

And an increasingly open and dynamic India does not see its socio-economic development in isolation. We see our fortunes linked to the prosperity and stability of our Asian neighbours, indeed, to that of the global community.

Friends, India's historic and civilisational role in Asia over millennia is well recognised. A large number of countries in Asia trace the roots of their cultural traditions to India. India has been, and continues to be, the link between West Asia and East Asia. In a sense, India is central to the Asian identity.

Much of the harmony and stability that we seek in Asia would depend on how India evolves and reflects its growing strength. It would depend on not only economic progress, but also how best we are able to nurture and strengthen our democratic way of life and plural society.

It will also depend on our success in ensuring peace and stability around us. In this great endeavour, I am sure we will derive strength and encouragement from our growing, co-operative relationship with the United States of America.

We are conscious that for all the promise of co-operative prosperity, Asia also faces risks and challenges to its future security environment. Asia is still striving to cement its various fault lines, reconcile past differences with future interdependence, confront the challenge to progressive and liberal values from terrorism and religious extremism that belongs to the medieval age, and cope with social strains caused by unequal development.

Asia faces future risks from possible aggressive assertion of interests and claims. Across the immense space and diversity of Asia, the challenges are sometimes similar, but often different.

The task of securing India's future in this complex scenario of risks and challenges is ultimately ours. We will exercise our judgement, witn responsibility and restraint, to meet our objective.

As I see it, Asia's collective peace and prosperity will be best secured only when nations on this continent develop common stakes and are no longer divided by narrow interests. And, common stakes can be developed only through close ties and friendly relations.

As the largest country in South Asia and the only one that shares borders with all other countries in the region, we are mindful of our special responsibility in taking the leadership in fostering co-operation. Indeed, India has consistently sought to build good neighbourly relations in the South Asian region. This is not only the policy of my Government, but is a reflection of our national consensus. We seek no undue favours, nor do we accept the right of others to seek unilateral advantages.

In pursuit of this approach, we have displayed a generosity of spirit that few countries can match. We have shown this in our dealings with all our neighbours. Again, this is as much a reflection of my Government's thinking as of our national genius.

All these have been an integral part of our approach to Pakistan, also. From the time of the Shimla Agreement—a generous agreement if ever there was one—we have sought to build friendly relations. Those of you who were present when I last addressed the Asia Society in 1998, will recall my emphasising India's faith in bilateral dialogue and accords in building peaceful relations with Pakistan.

In the spring of last year, I travelled to Lahore in search of a new quality of relations in the sub-continent and a new age of regional co-operation. That our initiative was not merely a gesture is reflected in the Lahore Declaration and the resumption of composite dialogue.

The rulers of Pakistan responded through Kargil in the summer of 1999. The history of that episode is well known. Pakistan suffered a military and diplomatic defeat. But instead of heeding international opinion, instead of responding to our offer to normalise relations, Pakistan responded by removing the last vestiges of democracy and embarking upon a yet more adventurous course of stepping up its terrorist campaign.

The hijack of the Indian Airlines aircraft to Kandahar in the winter of last year, the massacre of 40 innocent Indians during the visit of President Clinton in March, the carnage that left more than 100 men, women and children dead and whose purpose was to scuttle the nascent peace talks in Kashmir, are part of the painful record of this cross-border terrorist campaign.

In the face of extreme provocation, we have shown patience and restraint. Unfortunately, Pakistan has misread our generosity of spirit and our desire for friendly relations as weakness. It has consciously opted to pursue the path of hostility by promoting terrorism in different parts of India.

The protagonists of this terror campaign are known to the world. The proliferation of practitioners of medieval religious extremism in our neighbourhood is only one of the factors that have contributed to cross-border terrorism. But they have provided a convenient cloak to disguise the aggression on our civil society—the cloak of *jihad.*

This is nothing but an attempt by those who have adopted cross-border terrorism as an instrument of state policy to disown responsibility for their terrible crimes against humanity. We reject, and we call upon the international community to reject, attempts to cloak cross-border terrorism as *jihad.*

We are a patient people and have persevered in the search for a peaceful settlement with Pakistan in the conviction that war is in nobody's interest. We have displayed patience and restraint in order to discharge our higher responsibilities towards the region.

We are determined to preserve and protect our national interests. None should doubt that India has the means and the will to protect her territorial integrity, secular unity and communal harmony. We will continue to conduct ourselves in accordance with the great traditions bequeathed to us by our civilisational history in combating the terrorism and instability that is emanating from our neighbouring region.

Nevertheless, India remains committed to a composite dialogue process with her neighbour. But for any meaningful dialogue, that country must demonstrate its commitment to existing bilateral agreements and abjure cross-border terrorism. Unfortunately, the current leadership of Pakistan has time and again publicly repudiated both the Shimla Agreement and the Lahore Declaration.

Terrorism poses as much a threat to all countries that subscribe to open society and democracy, as to India. In fact, many a country in the West, including the USA, is seized of this problem.

Huge amounts of narcotics that form the mainstay of terrorist funding are today finding their way into the USA and European countries. Some terrorist groups have sought sanctuary in the West. Let there be no doubt that they will one day threaten the fabric of those very societies that have given them shelter today. Indeed, the USA is already facing this threat.

India has been in the forefront of campaigning for early adoption of the Comprehensive Convention Against Terrorism. We acknowledge with appreciation the USA's support on this front. We look forward to the Convention's adoption by the United Nations General Assembly.

When I addressed Asia Society in 1998, I had mentioned how India had raised, for five decades, her voice for universal verifiable nuclear disarmament. But not only was our voice disregarded, India's sovereign right to keep the nuclear option open was sought to be curtailed.

In the circumstances, we exercised our nuclear option. Our decision was as much influenced by national security concerns as to assert our objection to nuclear apartheid.

The multipolar world of the 21st century necessitates a plural society order that accommodates and acknowledges the growing strength and confidence of emerging economic and security players. We believe that in the emerging multipolar world, a plural society order alone can deal with the challenges of the new era.

Hence, our resolve to build a multipolar world where we have strategic space and autonomy in decision-making, instead of being subjected to the hypocrisy and hegemony of those who refuse to dismantle their nuclear stockpiles.

However, our decision to acquire credible minimum nuclear deterrent has not deflected us from our belief that peace between nations in this new century is best guaranteed by nuclear disarmament, and not nuclear deterrence. But there appears to be little inclination on part of nations that have acquired huge stockpiles and delivery systems to turn their swords into ploughshares.

Therefore, till such time weapons of mass destruction are dismantled, we will retain a credible minimum deterrent. Our experience has taught us that to defend peace, we have to be strong.

Above all, India's security, stability and prosperity are central to security, stability, democracy and prosperity in Asia. The security of a billion people will contribute to the security of Asia. Our strength and unity will be vital to the stability of Asia. Our prosperity will support prosperity in the region. And, the initiatives we take to uphold all that India values and symbolises will not threaten, but strengthen, the future of others.

I also believe that those who share our vision of Asia must show in the policies they formulate that they recognise our stakes in the region and the full sweep of our security concerns. I cannot imagine that any future paradigms or arrangements for security in the region can be effective if it does not include India.

Friends, as a nuclear weapon state, we acknowledge the responsibilities that come attached with it. Indeed, India has proved to the world, in more ways than one, that it is a responsible state.

We have maintained our unilateral moratorium on further tests. We have scrupulously adhered to export controls, unlike some countries in Asia. We continue with our "no first use" policy.

On CTBT, we have been involved in seeking a national consensus. However, pending the evolution of a national consensus on India signing the CTBT, my Government will not prevent the Treaty's entry into force. We also believe that all other countries that must ratify CTBT under article XIV of the Treaty, should do so without condition. My Government has agreed to participate in negotiations on a FMCT at the Conference on Disarmament in Geneva.

All this demonstrates that India's genuine concern is to secure her national interests without in any manner affecting peace and stability in the region. If I may quote one of your presidents, we believe that peace lies in strength.

We believe that economic restrictions serve little purpose other than being irritants in bilateral relations. We feel, as do your policy makers, that India and the USA are natural allies. Given the potential of mutual benefit of close co-operation between India and the USA, it is for you to judge how far such restrictions serve our mutual interests.

Before I conclude, I would like to comment on what is perhaps the most significant development in India-US relations since I last had the opportunity to speak to you.

Address at the US - India Business Summit

New York, September 13, 2000

I am happy to be with all of you this morning for the US-India Business Summit.

I congratulate the CII for arranging – or, rather, re-arranging – this event. I am sorry for the inconvenience caused to you because of the change in the date of this event.

I value this interaction with such a wide cross section of trade and industry. New York symbolizes the spirit of enterprise and innovation. It is this spirit that has driven the US economy with such distinction.

We have watched with admiration the longest period of economic boom in the United States. We have carefully assessed its impact on the global economy, including on our economy.

We are reinforced in our conviction that there is a natural synergy between our two societies in many spheres. This also includes the economic sphere.

What unites us is not only our common commitment to democracy, liberty, openness and pluralism. It is also a perspective on economic growth. A perspective in which private enterprise is given maximum encouragement by the State that limits its own role to that of a facilitator and impartial regulator.

For historical reasons, private enterprise in India was not assigned the desired role in the initial decades after Independence. Since the Nineties, we are correcting this situation by a comprehensive set of economic reforms.

My own Government is committed to further broaden, deepen and accelerate the process of reforms. We are convinced that this will unleash the full potential of economic growth and social development in India.

I am happy to note that the US Government and US enterprises have responded positively to the historic change being effected in the Indian economy.

The United States is today India's largest trading partner. The US companies are also the largest investors in India.

Most major US corporations, banks and financial institutions are present in India. We value their contribution to our economic growth.

Equally, I am sure, they value their business in India and the contribution that our expanding economy is making to their business profitability. We would like to deepen this relationship.

In the last ten years total approval for US investments to India is a mere 15 billion dollars. Actual flows are even smaller.

In the context of the new opportunities, we must dramatically alter this arithmetic. Let us accept a target of a 5 billion dollars of annual flow beginning next year and raise it to 15 billion dollars over the next three years.

This is ambitious. It is, however, achievable.

Let us also agree to at least double bilateral trade flows over the next three years. There is enough scope for that.

I realize that apart from motivating you, we also need to change. I am not unmindful that you often find our rules, regulations and procedures burdensome.

There is an image problem often described as "hassles of doing business in India". This is partly a communication problem.

The success stories do not circulate fast enough. One failure proves infectious.

Many approved projects are languishing. Assistance in project implementation is one area that needs to be strengthened.

I am, therefore, creating a Strategic Management Group in the Prime

Minister's Office where difficulties encountered by large investment projects will be speedily resolved. An Inter-Ministerial Team would assist this Cell. The Group would directly report to me once a month.

Many of the project problems concern State Governments. I would be urging the Chief Ministers to take a similar initiative. I am sure that this will impart some momentum and seriousness to address 'implementational concerns'.

Distinguished American businessmen, when you look at India, I urge you not to be overly influenced by the size of the present bilateral economic engagement between our two countries.

Rather, take a long-term view by looking at the magnitude of the opportunities and rewards as they will unfold in the future.

The interests of India and the United States are complementary. Let us harness this complementarity to the fullest.

India today is among the fastest growing economies of the world. Our annual growth of over 6 per cent in the Nineties makes us among the top ten fast growing economies in the world.

On our Independence Day this year, I have pledged my Government to a new target: The target of doubling our per capita income over the next decade.

This implies an annual GDP growth of 9 per cent and more. This is a daunting target, but a target that India will achieve.

The reform process in India is on an irreversible course. Discussions and differences within the party and across parties are natural in a democratic polity.

Open public discussion fortifies national consensus. It mobilizes social support and protects reforms from uncertainties of political change.

We also want to alter the focal points of change. As a result of our efforts, reforms are being perceived less and less as being 'elitist driven'.

We are taking concrete measures to cushion the impact of change on the weaker sections of the society. The trickle down effect of growth is often slow. Which is why, we are consciously trying to harmonize faster economic growth with equitable development.

We are determined to ensure that the benefits of reforms do not bypass the common man.

We have strengthened the focus on agriculture and rural development. Areas like rural connectivity, safe drinking water, shelter and sanitation are being given higher priority.

We are paying far greater attention to the development of the social sector – especially primary health and primary education. We know that this is critical for the enrichment of India's vast human capital. This is also the most important resource in the emerging era of the Knowledge Economy.

As a result of our initiatives, the constituency for reform is rapidly enlarging.

My Government has created many new opportunities for private investment. Let me illustrate this:

A. There has been a massive deregulation to create investment opportunities in infrastructure.

B. We now have a world class Information Technology Policy. The IT and other knowledge-based enterprises offer the greatest opportunity for mutually beneficial partnership between Indian and American businesses. We have already seen many successes of this partnership. But this is just the beginning. The future is going to be immensely more attractive and fruitful.

C. India now has the professional manpower to truly maximize the benefit from the "New Economy". We are doubling the number of professionals from our educational institutions in one year and tripling them in three years.

We shall encourage collaboration between Indian and American educational institutions for joint research and training. Further, private, NRI and foreign investment in education – especially in technical and higher education — will be promoted

D. In the telecom sector there is total deregulation —

- o On national long distance;
- o On freedom to choose from own under-sea optical fibre cable;
- o On basic telephony;
- o VSNL's monopoly on international long-distance telephony is being removed.

The Department of Telecommunications is being corporatised by 1st October.

A Telecom Convergence Bill is in the offing.

- We are also considering how best to deregulate cellular telephony completely.
- We are building 13,000 kilometres of new National Highway in seven years.
- Ports are being corporatised and private participation in port building welcome.
- There have been complaints about power projects in the past. We want to undo this. Power requires huge investment in India to meet our energy needs.

The de-politicization of tariff fixation and its acceptance by many State Governments create new opportunities. I expect several important commercial agreements to be signed even during my visit.

Several large power projects languishing for years should see financial closure over the next four to six months.

A new Electricity Bill 2000, which significantly deregulates the power sector, is on the anvil. It will enable much greater consumer freedom. It will also enable private sector to take decisions on generation, transmission and distribution by unbundling them.

The regime for Direct Foreign Investment has now been made automatic. Sectoral caps are under constant review by a Group of Ministers. I expect further relaxations in many areas shortly.

Financial sector reforms are an area of high priority. Our financial institutions have adopted prudential norms consistent with international norms. Banking supervision follows the Basel guidelines. The disinvestment of Government equity in banks will be accelerated. This will further improve their competitive efficiency.

Disinvestment in general is receiving our close attention. We now have a credible disinvestment programme. During the course of this year there will be a significant disinvestment of some major companies covering the sectors of oil, telecom, airlines and hotels.

The resources realized would be mainly utilized to retire debt or meet social sector obligations. The Cabinet Committee on Disinvestment under my Chairmanship has been activated to achieve tangible results with definite milestones.

In sharing my thoughts on many of these issues I do not want to gloss over difficulties. Serious problems do exist in many areas, particularly long-term fiscal management.

While our tax rates are internationally competitive, tax administration needs significant improvement. Tax reforms also require urgent attention and the Double Taxation Treaty needs to be revisited.

Government expenditure needs to be pruned. Sustained action in this area is planned on the basis of the recommendations of the Expenditure Commission. The Fiscal Responsibility Act before Parliament would reinforce these measures.

State finances also need attention. The Finance Commission has made some important recommendations and it is my intention to pursue them with seriousness.

In short, there are enormous opportunities. There are no doubt problems and risks of investment. I, however, venture to suggest that the opportunities far outweigh the risks.

The opportunities and a conducive environment will grow. The problems and risks will ease.

The extraordinary achievement of Indian Americans in this country is sufficient testimony to the human resource of skill and enterprise available in India.

We also have:

- A widespread use of English language;
- A transparent legal system and rule of law;
- Respect for sanctity of contracts;
- And, above all, an unbroken record of fully honouring all international obligations.

India is poised for high all-round economic and social development. Today I seek your partnership in fostering this change. Partnership in participating in our prosperity.

Having recognized each other as "natural allies", India and the United States are poised to vastly strengthen and deepen our bilateral relations in the new century. Let us build a strong foundation of Indo–US economic relations to support the beautiful architecture of our natural alliance.

May I leave you with the words of our great poet Rabindranath Tagore who said:

Once we dreamt that we were strangers, we woke up to find that we were dear to each other.

The Vision Statement signed between President Clinton and myself in March this year represents this new re-awakening. I seek your participation in realizing this common dream.

I thank you for the opportunity of sharing my thoughts with you.

Remarks during the Meeting with the Think Tank Scholars

Washington D.C.

September 14, 2000

I am delighted to have this opportunity to meet such a distinguished gathering of American scholars and thinkers. Through my many years of public life, I have known some of you personally, others through your writings.

That is why I say that this great wealth of American intellect, in Blair House today, is a tribute to India.

I am aware also of the unique role that the institutions that you represent play in the United States, particularly in the formulation of US foreign policy. My delegation and I welcome you most warmly on that account, too, and look forward to a stimulating evening.

India is a factor for stability, peace and growth in Asia. But not in Asia alone. The role that it will play, and the influence that it will have on international prosperity and security is, I believe, significant and that should engage the attention of foreign policy experts such as yourselves.

As for India and the United States of America, this March, President Clinton and I had the privilege of outlining a new vision for the future relationship between our two countries. It is a vision founded on our many shared values, but equally on our many converging and common interests in Asia and beyond. We jointly set a goal.

That is yet to be attained. Both countries have still some distance to travel in fulfilling that vision.

For that we need to more clearly define the terms of our engagement. Non-proliferation and security related issues have cast a shadow on our relations. I have spoken on these matters at the US Congress. Let me just say that we do not wish to undermine your non-proliferation efforts. We ask you in turn to understand our security concerns. We have held consultations with political parties on CTBT. These discussions will continue with a view to forging a national consensus.

I must share with you, in all candour, some concerns that have been articulated at these meetings. The public debate has placed them mainly in the context of security-related developments in Asia, particularly the rapid pace of modernisation and expansion of nuclear forces in our neighbourhood.

There are concerns at the continuing cooperation for nuclear and missile technologies in our neighbourhood. Many of these concerns are based on assessments made in this country. You are familiar with these developments; you have examined their implications for American security.

About India and its neighbourhood: What is India's neighbourhood? Do not see India in a limited geographical context, or in the routinely delineated South Asian identity alone or only when you think of our western neighbour — Pakistan. Uptill 1947, we had common borders with Iran, as indeed with Afghanistan, too. With Tibet and China we have our longest land border. These remain, amongst others, our geo-political determinants. I am, therefore, somewhat perplexed when "South Asia" is described as "a dangerous place", or "a nuclear flash point". I find in these phrases the echo of alarmist calls raised by our neighbour — Pakistan. But this amounts — paraphrasing what a former Prime Minister of UK had said, to supplying the "oxygen" of anxiety and publicity that terrorism needs. Do reflect whether your expressions, however well intentioned, not produce precisely the consequences that you seek to prevent.

I urge you, therefore, not to simply stick labels. Do distinguish between cause and effect, between the malaise and its symptoms.

The tensions that we are witnessing in our western region, focussed on Afghanistan and over spilling in all directions, are manifestations of the growth of extremism in our neighbourhood. This affects us directly In fact, it is directed against us.

This extremism is the consequence of anyhow justifying an untenable ideology; of a variety of medieval malevolence founded on a perverse interpretation of faith. It is an attempt to establish a point, through violence, that a pluralist, secular, all inclusive and democratic society cannot exist in the region. And all this for a profoundly important reason: because it challenges the proclaimed basis of nationhood of some.

When we hear calls for 'jehad' against India, when calls for the destruction and dismemberment of India are made and when international agreements like Shimla and Lahore are belittled, then the people of India wonder whether the problem lies in the valley of Kashmir or this constant attempt to define nationhood in terms only of compulsive animosity towards India.

India is, of course, capable, and is determined, and we shall do everything it takes to preserve India — its integrity, stability and security.

We have faced this challenge in the past. It is not a geographical India whose undermining is desired. It is the values on which our society — and yours — is founded.

But be assured: We have the strength, the maturity and the understanding to act with restraint and responsibility. As we demonstrated when we were challenged in Kargil, or in Kandhar, or in the massacre of a hundred innocents on their way to a time honoured pilgrimage in the Valley of Kashmir.

But we have another responsibility, too. India has to address itself to the questions raised by my countrymen and women in the State of Jammu & Kashmir. This State is not any "core issue" of territorial contention; it is at the core of India's nationhood.

Like any other integral part of India Jammu & Kashmir must get the full benefits of India's democracy, secularism and economic growth. All these expectations have not been fulfilled in full measure. A variety of reasons explain this. Cross border terrorism and efforts to undermine every initiative that India takes is also part of that totality.

We made a beginning in that direction in July this year. Our initiatives were welcomed by the large collectivity of citizens in the region. This welcome held promise of expanding the 'constituency of peace'. The hope that was generated, in all of India, and most particularly in Jammu & Kashmir, was sacrificed at the altar of inhumanity – of killing of innocents.

But hope for peace can never be killed. That is why we remain undeterred in our efforts. I have said so in our Parliament and I reiterate—we will talk to all those who give up the path of violence and embrace the path of peace.

Our approach is clear. It is based on five fundamental propositions: One, religion or sword shall no longer be used to redefine boundaries. Two, this is the age of reconciliation not of conflict. Three, whether it is Jammu or Kashmir or Ladakh the citizens of J&K are tired of violence and bloodshed. Four, it is time to stop the bloodletting and time for healing wounds in Jammu & Kashmir. And fifth, India is prepared to heal the wounds by the larger power of *insaniyat* – of humanity.

In this time and age the irrefutable need is for regional cooperation. India understands and accepts its responsibility as the largest country of the region. We have demonstrated this in our completely free access agreements, for example, with Nepal and Bhutan. We have a Free Trade Agreement with Sri Lanka. We are improving our concessional arrangements with Bangladesh. Greater growth and prosperity through greater economic integration is our announced policy. This rising momentum of integration in our region often goes unnoticed, in a world that is preoccupied only with the contours of relations between India and its western neighbourhood. There are other examples of cooperation: Like BIMSTEK or the recently announced 'Ganga-Mekong'.

For us in India economic growth, human development and eradication of crippling poverty, are not only the most important goals; they are, simply, the only worthwhile goals. They are my bounden duty.

My government is committed to constantly deepening economic reforms and to improve the relevant policy frameworks. We have laid the foundation for achieving an annual economic growth rate of 8-9 per cent. We remain conscious of the need to distribute the benefits of this progress to the widest sections of the people. Our growth, the size of our economy, our participative institutions, and our strengths in the new frontier areas of knowledge-based industries, will benefit Asia, and in the fullness of time, the world.

In a world still working itself through the changes brought about by the end of the Cold War, an economically strong, democratic, pluralist India will share its wider responsibility and confront larger challenges.

The future contours of Asia are by no means settled or certain. There are many challenges to its future. It is a continent still striving to cement the various fault lines, not the least between democracy and other forms of government.

But above all, Asia faces risks from aggressive assertion of national interests, if necessary to the exclusion of the interests and concerns of others in and outside Asia.

Many of these questions, I believe, will have to be faced by India and the United States jointly. That is why I believe that the US and India will have to work together in joint endeavours for the pursuit of regional and international peace, stability and prosperity.

I now look forward very much to your views on these and other issues.

Thank you.

Remarks at the India Caucus Lunch

Washington, D.C.

September 14, 2000

Mr. Co-Chairman Gary Ackerman and Jim Greenwood, Friends of India:

It is a great pleasure to be here with you today.

I would like to begin by thanking all of you. By promoting better Indo-US relations by focusing attention of the House on positive elements like growing trade and economic interaction, you have been friends in deed and friends in need.

The India Caucus is an outstanding example of participatory democracy. It serves as a bridge between the 1.5 million strong Indian American community and their elected representatives.

The Caucus took shape seven years ago with four members. I understand that today it has more than 120 members. This reflects both the growing confidence of the Indian American community and the increasingly close relationship between India and the US on wide-ranging issues.

We have noted with gratitude your support for India during last summer's intrusion by Pakistani Army regulars in India's Kargil sector. As we have your efforts to block certain amendments.

We share your commitment to promote democracy and protest its demise at the hands of military rulers.

Earlier today, when I addressed the Joint meeting of the US Congress, I began by recalling the adoption of the India Resolution by an overwhelming vote of 396 to 4, calling for the broadening of Indo-US relations into a strategic partnership. That Resolution's successful adoption owes much to Caucus members who co-sponsored it.

We believe that the challenge posed to open, plural and democratic societies by terrorism calls for concerted international action. We are greatly encouraged by the support extended by India Caucus members to our efforts in this regard. We know that we are not alone in voicing concern over and fighting the challenge of international terrorism.

Your support in expanding Indo-US economic and business relations also encourage us. India looks forward to American investors, industry and business to collaborate with their Indian counterparts in an environment that is conducive to growth, development and mutually enriching enterprise.

India and the US have much to gain from a close relationship between two natural allies. I am confident that the India Caucus will play a leading role in giving an impetus to this relationship, thus serving as a bridge between the peoples of our two great countries.

On behalf of the people of India and my colleagues in the democratically elected Parliament of India, I once again express my heart-felt thanks to all of you.

Thank you.

Remarks at a meeting with the US House International Relations Committee

Washington D.C.

September 14, 2000

Congressman Benjamin Gilman, Chairman of the House International Relations Committee,

Congressman Sam Gejdenson,

Members of the Committee,

Ladies and Gentlemen.

I am delighted to be here today to renew my friendship with some, to establish contact with others and to strike a dialogue with all.

Your Committee is at the cutting edge of the reach of the United States to the rest of the world. As a fellow parliamentarian, I am conscious of the need for a strong popular endorsement and backing for the foreign policy initiatives of government. You are the channel for the people's energy, endorsement or disapproval.

To the world of alliances, power politics, conflict and change, legislatures impart a ballast of morality, principles and ideals. It is not less important that you also control the purse strings of government. No taxation without representation is as relevant as no spending without authorization.

Members of the Committee, I salute your abiding contribution to the enrichment of Indo-US relations. Spanning different Administrations and times you have imparted to the relationship the stamp of continuity and predictability.

The challenges that confront us today have a strong moral dimension.

Afghanistan is an unfortunate example of a country processed into anarchy by outsiders. It has emerged as a world leader of terrorism, drugs and medieval bigotry that challenges civilized societies everywhere. As a neighbour, India is naturally concerned. As leading democracies USA and India must lead the effort to restore to Afghanistan a broad-based government.

Regrettably, we in India are at the frontline of the fight against terrorism. The area on our west has become the epicentre of this criminal enterprise. It is not only India's fight but yours as well. Experience has shown that hatred can explode bombs in New Delhi with as much ease as in New York or Moscow. Let us work together to fight these dangers and not accommodate them.

What happened in Fiji was not only a criminal overthrow of an elected government but the resurrection of racism. Unless checked, such tendencies lead to ethnic cleansing and further conflict.

Let me also reaffirm that India will work closely with the USA to address issues of international security. Our nuclear policy is transparent and restrained. We have in place a unilateral moratorium on nuclear explosive tests and a policy of no first use. Let us remain engaged and work together to free the world of all weapons of mass destruction.

Thank you.

Address to the Joint Session of the United States Congress

Washington, D.C.

September 14, 2000

Mr. Speaker,

Mr. President Protem,

Honourable Members of the United State Congress,

It is with a deep sense of honour that I speak to you today. I would like to thank you, Mr. Speaker, and the members of the Congress for giving me this opportunity.

In November 1999 a remarkable event took place in the House of Representatives. By a vote of 396 to 4, the House adopted a resolution congratulating India and my government on the successful elections completed in October 1999. This display of broad-based bipartisan support for strengthening relations with India is heartening.

It is a source of encouragement to both President Clinton and to me, as we work together to infuse a new quality in our ties. I thank you for the near-unique approach that you have adopted towards my country.

Those of you who saw the warm response to President Clinton's speech to our Parliament in March this year will recognise that similar cross-party support exists in India as well for deeper engagement with the USA.

I am also deeply touched by the resolution adopted in the House two days ago welcoming my visit and the prospect of closer Indo-US understanding.

Mr. Speaker,

American people have shown that democracy and individual liberty provide the conditions in which knowledge progresses, science discovers, innovation occurs, enterprise thrives and, ultimately, people advance.

To more than a million and half from my country, America is now home. In turn, their industry, enterprise and skills are contributing to the advancement of American society.

I see in the outstanding success of the Indian community in America, a metaphor of the vast potential that exists in Indo-US relations, and what we can achieve together.

Just as American experience has been a lesson in what people can achieve in a democratic framework, India has been the laboratory of a democratic process rising to meet the strongest challenges that can be flung at it.

In the half century of our independent existence, we have woven an exquisite tapestry. Out of diversity we have brought unity. The several languages of India speak with one voice under the roof of our Parliament.

In your remarkable experiment as a nation state, you have proven the same truth. Out of the huddled masses that you welcomed to your shores you have created a great nation.

For me the most gratifying of the many achievements of Indian democracy has been the change it has brought to the lives of the weak and the vulnerable.

To give just one figure, in recent years it has enabled more than a million women in small towns and distant villages to enter local elected councils and to decide on issues that touch upon their lives.

Two years ago, while much of Asia was convulsed by economic crisis, India held its course.

In the last ten years, we have grown at 6.5 per cent per year: that puts India among the ten fastest growing economies of the world.

Economic activity gets more and more diversified by the year: President Clinton and many among the friends gathered here have had occasion to glimpse our advances in information technology.

We are determined to sustain the momentum of our economy: our aim is to double our per capita income in ten years — and that means we must grow at 9 per cent a year.

To achieve this order of growth we have ushered in comprehensive reforms. We are committed to releasing the creative genius of our people, the entrepreneurial skills of the men and women of the country, of its scientists and craftsmen. At the same time, we in India, remain committed to the primacy of the State in fulfilling its social obligations to the deprived, the weak and the poor.

Important sectors of the country's infrastructure — power, insurance, banking, telecom — are being opened to private initiative, domestic and foreign.

Trade barriers are being lowered.

Mr. Speaker, ladies and gentlemen,

There are forces outside our country that believe that they can use terror to unravel the territorial integrity of India. They wish to show that a multi-religious society cannot exist.

They pursue a task in which they are doomed to fail.

No country has faced as ferocious an attack of terrorist violence as India has over the past two decades: 21,000 were killed by foreign sponsored terrorists in Punjab alone, 16,000 have been killed in Jammu and Kashmir.

As many of you here in the Congress have in recent hearings recognised a stark fact: no region is a greater source of terrorism than our neighbourhood.

Indeed, in our neighbourhood — in this, the 21st century — religious war has not just been fashioned into, it has been proclaimed to be, an instrument of State policy.

Distance offers no insulation. It should not cause complacence.

You know, and I know: such evil cannot succeed.

But even in foiling it could inflict untold suffering.

That is why the United States and India have begun to deepen their cooperation for combating terrorism. We must redouble these efforts.

Mr. Speaker, ladies and gentlemen,

There was a time when we were on the other side of each other's globes. Today, on the digital map, India and the United States are neighbours and partners.

India and the United States have taken the lead in shaping the information age. Over the last decade, this new technology has sustained American prosperity in a way that has challenged conventional wisdom on economic growth.

We are two nations blessed with extraordinary resources and talent. Measured in terms of the industries of tomorrow, we are together defining the partnerships of the future.

But our two countries have the potential to do more to shape the character of the global economy in this century.

We should turn the example of our own cooperation into a partnership that uses the possibilities of the new technologies for defining new ways of fighting poverty, illiteracy, hunger, disease and pollution.

Mr. Speaker, ladies and gentlemen,

We believe that India and America can — and should — march hand in hand towards a world in which economic conditions improve for all.

A situation that provides comfortable living standards to one-third of the world's population, but condemns the remaining two-thirds to poverty and want, is unsustainable.

The foremost responsibility that the 21st century has cast on all of us is to change this unacceptable legacy of the past.

It should be our common endeavour to overcome this legacy. I, therefore, propose a comprehensive global dialogue on development.

We would be happy to offer New Delhi as the venue for this dialogue.

In this Congress, you have often expressed concern about the future contours of Asia. Will it be an Asia that will be at peace with itself? Or will it be a continent, where countries seek to redraw boundaries and settle claims — historical or imaginary — through force?

We seek an Asia where power does not threaten stability and security. We do not want the domination of some to crowd out the space for others. We must create an Asia where cooperative rather than aggressive assertion of national self-interests defines behaviour among nations.

If we want an Asia fashioned on such ideals — a democratic, prosperous, tolerant, pluralistic, stable Asia — if we want an Asia where our vital interests are secure, then it is necessary for us to re-examine old assumptions.

It is imperative for India and the United States to work together more closely in pursuit of those goals. In the years ahead, a strong, democratic and economically prosperous India, standing at the crossroads of all the major cultural and economic zones of Asia, will be an indispensable factor of stability in the region.

Our cooperation for peace and stability requires us to also define the principles of our own engagement. We must be prepared to accommodate our respective concerns.

We must have the mutual confidence to acknowledge our respective roles and complementary responsibilities in areas of vital importance to each of us.

Security issues have cast a shadow on our relationship. I believe this is unnecessary. We have much in common and no clash of interests.

We both share a commitment to ultimately eliminating nuclear weapons. We have both declared voluntary moratoriums on testing.

India understands your concerns. We do not wish to unravel your non-proliferation efforts. We wish you to understand our security concerns.

We are at a historic moment in our ties. As we embark on our common endeavour to build a new relationship, we must give practical shape to our shared belief that democracies can be friends, partners and allies.

In recent years, through all the good and difficult times, we have spoken to each other more often than we have ever done in the past. I thank President Clinton for this leadership and vision in steering this dialogue. I sincerely thank members of this Congress for supporting and encouraging this process.

As we talk with candour, we open the doors to new possibilities and new areas of cooperation — in advancing democracy, in combating terrorism, in energy and environment, science and technology and in international peacekeeping. And, we are discovering that our shared values and common interests are leading us to seek a natural partnership of shared endeavours.

India and the United States have taken a decisive step away from the past. The dawn of the new century has marked a new beginning in our relations.

Let us work to fulfill the promise and the hope of today.

Let us remove the shadow of hesitation that lies between us and our joint vision.

Let us use the strength of all that we have in common to build together a future that we wish for ourselves and for the world that we live in.

Thank you.

Toasts given by US Vice-President Al Gore and Prime Minister Vajpayee at the Luncheon Hosted by Vice President in his Honour

US State Department, Washington D.C.

September 15, 2000

Vice President Gore: Prime Minister Vajpayee, Members of the Indian delegation. Members of Congress. Distinguished guests. Ladies and gentlemen.

Welcome. It is a true privilege and pleasure for me to host you, Mr. Prime Minister, for today's luncheon.

In today's world, it is rare to find a leader who combines the qualities of idealism and pragmatism, confidence and humility. In you, Mr. Prime Minister, we find such a leader.

As a poet, you have inspired the imagination of your people with your eloquence. As Prime Minister, you have challenged your people to act on their imagination, to create a shared vision for a united, democratic, prosperous and peaceful India, and then to make that vision a reality. You are truly a leader in both word and deed.

President John Kennedy once said, in our country, "If more politicians knew poetry, and more poets knew politics, I am convinced the world would be a little better place to live." I cannot translate that into Hindi, but Mr. Prime Minister, you embody President Kennedy's words. You know both poetry and politics, and through your inspired leadership, you are indeed making the world a better place to live. In your poem *Oonchai* — or "height" in English — you speak of the importance of not losing touch with humanity as one rises in life. Your poem ends with a stirring line, which I would like to quote: "Never let me climb so high that I cannot bend down to embrace another human." You have dedicated your life to this noble ambition.

I am confident that India is destined for great heights. One of the World's great civilizations, India has emerged, of course, as one of its great democracies. India's history has been turbulent at times. But your nation is on the way to overcoming these challenges by embracing change, uniting all, and setting a course for the future.

The United States, Mr. Prime Minister, joins India as a partner on this journey. Our two nations share a special bond. As the world's oldest democracy and the world's largest democracy, we are, in your words, "natural allies." Our cultures and customs differ, but we share a strong commitment to democracy and equality for all. We are proof that diversity is strength, and that freedom is power.

The success of the Indian-American community testifies to the potential for our partnership. Many distinguished members of this Indian-American community join us here today. Indian-Americans have excelled in all fields of endeavour, from medicine to movies, science to airlines, and everything in between. And they have been at the forefront of the information revolution. Many Indian-Americans have found a home in

Silicon Valley, leading some of the most successful internet companies. They have made an invaluable contribution to America's prosperity and democratic life.

As the world's two leading democracies, we bear a special responsibility to take the lead in meeting the challenges that all democracies face. We must work together to ensure democracy's promises are realized by all our people, that all benefit from freedom. Quality education, public health, a clean environment — these are the goals we share and which together we can achieve. Threats that undermine democracy — such as terrorism and the proliferation of dangerous weapons technologies — are concerns we also share, and will work together to address.

When you were sworn-in as India's sixteenth Prime Minister two years ago, you said that you "have a pledge to redeem and a promise to fulfill." On behalf of all Americans, I pledge to you America's continued support, and promise you our lasting friendship.

Please join me now in raising our glasses in honour of Prime Minister Vajpayee and to the friendship between our two great nations.

Speech at the Lunch Hosted by US Vice President Al Gore
US State Department, Washington D.C.
September 15, 2000

Let me, on behalf of the Indian delegation, thank you for the warm welcome that we have received in the United States.

I also thank you, Mr. Vice President for your generous hospitality today, despite the responsibilities of your office and the obligations of your campaign.

Five decades ago as we took our first steps into freedom, President Harry Truman had written in his message of congratulations, "I earnestly hope that our friendship will in the future, as in the past, continue to be expressed in close and fruitful co-operation in international undertakings and in cordiality in our relations with one another."

In October of 1949, India's first Prime Minister Jawaharlal Nehru had stated, "it was necessary, even desirable, and, perhaps, inevitable that India and the United States should know each other more and co-operate with each other more."

In March this year, President Clinton and I outlined the vision of a closer and qualitatively new relationship in the 21st century between the world's two largest democracies. This morning he and I reaffirmed that vision.

The foundation of our relationship is cast in our many shared values.

It is reinforced by our many common aspirations. And, from what I have experienced over the past few days and yesterday at the Capitol Hill, this foundation rests on the broad support of the people of our two societies.

Today, Indians and Americans are driving innovation and defining partnerships in areas that will increasingly determine the process of wealth creation and global economic relations. It is our common responsibility to show leadership and vision to foster an environment in which the natural skills and talent that Americans and Indians have for the digital world can thrive and prosper.

It is important not only for our economic future, but also because it gives the chance to find new ways of fighting hunger, disease, illiteracy and pollution.

As should have been natural to us all along, we have in the recent years expanded and deepened our co-operation in pursuit of our common vision of shaping a future of peace, prosperity, democracy, pluralism and freedom.

There are many people in India and the United States, who are devoting their resources, energy, expertise, foresight and insight to build a closer relationship and stronger partnership between India and the United States.

The transformation that we are witnessing in Indo-US relations is in many ways a tribute to their efforts and vision. The Indian-American community is an important part of the process.

It is up to us, the leaders of our two countries, to support and consolidate this process. I thank you Mr. Vice President for your contribution to the strengthening of our ties.

Excellencies, Ladies and Gentlemen, may I invite you to join me in raising a toast

- to the good health and well-being of Vice President Albert Gore,
- to the great people of the United States,
- to the friendship between the peoples of India and the United States and,
- to the vision that we share of our partnership for the larger cause of peace and prosperity in the world.

Remarks by President Bill Clinton and Prime Minister Atal Bihari Vajpayee at Welcoming Cermony

South Lawn, The White House, Washington, D.C.

September 15, 2000

President Clinton : It is a special honour to welcome to the White House the prime minister of the world's largest democracy. Prime Minister

Vajpayee, America always has had a great fascination with India, for its rich history, culture, great religions. And increasingly, we are fascinated by India when we think in terms of the future. We see in India today a rising economic leader, making breathtaking strides in information technology; an emerging environmental leader promoting ambitious goals for energy efficiency; a pioneering health leader, recently immunizing 140 million children against polio; a leader in our community of democracies, reminding the world that freedom is not a Western value, but a universal longing.

Mr. Prime Minister, it is not only India's democracy, but India's manner of achieving democracy that will forever inspire America. On my recent trip to India, I was profoundly moved by the visit that my daughter and our party and I had to the Gandhi Memorial. Tomorrow I will be proud to join you as you dedicate another Gandhi memorial right here in Washington, D.C.

It is altogether fitting that both our nations honour him. Martin Luther King used Gandhi's teachings to show America that while we held principles of equality we knew to be right, we permitted practices of inequality we knew to be wrong. And we have been changing for the better ever since.

Mr. Prime Minister, from very different histories, India and the United States have forged a common bond arising from our common commitment to freedom and democracy. Our challenge is to turn our common bond into common achievements. Today we will continue our work in areas where the world needs both America and India to lead if we are to defeat AIDS, reduce poverty, protect the global environment and open the global economy.

We will discuss our common desire to see peace through dialogue in South Asia. We will talk about our common interests in slowing the spread of nuclear weapons, and the broader consequences of proliferation in South Asia. At the same time, we welcome India's commitment to forgo nuclear testing until the treaty banning all nuclear testing comes into force.

No matter our differences — and two such large and diverse countries will always have some differences, as long as we are thinking — if we speak with care and listen with respect, we will find common ground and achieve common aims.

Prime Minister Vajpayee, in your speeches you talk of India's ability to cherish its own marvelous diversity. In your poetry you write of the importance of unity; saying that people of many faiths can have one dream in every eye. In America, we too have a dream of unity amidst our diversity. If people as diverse as we can affirm our common humanity and share common dreams, surely we should and can embrace common endeavors.

Mr. Prime Minister, I thank you again for the wonderful welcome you and your people accorded to me, the members of my family and my delegation on our unforgettable trip to India. I hope this too will be a great trip for you, and that you will feel the warmth of America's welcome in return. But more than anything else, I hope this is the beginning of a long line of common endeavors.

Thank you for coming here, sir, and welcome to America.

Prime Min. Vajpayee: Mr. President, ladies and gentlemen. I am very pleased to be here at the White House today as the guest of the American people and as yours. Thank you for your kind words and your generous hospitality.

This is a part of a continuing dialogue between the world's two largest democracies. We will carry forward the talks that we began in New Delhi in March this year during President Clinton's landmark visit to India. This is a time of new hope and new opportunities in Indo- American ties. The Indo-US Vision Statement, which we signed in March this year, embodies the aspirations and responsibilities of our two countries for the 21st century. Yesterday was an historic and memorable day on Capitol Hill. This day in the White House promises to be the same.

Our dialogue will embrace economic cooperation, science, technology, as well as in-depth discussion on regional and global issues. I pay tribute to the Indian-American community, which has been such an effective bridge in strengthening indo-US ties.

My sincere thanks to the people of America for the gracious welcome extended to me here.

Thank you.

Speech after Dedicating the Mahatma Gandhi Memorial in Washington, D.C.

September 16, 2000

Ladies and Gentlemen:

I am delighted to be with all of you this morning.

Today is, indeed, a memorable day for all of us. I have arrived here after unveiling a statue of Mahatma Gandhi in front of the Indian Embassy.

I am grateful to President Clinton for taking time out of his schedule to join me at the function. This extraordinary gesture, along with the glowing tributes he paid to the Mahatma in his opening remarks at the White House ceremony yesterday, have further endeared America and its President to our people.

With the unveiling of Gandhiji's statue in Washington, one of the greatest apostles of peace has, in a sense, arrived physically in the capital of the world's eldest democracy.

But the Mahatma's spirit has been with the people of America for the greater part of the last century.

Indeed, he was with Americans, not too far from here, 37 years ago. On that occasion, a quarter million Americans marched to Lincoln Memorial to hear Martin Luther King outline his dream of a truly emancipated America.

King's guiding light was Mahatma Gandhi. As he said: "The Christian doctrine of love, operating through the Gandhian method of non-violence, was for me the most potent weapon available to the oppressed people in their struggle for freedom."

Gandhiji's unique method of passive resistance proved to be an enormously active force against colonial oppression.

His use of non-cooperation, civil disobedience and non-violence as instruments in the struggle for freedom touched the American people as much as it did people all over the world.

America's own struggle for independence had an important influence on India's freedom movement. Gandhiji has acknowledged that the great American philosopher Thoreau was his teacher in "the science of civil disobedience."

Gandhiji's personality had a magnetic effect on many people in this country. All of us know about the incomparable homage paid to him by Albert Einstein.

But not so well known is the effect he had on ordinary Americans. For example, Samuel Evans Stokes, a wealthy American from Philadelphia, gave up everything to become a soldier in the Mahatma's army of Satyagrahis in India.

He even changed his name to 'Satyanand' Stokes and had the rare honour of being the only American to become a member of the All India Congress Committee.

His recent widely acclaimed biography, American in Khadi, shows how there has always been a natural affinity between India and America.

Friends, what is it about Gandhiji that makes him a man not just of the past, but equally of the present and the future?

What is it about him that makes him not just an Indian, but a man who belonged to the whole humanity?

The answer to these questions is obvious: The universality of the man. And the immorality of his message.

What is more, Gandhiji lived his own message. As he himself famously put it , "My life is my message".

It is the message of truth and non-violence.

Of brotherhood of all human beings.

Of cooperation among nations.

Equally, it is the message of tolerance and respect for diversity, which are the basic tenets of democracy.

Gandhiji saw both these tenets as the art and science of mobilising the physical, economic and spiritual resources of all sections of the people in the service of the common good.

It is the proud privilege of both India and the United States that our two countries are models—one in the East and the other in the West – of democracy as well as unity in diversity.

We both cherish, preserve and promote universal human rights such as freedom of speech, political choice and religious belief.

These are universal values that form the foundation of more tolerant and compassionate societies, a more non-violent world free from tensions and fear.

They form the foundation of a world where the liberty of people living in open societies is not threatened by extremism and terrorism.

These are values enshrined in the American and Indian Constitutions and handed down to us by great men like Abraham Lincoln, Mahatma Gandhi and Martin Luther King. It is not a coincidence that all three of them fell to the bullets of assassins.

Inspired by the Mahatma, we believe that non-violence requires faith in God and faith in man. Hence, we remain hopeful of a world where the conscience of humanity will never allow forces of bigotry and violence to succeed.

Gandhiji's statue here in the heart of Washington will be a symbol of the triumph of the human spirit against oppression, just as the Statue of Liberty in the New York has been the beacon of freedom, for the whole world.

Distinguished guests,

Today is the penultimate day of my visit to this great country. It has been a very satisfying and fruitful visit.

I thank President Clinton for the enormous personal commitment he has brought to bear on the success of the Indo-American dialogue.

Just as his visit to India earlier this year was a memorable one for him, my own visit to America now has been equally momentous.

It has taken a very short time—from March to September – for our two countries to come a long way.

At the same time, it seems that New Delhi and Washington are not a long way off from each other.

I describe this period as "Six Months That Cemented the Natural Alliance Between India and America".

The Vision Document we signed in New Delhi has been translated into a specific forward movement in a number of areas in the Joint Statement adopted in Washington.

It reflects the synergy of our manual interests.

We have laid a solid foundation for stronger and more broad-based economic cooperation between our two countries. I am confident that this foundation will support the attractive architecture of Indo-American relations in the coming years.

But going beyond the mutuality of economic opportunities, our two sides have talked candidly about several important issues that form the texture of our bilateral relations.

We have talked about security matters. We have talked about the situation in South Asia.

We have also talked about threat of terrorism to civilized world order.

Of course, differences are bound to be there between the two countries. But dialogue between democracies, in an atmosphere of candour and trust , never fails to dissolve some if not all differences.

And that is what has happened on account of the continuing dialogue at various levels between our two democracies.

From divergence, we have moved to a convergence of thinking and outlook on a broad range of issues.

I heartily thank all those who have contributed to the success of this dialogue.

I especially applaud the consistent efforts of the Indian-American community. Your patience and hard work are paying off. Keep it up.

I thank all of you for the opportunity of sharing my thoughts with you.

Thank you.

Opening Remarks at the Meeting with Indian American Entrepreneurs

Blair House, Washington, D.C.

September 16, 2000

I am very happy to meet you all here today.

I have had the pleasure of meeting several of you in Delhi. I have benefited from my interaction with you.

I regret that I could not come to the West Coast.

I thank you for taking time out to come to the East Coast for this meeting.

A famous writer once wrote, "East is East and West is West, and the Twain Can't Meet".

You, Indian-American entrepreneurs, have shown with your successes in Information Technology that East and West can not only meet, but they will meet on equal terms!

You have truly done India proud.

Your success stories have had a positive impact both in America and in India.

In America, you have helped change the image of India in the American mind.

In India, you have inspired tens of thousands of young Indians to achieve similar successes in IT.

I am amazed by the activities of the TIE (The Indus Entrepreneurs) Group. I congratulate you for your vision of bringing the glory of the Indus Valley civilization back to India.

You know the many initiatives our Government has taken to promote IT and telecom.

We welcome your suggestions and ideas for carrying these efforts forward.

Our dream is to create world-class conditions and facilities in India, so that talented Indians can achieve the same success while living and working in India as they do when they come to the United States.

Already, Bangalore is being described as the Silicon Valley of the East.

But we want many Bangalores to bloom in India. Indeed, many centres of IT are coming up very fast.

I would like to especially congratulate the community of Indian American IT entrepreneurs for the spirit of philanthropy you have demonstrated in recent years.

The GIST initiative, the IIT initiative, and other such efforts are all highly commendable.

These, too, I am sure, will inspire businessmen and professionals back home.

I assure you that our Government would assist you in every possible way in your patriotic desire to contribute to India's rapid and all-round development.

Thank you.

Statement on Returning from the Visit to the United States

New Delhi, September 19, 2000

I return home after an extremely satisfying visit to the USA.

During my visit, I addressed the UN Millennium Summit in New York. In Washington, I had the privilege to address a joint meeting of the US Congress, discuss bilateral issues with President Clinton, and meet a large number of US Congressmen. I also met a cross-section of intellectuals, representatives of American business and industry, Indian American and policy-makers in both New York and Washington.

The outcome of these discussions is cause for satisfaction. This visit of mine has served to consolidate the momentum of Indo-US relations. The joint initiatives and the understandings reached represent a major step forward.

The substantive engagement between the world's two largest democracies marks the beginning of a new era in bilateral and global affairs. As I have said before, this is a period of new hope and new beginnings in ties between the people of India and the people of America.

We have agreed that, as our dialogue proceeds, we will listen with respect to each other and seek to accommodate our mutual concerns. This is as it should be between two countries whose friendship is rooted in the hopes and aspirations of the present as well as the future.

Today, we can say that there is better understanding between the two countries on issues of mutual concern. Specifically, there is better understanding of the threat posed by international terrorism and India's security perspectives.

There is also greater appreciation of India's matured handling of challenges posed to her internal and external security. There is recognition of India's role as a factor of stability in Asia. We have also projected our willingness to shoulder our responsibilities as a global player.

There is increasing convergence of our perceptions of non-proliferation issues. While we remain committed to our unilateral moratorium on explosive tests, we will not allow this to stand in the way of our protecting India's supreme national interests.

We will continue to seek a national consensus on CTBT. In accordance with our stated position, we will not stand in the way of the Treaty's entry into force; we also expect that all countries that are required to ratify the

Treaty under Article XIV, should do so without conditions.

We have projected our position on resumption of dialogue with Pakistan. Meaningful dialogue will be possible only when the right atmosphere is created by Pakistan's cessation of abetting cross-border terrorism and hostile propaganda against India.

The Joint Statement issued after our bilateral talks with America reflects the beginning of the fruition of the agenda which India and the USA had set for themselves in the Vision Statement that President Clinton and I signed in March.

I am confident that the coming months will witness an upswing in Indo-US trade and economic cooperation, apart from increasing collaboration in critical socio-economic development-related areas like power, e-commerce, HIV/AIDS and agriculture.

I am equally confident that India and the USA will make full use of all opportunities to emerge as natural allies. We will be partners in international peace, progress and prosperity in the 21st century.

Speech at the Asia Society, New York - September 28, 1998

Mr. Greenberg, Mr. Platt, Mr. Bouton, Distinguished members of the Asia Society, Friends,

It is a great honour for me to be invited this evening to speak at this renowned institution. Its well-deserved fame is the result of many years of sustained and dedicated work by some of the most eminent minds of the United States of America. The Asia Society has provided a forum for the East and the West to meet, for Asia and America to meet and, on many occasions, for India and the USA to meet.

As all of us know through experience, the most productive meetings between nations are often those that take place outside the formal framework of diplomacy and summitry. It is when political leaders, intellectuals and policy makers of two or more countries meet and interact in informal and friendly settings that trust develops and understanding deepens.

I would, therefore, at the outset like to compliment the Asia Society for its excellent work in the field of what is called popular diplomacy.

March Elections Mirror India's Democratic Pluralism

Friends, this is my first visit to the USA after assuming the office of the Prime Minister of India. In March this year, we completed what have been described as the largest elections in the history of the world, with an electorate of over 600 million people. To Indians today, the vast majority of whom were born in freedom, democracy is the natural and the only acceptable form of governance. This very fact characterises the remarkable journey that India has travelled in fifty years during which India has remained true to its values, and has succeeded in knitting together its many diversities into a strong, coherent, pluralistic society.

Despite changes in government the political system itself has remained remarkably stable. This testifies to the inherent strength and stability of democratic traditions in India. India's commitment to democratic pluralism is also reflected in the Government, which I head. Ours is a Coalition Government led by the Bharatiya Janata Party. We have prepared a common programme, which defines the National Agenda for Governance. We are convinced that maturing of coalition politics is what India needs at the present juncture.

Our objective is clear, to build a strong, prosperous and self-confident India, which occupies its rightful place in the comity of nations. We know that India has what it takes to achieve a far higher—7-8 per cent — rate of annual GDP growth. We know that India has what it takes to emerge as a major manufacturing, trading and exporting power, by achieving global competitiveness in cost and quality. We also know that faster economic growth is the key to overcoming the historical legacy of unemployment and material backwardness afflicting large sections of our population. We are fully aware of the problems that lie in the path of achieving these goals. But we are also convinced that we can make light of these problems if we act in the national interest in all matters.

Personally speaking, I have always held the national interest above party and personal interest. This is the pledge I made to the people of India on August 15, in the concluding celebrations of India's fiftieth anniversary of independence. It is a pledge that I am determined to honour.

India's Bifocal Vision: Nationalism and internationalism

Friends, India's preoccupation with the imperatives of national reconstruction has never blinded us to our duties towards the world. As Pandit Jawaharlal Nehru, India's first Prime Minister, once vividly said, nationalism and internationalism are the two eyes of our national body. India has never seen what is good for herself without having simultaneously seen what is good for the whole world. India's freedom movement, led by Mahatma Gandhi, was without parallel in its endeavour to harmonise a nation's legitimate aspirations for political independence with the universal values and concerns of the human race.

In my lecture before this august audience today, I therefore wish to talk about both India and the world standing expectantly on the threshold of the 21st century. I do so from an Indian point of view. But I make bold to claim that the Indian point of view is broad enough to command respectful attention of every progressive opinion in America and the world.

The 20th century has been a time of unprecedented changes. The scale and newness of changes in this century have far surpassed anything recorded in known history of mankind. Of this century can it be truly said that "it was the best of times and it was the worst of times."

It has been a century of world wars and conflicts, of stockpiling of weapons of mass destruction, of colonialism, hegemonism, terrorism and religious fanaticism. At the same time, it has also been a century of freedom, relative peace, prosperity, advance of democracy, spectacular progress in science and technology, especially the recent advances in information and communication technology, and unprecedented levels of global cooperation.

The challenge before the world is: how can the worst features of this century be held in check, reversed and their non-recurrence ensured? The challenge also is: how can we better the best features of the 20th century for the benefit of all sections of humanity—and not just some select, privileged nations and classes, as has happened so far? Will the new century be really new for humanity, or will it be a continuation of the old problems and crises and conflicts that we have seen in our times?

Will the world move decisively in the direction of peace and disarmament? Will mass poverty, undernourishment and starvation be things of the past? Will the world financial system become less volatile and more predictable? And will there be a just and equitable global economic order? Will we able to overcome terrorism, ethnic strife and religious hatred in the coming century? These are the questions that confront the leaders of the world in the twilight days of the 20th century. By leaders I do not mean only heads of governments. No. History has thrown this challenge before all of us—leaders in government, politics, business, international agencies, academic institutions, media and cultural organisations. Will we be able to rise to the occasion?

Today, India, USA and the world stand at a unique moment in history. As we peer into the future, we find that it is not so far away at all. In less than 500 days, we will leave the 20th century behind, the second millennium behind and enter into a new century and a new millennium.

As we all know, computer professionals around the world are busy grappling with what is famously called the Y2K problem. The problem basically is to re-programme the software to let the computers know that the Year 2000 has begun. Computers will behave funnily and totally unreliably if the Y2K problem is not solved. Drawing from the computer terminology, let me pose the question: Have we—the political leaders, heads of governments, policy makers and intellectuals of the world—begun to re-programme our political and economic minds to take note of the fact that we are all soon going to enter a new era? I call this the PE-Y2K— the Political Economic Year 2000 - problem.

World Peace: The Need to Move from Deterrence to Disarmament

Friends, in order to successfully meet this challenge, leaders around the world need a new mindset, And the mindset necessary to sustain the world in the 21st century demands that all of us must first learn the lessons of the 20th century. The greatest lesson of this century is that peace is the highest ideal. The 20th century witnessed two World Wars, each more ferocious than all the previous wars. The price humanity paid in these two global conflicts has been so frightening that the option before the world today is stark: another world war, which will be a nuclear war, and extinction; or peace, survival and progress. For fifty years, world peace has been secured on the tenuous principle of nuclear deterrence. But this cannot be the durable basis for peace. The conscience of humanity demands that the world move away from deterrence to disarmament.

Unfortunately, however, traditional nuclear powers have paid little heed to this universal demand. They first used the Cold War as a pretext for a costly arms race. Now, even though the Cold War is over, they have sought to perpetuate their hegemony through discriminatory non-proliferation treaties, which are bound to fail.

It is this hypocrisy and hegemony, which forced India to rethink our nuclear policy recently. As you well know, my country has championed the cause of peace and disarmament with consistency and conviction for the past five decades. We raised our voice for disarmament, both on our own behalf and on behalf of members of the Non-Aligned Movement, in every multilateral and bilateral forum. Not only was our demand disregarded, but also India's sovereign right to keep the nuclear option open was sought to be curtailed. In the circumstances, we were forced to exercise our nuclear option both for reasons of national security and as a powerful challenge to the practitioners of nuclear apartheid. With this firm action, we have reminded the nuclear club that the voice of one-sixth of the humanity cannot be ignored.

The lesson of the late 20th century is, thus, simple: Disarmament—

real, visible, verifiable disarmament — is the only way to achieve the goal of non-proliferation.

I do hope that the leadership of America, the country with the largest stockpile of nuclear weapons and delivery systems and hence carrying the greatest responsibility for peace on earth, takes the right course of action in the coming years. Apprehensions have been expressed in some quarters that recent developments in South Asia raise the spectre of an arms race and heightened tensions. These apprehensions are misplaced. Those who voice this apprehension argue that India and Pakistan have fought three wars in the last fifty years. They forget to add that there has been no war for the last 25 of those 50 years. And that is because of the bilateral Shimla Agreement arrived at between India and Pakistan in 1972. Contrary to what some may believe, bilaterialism works. It is the intrusion by third parties, however well intentioned, that creates complications.

Democratisation of the World Order

Disarmament in turn demands democratisation of the world order. And this brings us to the second greatest lesson of the 20th century. This has truly been a Century of Democracy. More and more countries around the world have embraced democracy, of course with necessary local variations. But we see a strange dichotomy here. Democracy at the global level, as a framework for setting the norms for international relations, has not kept pace with the march of democracy as a system of national governance. The rich and the powerful make and unmake rules to suit their partisan interests.

As the world moves into the 21st century, this situation is totally unsustainable. No nation, however rich and militarily powerful, can for long pursue interests that do not harmonise with the interests of the global community. The age of colonialism, which was the curse of the past few centuries, is over forever. In no way can the unequal relations that marked this age be revived without deeply endangering peace and stability. I do hope that America, the land that cherishes democratic values, takes concrete steps to promote democratisation of the world order. The process could begin with democratisation of the UN system.

Need to Restructure Indo-US Ties for the Good of Global Democracy

Friends, we in India believe that Indo-US relations, restructured on an equal footing, constitute the key element in the architecture of tomorrow's democratised world order. However, I must confess to being baffled by the unsatisfactory current state of relations between our two countries.

We are the two largest democracies in the world, and have similar political cultures, a free press and the rule of law. We both have a tradition of private enterprise and free markets. Above all, I see no conflict of interests between the two countries in the foreseeable future and yet all of us here would agree that the full potential of our relationship has not been realised in the last 50 years. I have been trying to analyse the reasons and I think I can at least indicate where the shoe pinches us. First and foremost, it is American reluctance to accept us as a responsible member of the international community.

Whether it is regional arrangements dealing with Afghanistan, where we have vital security and other interests; whether it is cooperative arrangements in the Asia-Pacific region, where we have a clearly positive, moderating and stabilising role to play; whether it is global organisations like the UN Security Council or the discriminatory Non-Proliferation Treaty; in all of these the United States does not appreciate and accommodate India's interests and concerns.

Secondly, we have been subjected to technology denials virtually from the time of our Independence. Our own export control regimes are extremely stringent and there has been no leakage of equipment or technology from India. Despite this, we find the US unwilling to accommodate us in terms of technology transfers. Similarly on South Asian issues, where our supreme national interests are involved, we encounter policy approaches from America that go contrary to our basic irreducible security needs.

An even more serious case of incomprehension in India are the public statements made by American leaders where our sensitivities are involved. The statement issued on South Asia during President Clinton's visit to China, and American attempts at putting pressure on Russia to end its defence and scientific cooperation with India are two prime examples of recent vintage. For democratic governments like ours, which desire closer understanding with the USA, it becomes extremely difficult to move forward in the face of such public declarations.

Friends, I have argued for restructuring of Indo-US relations not just because they will help India—but also because they will help the US itself. Let me repeat what I have said earlier: Indo-US ties based on equality and mutuality of interests is going to be the mainstay of tomorrow's stable, democratic world order.

Reforming the Global Financial System

Friends, by now it is well recognised that economic democracy is at the very core of democracy, both in a domestic set up as well as in international relations. But the financial system that has come into being in the post-World War II period has proved itself to be anything but democratic. The intrinsic inequities in this system cannot be rationalised by saying that they are the result of market forces that brook no governmental intervention. The 20th century has seen the heavy price that the dogma of communism extracted.

The world is today paying the price for another dogma: the dogma of the Invisible Hand of the market forces. We have seen how irrationally volatile the markets have been. We have also seen how market instability in one part of the world quickly travels, like a seismic wave, to other parts of the world through the fault lines of the global financial system. With market instability comes social and political instability. Overnight ordinary people lose—see their hard-earned savings evaporate, investors lose their market capitalisation and countries lose the value of their currencies.

There is no doubt that nations that do not manage their economies on sound principles invite a penalty in this system. But often they and their innocent people pay the penalty of unemployment and price rise for no fault of their own. It is rightly said that in the era of globalisation, the global market for goods, services, investments and human labour is one and indivisible—much like tile atmosphere that surrounds our planet. Any damage to the atmosphere at one place adversely affects all the people inhabiting this planet.

Rich nations of the Western Hemisphere, therefore, should not be under the illusion that they are immune from the crisis that is currently rippling through the Asian markets. There is an urgent need for collective global action to reform the world's financial system by refocusing it to meet the priority growth needs of the human race.

We in India have taken a principled stand towards globalisation—cautious, calibrated and steady integration. This approach has served our national interests well. We have remained largely unaffected by the turmoil in the Asian markets. We know we have to implement many more internal and external reforms to harness the full potential of our economy. We shall definitely do so. At the same time, we shall continue to raise our voice for radically reforming the global economic order as the main guarantor for a stable and peaceful 21st century.

Managing Diversities: Key to Peaceful World Order

There is a fourth important lesson of the 20th century and it has to do with how we manage diversities. All of us on this planet belong to different races, regions, religions, cultures and nationalities. We speak different languages and hold different views on politics and life. But we all share the same common home because we are all part of the same human family.

India's Vedic seers extolled this value by stating that, whereas the Truth is one, wise men express it differently—*Ekam Sat Viprah Bahudha Vadanti.*

This was always true. But in the age of globalisation, when interaction and interdependence is a law rather than an exception, acceptance of the truth of 'Unity in Diversity' and 'Diversity in Unity' is not just an option. It is an inescapable necessity. Sadly, unwillingness to accept this truth is at the root of much violence and strife in many parts of the world today. When such exclusivism and intolerance are wedded to narrow political goals, they even give rise to terrorism.

Friends, terrorism has become one of the gravest threats to civil society, and national security. Here again, both India and the USA have been its victims. We were shocked and horrified at the wanton loss of innocent American and African lives in the recent attacks on the US Embassies in Nairobi and Dar-es-Salaam. We shared the anguish and anger that you felt. The forces of international terrorism that launched these cowardly attacks are active in our region also. India has been a target of relentless terrorist violence. You have Lockerbie, We have Kanishka. You have the World Trade Centre, we have Wandhama.

The threads lead back to one and the same source. It is contemptible that this is being sponsored and abetted from across our borders. One country in our region has already fallen to obscurantism. The international community must act determinedly to prevent the contagion from spreading. As the world moves into the next century, we must accept multiculturalism and respect for diversities as a way of life. I am happy to note here that both India and the United States, which have a rich experience in peacefully managing diversities, can work together in this area for the benefit of mankind.

India and America: Natural Allies in the Quest for a Better Future

Friends, on all these major challenges facing mankind today, my belief is that progressive people all over the world have convergent views. I see this convergence especially among the forward-looking leaders, policy-makers and intellectuals of India and America. It is this convergence, it is this commonality of concerns and cognition, which reinforces my belief that India and the United States are natural allies in the quest for a better future for the world in the 21st century.

Thanks to the initiatives of non-governmental and non-partisan institutions like the Asia Society, I am sure this alliance will become stronger and stronger in the coming years.

In conclusion, as an ode to this natural Indo-American alliance, let me quote a few lines from the poem written by Swami Vivekananda, one of the greatest Indian sages of modem times. It is called "TO THE FOURTH OF JULY". It was written a hundred years ago, on July 4, 1898 when he was travelling with some American disciples through the woods of Kashmir.

Move on, O Lord, in thy resistless path!
Till thy high noon o'erspreads the world,
Till every land reflects thy light,
Till men and women, with uplifted head,
Behold their shackles broken, and
Know, in springing joy, their life renewed!

Thank you.

Visit to USA

I am happy to participate in this business event organized by the National Association of Manufacturers and the Confederation of Indian Industry.

My interaction with industry began in New York. It is in the fitness of things that it concludes in Washington. It comes towards the end of my visit to the United States. This interaction convinces me that there is great scope for economic partnership between India and the United States.

In March this year, President Clinton and I had signed a Vision Statement on Indo-US relations in New Delhi. That Statement had pledged to make a new beginning for India and the United States to realize the full potential of our relationship.

I came here to carry this process further. I came to explore the opportunities for realizing this full potential of our partnership.

The Joint Statement issued today reinforces this. It reflects the considerable progress made between the two countries even in a short period of six months.

Economic and business cooperation is the critical pillar of our relations. Business within and between nations is not only about market share and margins. It is prompted by mutuality, fostered by partnership and realized through trust.

All commerce is an endeavour to enhance human comfort.

All investment is an investment to promote human happiness.

All development is about improving the quality of life.

Both for India and the United States this is the vision for any development process. Distinguished businessmen, you have a noble calling to realize this common vision.

The continued US prosperity is almost a miracle. Your economic performance has evoked global admiration. It has also inspired India.

We are gratified that the Indo-Americans have made an important contribution in your economic success. Their significant achievements in Information Technology are a glowing chapter in the growth of the "New Economy".

Less well known than the stellar performance of the US economy is the story about the Indian economy. At an average GDP growth of 6.5 per cent per annum, India in the Nineties has been among the ten fastest growing economies of the world.

We want to do even better in the decade that has just begun. We have pledged to double our per capita income in the next ten years. This implies a growth rate of around 9 per cent.

Although it is a difficult challenge, India can achieve it. India will achieve it.

In the last decades of our development, we have built a strong and resilient India. But we have also drawn lessons for the future. We have re-thought about the respective roles of the State and the private sector for economic development.

The first point of change has been to free Government from providing private goods and services to use its resources to provide public goods. This has involved far reaching changes in fiscal, financial, social and institutional arrangements. While significant progress has been made, considerable work remains to be done.

Second, to create an environment where private initiative can flourish and where entrepreneurship and innovation rewarded. That is why through progressive liberalization we are expanding business opportunities – both domestic and foreign.

Rules, procedures and policies which hinder private initiative are being changed or re-adapted. In the process, reforms have touched most areas of the economy industry, infrastructure, international trade, foreign exchange market, financial system and taxation.

Let me enumerate some of our important initiatives.

We shall complete a project to build 13,000 kms of improved and expanded National Highways by 2007. The first component of 7, 000 kms, involving the four major metros, would be completed by 2003 itself.

A massive rural road connectivity programme to connect all the villages with populations of more than 500 with all-weather roads by 2007. An accelerated programme is being worked out to connect villages with populations of more than 1000 by 2003.

The deregulation in the area of telecommunications is more or less complete.

- We have fully liberalized National Long Distance, Basic Telephony and under-sea optical cable.
- We are considering how best to fully deregulate cellular telephony.
- The monopoly of the VSNL will end by nearly 2002.
- The new Telecom Convergence Bill is in the offing.

Our Internet Service Policy is about the most attractive anywhere in the world. We are placing emphasis on human resource development to support our IT Policy. We propose to dramatically increase the number of IT professionals in the next two or three years.

In this context, I applaud the initiative taken by a group of successful Indian-Americans to set up a Global Institute of Science and Technology in India in collaboration with University of California, Berkeley.

Financial sector reforms are being continued. New measures are being adopted to minimise the Non-Performing Assets.

- We have opened up the insurance sector. The Insurance Regulatory Authority informs me that the first batch of private licences will be issued by the first of October this year.
- The Reserve Bank is willing to consider further expansion of foreign private banks in India.
- Our tax rates are moderate and compare with the best you have anywhere in the world. We recognize that further tax reforms are necessary. We have, therefore, decided to constitute a Tax Reforms Commission to lay down the roadmap of further tax reform and what is more, reform tax administration.
- In the Joint Statement, we have decided to modify the Double Taxation Treaty so that on a reciprocal basis some of the present tax irritants on both sides can be eliminated.

A new Civil Aviation policy is on the anvil. This would be based on the principle of making India an easier destination. It would not be driven by a mere bilateral consideration of trade-off in slot sharing. I am sure that this will enable American and other foreign airlines to bring more flights, and business, to India.

Disinvestment of Government's holding in Air India is well on course. The necessary advertisement will be issued within a fortnight's time.

Milestones have been determined for long-term lease of our five major international airports.

The corporatization of ports and private participation in port building is being aggressively encouraged.

We need to attract large investments in the power sector. We shall speed up reforms in this crucial sector, both at the Centre and in the States. We now have a regulatory framework that depoliticises the fixation of tariffs. This has been emulated by 14 State Governments. Financial institutions have worked out alternative arrangements that will enable them to lend more easily.

Yesterday we have signed four large power projects involving an investment of nearly 7 billion dollars. The next few months will see the financial closure of many power projects, which have been languishing for several years.

On Foreign Direct Investment, our policy is to make our climate more hospitable and competitive. The approval process for Foreign Direct Investment is more or less automatic for most types of investments.

Even last week, we have substantially relaxed sectoral caps in respect of a number of areas. We believe that India needs large flows of capital and technology to achieve the required growth targets. The thrust of our policy will be automaticity, transparency, simplicity, speed and removal of conditionalities.

The disinvestment and privatization programme of a large number of public corporations and selected utilities is moving ahead with full speed. Only a week ago, we have finalized definite milestones that will enable the privatization programme to cover many large undertakings.

We confront major challenges. There are many problems to be resolved. There are issues concerning fiscal rectitude. We are determined to ensure that the reforms benefit the average man. We have also resolved to address social concerns like rural connectivity, housing, drinking water, primary education and health. These will further expand the social base of prosperity in India.

Distinguished businessmen, Corporate America has reaped the rewards of a record ninth year of domestic economic expansion. Today, I invite you, captains of US industry, to grasp many new opportunities India offers. Your choice is diverse. It ranges from infrastructuring to manufacturing, from financial services to knowledge-based enterprises.

Let us forge a new economic partnership. A partnership reinforced by a common desire to derive mutual benefit.

I look forward to this US-Business India Summit heralding a new era of business to business relationships. An era that will bring growth, prosperity and liberation from deprivation.

Thank you, Ladies and Gentlemen, for enabling me to share that vision of a better tomorrow.

16
Flays Attack on Christians

PM Flays Attack on Christians

Prime Minister Atal Bihari Vajpayee today strongly denounced what he termed as 'condemnable acts against the Christian community in recent months by anti-social elements'. "India is a secular nation. *Sarva Pantha Samabhav*—equal respect for all faiths—has been the cornerstone of our culture and nationhood. My Government is fully committed to upholding this principle," Mr. Vajpayee said. Elaborating on the imperative need of strengthening communal harmony and secular fabric of India, the Prime Minister asserted that every citizen had the fullest freedom to practice his beliefs so long as these did not interfere with another person's right to do the same. (*Hindustan Times* - December 5, 1998)

The National Commission for Minorities Welcomes Prime Minister's Statement

The National Commission for minorities has welcomed the statement of the Prime Minister expressing grave concern over the communal violence in Gujarat in a press statement. The Commission said the Prime Minister's directions for curbing the anti-minority violence would go a long way in saving the fair image of the nation at the global level and rebuild the confidence of the minorities. (December 31, 1998)

Vajpayee Orders Punishment for Anti-Christian Acts

Prime Minister Atal Bihari Vajpayee has directed the Gujarat government to take action against those disturbing communal harmony and peace in the state. (*Rediff on the net*, December 30, 1998)

No Place for Religious Bigotry : PM

New Delhi : Prime Minister Atal Bihari Vajpayee on Thursday asserted that there was no place for religious bigotry and that his government was committed to maintain social amity and peace in the country.

In a New Year message to the nation, Mr. Vajpayee said he wanted India to step into the next millennium as a strong and powerful country where every citizen, irrespective of his caste or creed could live in a prosperous, peaceful and amicable atmosphere. He reiterated the government's commitment to the people and said it would live up to their expectations and discharge its responsibilities to the best of its capability. (*The Times of India* – January 1, 1999)

President Calls for Religious Tolerance

President K.R. Narayanan on Friday urged the people to make 1999 a year of "peace, amity and happiness" and prove themselves to be worthy of "a tolerant and secular heritage." In his New Year greetings, he quoted Swami Vivekananda who had said that India was "the only country where people have built temples for Mohammedans and Christians."

The message, coming in the backdrop of the recent attacks on Christians in Gujarat and other parts of the country, recalled Swami Vivekananda's words: "I am proud to belong to a religion which taught the world both tolerance and universal acceptance. We not only believe in universal tolerance, but accept all religions as true."

Home Minister L.K. Advani, who has not minced any words in attacking the violence against Christians, may take the national executive into confidence and brief his colleagues on the findings of an official committee that is believed to have submitted to him a report on the incidents. (*The Times of India* – January 2, 1999)

More than 100 People Arrested

According to an official spokesman of the State Government, 30 offences have been registered from December 25 till yesterday and 116 persons belonging to both the warring communities arrested in connection with the 25 cases detected. In addition, 44 persons were taken into custody under preventive detention. Seven persons were arrested in connection with the attack on the Deepdarshan School hostel in Ahwa and another six persons for the attack on the Navjyot School in Subbir, about 30 km from Ahwa, the district headquarters. (*The Hindu* – January 5, 1999)

Vajpayee to Visit Dangs

Prime Minister Atal Bihari Vajpayee will leave for Gujarat tomorrow to see for himself the situation in Dangs district where Christians were allegedly under attack. He will also visit the state capital Gandhinagar where he will hold discussions with Chief Minister Keshubhai Patel and senior officials. Vajpayee is likely to meet some Christian leaders as well during the visit.

17
Emphasis on Indianness

Address by Shri Atal Bihari Vajpayee, Prime Minister of India at the Pravasi Bharatiya Divas Celebrations

New Delhi, January 9, 2003

My simple greeting to all of you here today is: Welcome home.

Many of you are citizens of your adopted countries. Over 20 million of you have set up home in scores of countries, near and far. But each one of you shares a common identity—your Indianness—and a common origin – this Motherland of your forefathers. Therefore, this great gathering, which is the first of its kind, is truly a homecoming.

It is also a grand occasion for the country to pay tribute to its sons and daughters who have succeeded in reaching the pinnacle in so many diverse fields of human endeavour all over the world.

There is yet another important aspect of this unique celebration of the Pravasi Bharatiya's Association with his land of origin. Many of you – or your forefathers – left India in search of fortune for a better livelihood. Today, India has itself become a land of opportunity. We want to share with our extended family our achievements, hopes, concerns, aspirations and goals. Your awareness of our current national course and understanding of our perspectives would enrich your bonds with India and heighten your sense of belonging to the global Indian family.

The odyssey of our people to the four corners of the globe has been a saga of courage, enterprise and character. In ancient times, our forefathers went to distant lands as traders, monks, teachers and temple builders. A century and a half ago, Indian indentured labour was sent forth to sugar, tea and rubber plantations in near and far-flung parts of the British Empire. They worked on lands as far apart as Fiji and Mauritius, Surinam and Sri Lanka, Trinidad and Burma, Guyana and Malaysia.

The next wave of emigration was of entrepreneurs and traders who sailed intrepidly into uncharted waters for unknown countries. Since the 70's, young Indian professionals have been migrating abroad to corporate boardrooms, research laboratories, engineering workshops and university faculties. The emigration of doctors, nurses, engineers, managers, plumbers, and electricians to West Asia and the Gulf, has been a steady growth.

Today, the success of every category of these emigrants all over the world testifies to the indomitable spirit, which they carried from Indian soil. It is a tribute to their patience and forbearance in the face of hardship, rebuke and denial. It speaks of their dedication to their chosen professions, overcoming various trials and tribulations.

On this day, 88 years ago, Mahatma Gandhi returned to India after nearly 20 years as a Pravasi Bharatiya in South Africa. His struggle against discrimination, deprivation and exploitation of Indians in South Africa not only fired the imagination of Indian patriots, it also inspired a spate of freedom movements right across the African continent. Out of those freedom movements emerged Pravasi Bharatiya heroes like Seewoosagar Ramgoolam of Mauritius; Yusuf Dadoo and Monty Naicker of South Africa; Cheddi Jagan of Guyana; Jagennath Lachmon of Surinam and many others.

Not many people today remember the painful Kamagatamaru episode of the early 20th century, when a boatload of Sikhs from India were most brutally left to fend for themselves on the high seas off the coast of Canada. Today, Sikhs are among the most prosperous Canadians and are increasingly influential in Canadian politics. In Ujjal Dossanj, we have honoured one such prominent Canadian figure.

Even the illiterate indentured plantation labourers empowered succeeding generations through a determined pursuit of education. Sir Vidia Naipaul, Sir Anerood Jugnauth, Dato Samy Vellu and millions of others are living symbols of the transformation of an oppressed community to leaders of society in the space of a few generations.

Let us remember that, unlike the British, the French, the Dutch and the Germans, India was never a maritime power. All the same, Indians ventured forth across the seas to set up new homes in new lands. They went in peace, often with nothing more than faith in their destiny. No country can claim that Indians entered its territory in the spirit of colonialism. This also is a glorious tribute to you and your forefathers. Few people who entered foreign lands can claim such a testimony.

Pandit Nehru once remarked that wherever there is an Indian, a bit of India goes with him. Pravasi Indians have truly taken India abroad – Indian culture, Indian society and Indian traditions, not to mention Indian films and Indian cuisine!

The outside world has also attracted the best Indian talents, skills, brains and abilities – like Amartya Sen and Jagdish Bhagwati; E.C.G. Sudarshan and S. Chandrashekhar; Hargobind Khorana and Zubin Mehta. The Pravasi Bharatiya family today also includes.

Indian writers in English with an international readership;

Entrepreneurs and industrialists with a global reach of operations;

Management and lifestyle gurus with a huge following; and, Filmmakers, sportspersons, artists and performers of great popularity.

They have dramatically changed the world's perception of Indians, and hence of India. They have provoked a new appreciation of this land, which has produced and exported so many achievers. They have built bridges of understanding between the international community and India.

The benchmarks for success, which the Pravasi community has set, are a challenge for us in India. They make us examine why the Indian is so much more innovative, productive and successful abroad than in his own country. They prod us to create a business, investment and economic climate, which is as conducive to success as anywhere else in the world.

I assure you that we are fully committed to creating such an environment in India.

We are modernizing our infrastructure. Our telecom facilities are already as good as anywhere in the world. The combination of India-based IT companies and Indian professionals abroad, have made India a premier software power. We are building world-class highways through our National Highway Development Project. Our rural roads network is being upgraded. We have ambitious plans for airports, ports, and railways. Housing construction has acquired an unprecedented speed. Literacy, especially women's literacy, has registered a marked rise over the last decade.

We are aware of the slow progress in several areas of our social sector development, but we are determined to move faster than before. All in all, we are guided by the ambitious goal of making India a Developed Nation by 2020, free from all vestiges of poverty and full of opportunities for all our one billion people.

We would like to create an environment in India which will make you want to return, not just for sentimental or emotional reasons, but in the conviction that you can excel in this country as much as you could anywhere else in the world.

I believe that the Pravasi Bharatiya can be a catalyst for rapid change in this direction. Each of you, through your network of friends, relatives and acquaintances can create a strong urge for change in India. Our collective attention needs to be rescued from the sterile controversies and trivial issues that dominate the headlines, and focused on the real tasks to be accomplished, so that India can catch up with the developed world.

At the same time, you can project the truth about India to the world in a credible and effective manner. Misleading, one-sided and negative pictures are often put out due to bias, ignorance or design. Your familiarity with the Indian reality and with the perspectives of your adopted society equips you to correct such misrepresentations. You could project a positive image of India — not as propaganda, but as a true reflection of the reality on the ground.

For example, India continues to have one of the fastest growing economies, at a time when most developed economies have slowed down.Our exports grew by 19 per cent, in spite of a global slowdown and a strong rupee.

Till recently, India needed to import food grain to feed its population. Last year, we exported food grain worth over 60 billion rupees to 25 countries.

About a decade ago, we had to mortgage our gold to tide over a difficult Balance of Payments crisis. Today, we have record foreign exchange reserves of nearly 70 billion dollars.

How often have we seen such facts quoted outside the country? It is far more likely that mindless political gossip or isolated acts of crime and violence would dominate the headlines around the world.

India has been deeply appreciative of the support of the Pravasi Bharatiya community, at times of need. Whenever India has faced a challenge to its security or to its territorial integrity, you have tirelessly championed its cause. When there was an effort to isolate India after our nuclear tests of 1998, you came forward to stand by India. Your enthusiastic response to our Resurgent India Bonds in 1998 helped us raise over 4 billion dollars, when we needed it most.

Many of you have been generously helping the schools, colleges, IITs and universities, as their grateful alumni. I commend this gesture of Guru Dakshina. Some of you have met me with interesting suggestions on how to expand the scope of Pravasi Bharatiya involvement in the development of India's educational infrastructure. The Ministry of Human Resource Development has also taken some initiatives in this direction. Since education is going to be one of the main competitive strengths of India in the emerging Knowledge Society, let us work together to seize the opportunity.

In this context, I will take the luxury of offering a word of advice. The Indian community abroad often reflects the diversity—which is the hallmark of our society here. We are proud of this diversity - whether it is linguistic, religious or regional. Groupings like the Telugu, Tamil, Punjabi and Marathi associations serve a useful purpose in preserving linguistic skills and regional cultures. But it is also necessary to strengthen the broader Indian identity in the country of your residence. When you are united as Indians, your voice carries greater weight: both for highlighting issues of your concern in your host country, and for promoting Indian causes. This is a truth of great long-term significance for Indian communities everywhere.

I have always been conscious of the need for India to be sensitive to the hopes, aspirations and concerns of its vast diaspora. It is like a parental charge. It is also an obligation derived from our civilizational heritage.

It was with this perspective that we set up a High Level Committee, headed by Dr. Laxmi Mall Singhvi, to examine all matters relating to the interaction of the community with India. I would like to congratulate Dr. Singhvi and his colleagues for the thorough and exhaustive nature of their report.

The idea of celebrating the Pravasi Bharatiya Divas annually flows from the recommendations of the Committee. The revised and improved scheme for PIO Cards is also based on the ideas of the Committee.

Indians who have chosen to settle in foreign lands should be loyal to their country of adoption. The biggest challenge facing every immigrant community is to integrate harmoniously into the political, economic and social life of the host society, while preserving and cherishing its civilizational heritage. Over the years, Indians have achieved this delicate balance virtually everywhere, without a contradiction between their adopted citizenship and their original Indian identity.

It is in this background that my government has decided to accept the High-level Committee's recommendation to permit dual citizenship for People of Indian Origin living in certain countries. We are now working on the administrative regulations and procedures governing dual citizenship. We will introduce the necessary legislation during the Budget Session of Parliament.

The NRI of today is the Pravasi Bharatiya of tomorrow. The welfare of NRIs in the Gulf region is of utmost concern to us. A compulsory insurance scheme for Indian workers migrating to this region will be unveiled shortly. Parliament is already considering a bill to establish a welfare fund for the overseas Indian workers. To meet the educational needs of children of workers in the Gulf, we plan to reserve a certain proportion of seats in our academic institutions for the children of the GulfNRIs.

Our preparations for this first Pravasi Bharatiya Divas, and the encouraging response to it, have convinced us of the fruitfulness of this event. We will continue to engage closely with the communities of Indian origin. For this, we are setting up an Advisory Committee, which will meet periodically to suggest new initiatives to the Minister of External Affairs.

We are prepared to respond to your expectations from India. We invite you, not only to share our vision of India in the new millennium, but also to help us shape its contours. We do not want only your investment. We also want your ideas. We do not want your riches, we want the richness of your experience. We can gain from the breadth of vision that your global exposure has given you.

When you left the country, you carried with you the primary colours of the Indian ethos. A cross-fertilization of cultures over time has added new shades to those vibrant hues. Today we invite you to brush in some of these new colours into the ever-evolving canvas of India's development.

Let us Celebrate and Strengthen out Indianess
Prime Minister's musings from Goa
January 31, 2002

Hearty New Year greetings to all my dear countrymen and to all members of the Indian diaspora living in far-flung corners of the world. I also send my greetings to our brothers and sisters both in the neighbouring countries and in countries far and wide. May the New Year bring greater peace, prosperity and happiness to the entire humanity.

I have come to Goa to see the sun set on 2002 and to welcome the first morning of 2003. I had come here more than four decades ago to participate in the Goa Liberation Struggle, which saw the sun set on this last enclave of colonial rule in India. Since then, Goa has progressed in many ways, retaining its old charm, which is the alchemy of diverse historical influences, and yet adding many new features that heighten the appeal of its original attraction: the unique combination of the sun, the sand, the sea, swaying coconut trees, the rivers and forests, and of course the natural hospitality of the Goan people.

The sight of the sea and the sound of its waves can easily make one's mind wonder about the eternal and the infinite. My wandering thoughts, however, return to India. How many waves of history have crashed at the shore of our Motherland! How many New Year suns have dawned on its vast expanse! In our preoccupation with the Here and Now, we sometimes tend to forget how ancient, and yet how enduring and self-renewing is our civilization, indomitable, inclusive, absorbing all the positive influences brought ashore by the tides of history and making them its own.

I recall here the ringing words of Swami Vivekananda in his essay 'The Future of India' : "It is the same India which has withstood the shocks of centuries, of hundreds of foreign invasions, of hundreds of upheavals of manners and customs. It is the same land which stands firmer than any rock in the world, with its undying vigour, indestructible life. Its life is of the same nature as the soul, without beginning and without end, immortal; and we are the children of such a country."

Our diversity is as much a source of India's greatness – and of Indians' pride in their nation — as her antiquity. Foreigners have always wondered how we can embrace so much diversity in religion, ethnicity, language and lifestyles, and yet remain a united nation. What they may not understand, and which we must never forget, is that living with diversity, and yet weaving a thread of unity and harmony through it, has been a way of life throughout India since time immemorial. This is as true in Goa as it is in Gujarat, in Jammu & Kashmir as much as in Kerala, in Manipur as much as in Madhya Pradesh.

From time to time, the theme of unity in diversity provokes intense debate, even controversies. I wish to comment on two distinct voices, which have become louder after the Gujarat elections. On the one hand, secularism is being pitted against Hindutva, under the belief that the two are antithetical to one another. This is incorrect and untenable. Secularism is a concept of the State, enjoining upon it the duty to show respect for all faiths and to practise no discrimination among citizens on the basis of their beliefs. In this sense, India has been secular since the beginning of her known history. We chose to remain wedded to secularism even when Pakistan was carved out on the basis of the spurious and communal Two-Nation Theory. This could not have been possible if the majority of Indians were not secular.

Gurudev Rabindranath Tagore has explained it very well. "India has all along been trying experiments in evolving a social unity within which all the different peoples could be held together, while fully enjoying the freedom of maintaining their differences. The tie has been as loose as possible, yet as close as circumstances permitted. This has produced something like a United States of a social federation, whose common name is Hinduism."

Hinduism's acceptance of the diversity of faiths is the central feature of secularism in India. As Maharshi Aurobindo points out, "Indian religion has always felt that since the minds, the temperaments and the intellectual affinities of men are unlimited in their variety, a perfect liberty of thought and of worship must be allowed to the individual in his approach to the Infinite."

On the other hand, Hindutva, which presents a *viraat darshan* (broad, all-encompassing view) of human life, is being projected by some people in a narrow, rigid and extremist manner – an unfortunate and unacceptable interpretation that runs totally contrary to its true spirit. Hindutva is an integral understanding of the entire Creation, showing the way both to the Here and the Hereafter. It emphasizes the inseparable relationship between the individual and society, as well as between man's material and spiritual needs. Hindutva is liberal, liberating and brooks no ill will, hatred or violence among different communities on any ground.

We need to affirm and promote that true understanding of Hindutva which is forward-looking, not one that seeks to take us back; that which makes us capable of meeting the challenges of the modern world, not one that is stuck in the grooves of the past; that which is reform-minded, and not one that protects obscurantism and injustice, against which all the reformers of the past have fought. If understood and practiced in this enlightened sense, which is how Swami Vivekananda and other great patriots propounded it, the current controversy over Hindutva will be seen as wholly unnecessary.

There is no difference between such Hindutva and Bharateeyata, since both are expressions of the same *chintan* (thought). Both affirm that India belongs to all, and all belong to India. It means that all Indians have equal rights and equal responsibilities. It entails recognition of our common national culture, which is enriched by all the diverse religious and non-religious traditions in India. For centuries, both have synonymously pointed to our national identity. Even the Supreme Court has held that Hindutva is neither a religious nor a political concept, but connotes a noble and elevating way of life.

This Indianness is what we should all celebrate and further strengthen. It is obvious that we have to remain committed to the task of strengthening our common Indianness in spite of every provocation, big or small, coming from our western neighbour. I often find it odd that whereas India reconciled itself long ago to the creation of Pakistan, the latter continues to find it difficult to accept the unchangeable reality of a united and secular India. Pakistan, even after five and a half decades of failed pursuit, seems to be unready to face the truth that Jammu & Kashmir is an integral part of India and will always remain so.

For the past several years, the rulers in Islamabad have, almost as a last resort, surrendered to the temptation of targeting India with terrorism, inspired by religious extremism. Innocent children, women and men are being routinely killed, temples are stormed, our symbols of democracy are attacked, and our security forces are challenged – all in the name of a "holy religious war" and "freedom struggle". This campaign of *jehadi* terrorism, too, is doomed to fail.

By rejecting Islamabad's call for boycott of polls, and participating enthusiastically in the free and fair elections to the State Assembly held in October, the people of Jammu & Kashmir have yet again expressed their will and preference. I am convinced that someday – hopefully soon — the people and rulers of Pakistan will realize the futile and counter-productive nature of its Kashmir policy. Pakistan cannot fight religious extremism and modernize itself as long it chooses to be in a position of permanent confrontation with India. Therefore, it must stop cross-border terrorism and abandon its insistence on the "centrality" of the Kashmir issue. Let our two countries agree to promote mutually beneficial trade and economic ties, strengthen cultural relations, and encourage greater people-to-people contacts. Once our two peoples experience the fruits of a tension-free and cooperative environment, we will be able to see the Kashmir issue in its proper dimension and arrive at an amicable and lasting solution.

Dear Countrymen, many pressing tasks confront us in the New Year and in the years ahead. As far as the Government is concerned, we are determined to accelerate the pace of implementation of numerous developmental initiatives that we have begun in recent years and to unveil several new ones in the New Year. I would like to characterize many of these initiatives as various components of the "Connectivity Revolution".

Highway connectivity and rural roads connectivity are two of the most ambitious infrastructure projects since Independence. We are also strengthening the rail and air connectivity in our country. Telecom connectivity, Internet connectivity and the attendant IT revolution have rapidly modernized our economy and society. I must also add here that our many foreign policy initiatives have yielded a better connectivity between the international community and an India that is today stronger and more self-confident than ever before. Another important endeavour will soon be added to this revolution. It is the River Connectivity project.

I would, however, place a far bigger importance on another connectivity effort, one to which I referred earlier – Connectivity of the Hearts and Minds of One Billion Indians. No nation has ever attained greatness without first attaining success in the awakening and organizing of the whole strength of its people. Unity of minds, unity of purpose, and unity in action – this is what we have to demonstrate in every sphere of our national life. We have to strengthen the spirit of nationalism, and make it an inspiring and motivating force to drive all our endeavours.

This is how India won the struggle for becoming a Free Nation. And this is how India will have to win the struggle for becoming a Developed Nation – free at last of poverty and unemployment, of illiteracy and disease, of poor shelter and sanitation, and of all other curses of underdevelopment. For this, we have to expand the area of consensus on economic and other urgent reforms, so that these can be implemented speedily and effectively. To me, the true test of reforms is when they beneficially touch the lives of all Indians – especially the poorest and those living in backward regions.

We are making progress on all these fronts. But the progress is not always as rapid – and as regionally and socially balanced – as we desire. There is a lot that the Central and State Governments have to do to speed up this process. I appeal to all our legislators, both at the Centre and in States, to show the same dedication to doing their duty as was seen in the last session of Parliament, when a record number of Bills were passed.

But there is an even larger area where people's own self-initiated and self-organized effort will produce the desired results. I am convinced that there is an immense untapped energy in our society, which can and must be channelised for constructive purposes, in order to bring about a positive change, even if such change is on a small scale and its impact is felt only locally. I would like our people to reduce their dependence on Government for everything.

For example, why should our cities and villages be so unclean and unhygienic? Can this not be changed visibly by changing the habits and the mindset of each one of us? Shouldn't citizens themselves initiate a drive for water conservation, energy conservation, and conservation of our precious cultural heritage? Shouldn't our society come down heavily against those who commit atrocities against women, dalits, adivasis and other weaker sections? Shouldn't our rich people provide more philanthropic resources for the care of the orphans, disabled, destitute, and senior citizens? My thoughts especially go out to our children, who are the future of our nation. The Government and society should work together with greater commitment to make all the emotional and material investment we can, to ensure that every Indian child is well fed, well educated and well looked after.

As a matter of fact, there are tens of thousands of unsung or little-sung heroes of development, both individuals and organizations, all over the country. They are inspired by the spirit of nationalism and the true meaning of religion as service to society – *Nar Seva* is *Narayan Seva*. Many of them are young people. Few things bring me greater joy than when I get to meet these selfless volunteers with soaring idealism. May the number of such individuals and organizations increase a thousand fold, and may they inspire each of us to do something more for our country in the New Year.

These are some of the thoughts and reflections that the idyllic setting in Goa has triggered in my mind, and which I wish to share with you.

Once again, I wish you all a very Happy New Year".

Statement before Departing to India

New York, September 15, 2002

Today, I conclude a satisfying visit to New York. Besides attending the 57th Session of the United Nations General Assembly, I met a number of Heads of State and Government, US Congressmen and Senators, and representatives of US and Indian community organizations.

I had the pleasure of meeting President Bush in New York. We re-affirmed our commitment to a long-term relationship of trust and transparency between India and USA. President Bush reiterated the total commitment of USA against terrorism and condemned the recent killings in Jammu & Kashmir, aimed at sabotaging the election process in that State. We reviewed our bilateral relations and agreed to intensify contacts and exchanges in high technology, space and nuclear energy.

I welcomed the opportunity to meet a group of US Senators and Congressmen. There is broad political support both in the Senate and the House of Representatives for strong India-US relations. I expressed our appreciation for this. We discussed areas where the US Congress could support the initiatives of our two governments to further intensify India-US relations.

A delegation of US Jewish organizations called on me. The Jewish community in USA has been strongly supportive of India in the US Congress and outside on terrorism and other important issues.

In a cordial meeting with the President of Afghanistan, I conveyed a strong message of our support for the unity and independence of

Afghanistan. The President appreciated India's financial, economic and technical assistance to his country.

Our traditionally close ties with Mauritius were re-affirmed in my meeting with the Prime Minister Sir Anerood Jugnauth. Our cooperation with Mauritius is strong and vibrant. A Union Cabinet Minister would shortly be visiting Mauritius to lay the foundation stone of their Cyber City, which is being built under Indian financial assistance of US$100 million and with our technical cooperation. I invited the Prime Minister to the inaugural Pravasi Bhartiya Diwas celebrations in Delhi in January next year.

In my meeting with the Prime Minister of Denmark, we discussed the intensification of the India-EU cooperation in the context of the forthcoming India-EU Summit in Copenhagen. We agreed to jointly attend a session of the India-EU Business Summit on the eve of the Heads of Governments Summit.

With the Prime Minister of Japan, I discussed follow-up on initiatives which we had announced during my visit to that country late last year. Economic cooperation has made satisfactory progress, including work on the Delhi Metro and preparatory action on the cleaning of the Ganga and the Yamuna rivers.

I had the opportunity to meet the newly elected President of Zambia and to reiterate to him India's commitment to further strengthening our historical relations. I reiterated my invitation to the President to visit India and we expect his visit to materialize in the near future. A number of areas of India-Zambia cooperation were identified for future cooperation, including small-scale industries and agricultural development.

We have had relations of close cooperation with Bulgaria, both bilaterally and in the UN In my meeting with the President of Bulgaria, we reviewed our bilateral relations in all areas. I conveyed our appreciation to Bulgaria for their support to us in matters of concern in the UN Security Council. Bulgaria has also extended its support to India's permanent membership of the UN Security Council.

A common theme running through all these meetings was that of international terrorism. Every single world leader whom I met condemned the terrorist attacks in Jammu & Kashmir and elsewhere in India. The Prime Minister of Mauritius called for an end to cross-border infiltration in his UNGA statement. Meeting in New York during the first anniversary of the horrible tragedies in USA, I naturally discussed with all these leaders the imperative need for democracies to cooperate in rooting out terrorism effectively and without discrimination.

It was a poignant experience for me to meet some of the relatives of the Indian victims of the brutal terrorist attacks of September 11. I attended the simple, but evocative, remembrance ceremony at Battery Park to express solidarity with all those who have suffered from terrorism.

It was a special pleasure to pay homage in New York to the memory of Swami Vivekananda.

The diverse groups of Indian community representatives whom I met on various occasions gave me a good idea of the outlook and perspectives of the Indian Diaspora in this country.

18

In General Assembly of the UNO

Address by Shri Atal Bihari Vajpayee, Prime Minister of India at the 57th Session of the United Nations General Assembly

New York, September 13, 2002

Mr. President,

I congratulate you on your election as President of the 57th General Assembly. We wish you success and pledge our whole-hearted support.

I also extend my best wishes to Secretary General Kofi Annan in this first year of his second term in office.

Mr. President,

Two days ago, we commemorated the first anniversary of a terrible event, which focused the collective global consciousness on international terrorism. Terrorism did not start on September 11. It was on that day that it brazenly announced itself on the global stage, flaunting its immunity from distance and power.

As a country exposed to the depredations of terrorism for decades, India empathized with the pain of the American people, admired their resilience in coming to terms with the consequences, and supported the bold decision to counter-attack terrorism at its very source.

The international community has taken some collective decisions in the global effort to combat terrorism and to choke off its lifelines. The UN Security Council Resolution 1373 contains the essence of these decisions. Its Counter-Terrorism Committee should now move beyond information compilation and legal assistance to enforcing compliance by states known to be sponsoring, sheltering, funding, arming and training terrorists.

In our South Asian region, nuclear blackmail has emerged over the last few months as a new arrow in the quiver of State-sponsored terrorism. Dark threats were held out that actions by India to stamp out cross-border terrorism could provoke a nuclear war. To succumb to such blatant nuclear terrorism would mean forgetting the bitter lessons of the September 11 tragedy.

As far as India is concerned, we have repeatedly clarified that no one in our country wants a war — conventional or otherwise. Nor are we seeking any territory.

But absolutely everyone in India wants an end to the cross-border terrorism which has claimed thousands of innocent lives and denied entire generations their right to a peaceful existence with normal economic and social activity. We are determined to end it with all the means at our command. Let there be no doubt about it in any quarter.

Mr. President,

Yesterday we heard the extraordinary claim in this Assembly that the brutal murder of innocent civilians in Jammu & Kashmir is actually a "freedom struggle". And that the forthcoming elections in that state are a "farce", since they cannot be a substitute for a plebiscite demanded over 50 years ago.

It requires an effort of logical acrobatics to believe that carnage of innocents is an instrument for freedom and elections are a symbol of deception and repression!

If the elections are a mere fraud, why are terrorists being trained and infiltrated into India at the command of the Inter-Services Intelligence Agency of Pakistan to kill election candidates and to intimidate voters?

If Pakistan claims to be a crucial partner in the international coalition against terrorism, how can it continue to use terrorism as an instrument of state policy against India?

How can the international coalition condone Pakistan-directed killings of thousands of innocent civilians — women and children included – to promote a bizarre version of "self-determination"?

Those who speak of "underlying" or "root" causes of terrorism, offer alibis to the terrorists and absolve them of responsibility for their heinous actions – such as the September 11 attacks on the United States or the December 13 attack on our Parliament.

General Musharraf has himself admitted that rigging was responsible for his winning the referendum by a dubious margin of 90 per cent in April this year. As for the "true" democracy he intends to establish in Pakistan, he has rendered it impotent even before the elections are held next month.

Those who had to "adjust" voting and counting procedures to win a referendum – and achieved constitutional authority by the simple expedient of writing their own constitution – are ill-placed to lecture others on freedom and democracy.

Mr. President,

Yesterday we heard yet another patently false and self-serving claim that in India, Muslims and other minorities are the target of "Hindu extremists". With 150 million, India has the second largest Muslim population in the world, more than in Pakistan. We are proud of the multi-religious character of our society. Equal respect for all faiths, and non-discrimination on the basis of religion, is not just our Constitutional obligation. As the whole world knows, it is the signature tune of India's civilisation and culture.

Mr. President,

We have to recognize that the developmental divide between the North and the South is becoming wider and deeper by the day. The challenges that face us are stark and there is no alternative to all the countries of the world joining hands to face them together.

Over the last decade, 10 million people have been joining the ranks of the poor each year. A quarter of the world's population lives in extreme poverty.

A million lives are lost to malaria each year. Tuberculosis claims twice as many lives annually. One-fifth of humanity does not have access to safe drinking water.

We have to find US$ 24 billion annually for investment in poor countries if we are to achieve the World Food Summit goal of halving hunger by 2015.

It was this bleak picture that we addressed in our Millennium Declaration in 2000 with a time-bound road map for poverty eradication, with goals and targets to be achieved by 2015. The Monterrey Conference on Financing for Development was an encouraging beginning in the effort to enhance international financing for development.

Continuation of widespread poverty, at a time when unimaginable wealth is concentrated in a small social layer, is totally unacceptable. The 21st century has all the means to end this sad legacy of the past centuries. What is lacking is the political will among the developed countries to sincerely and speedily address the legitimate developmental needs of the developing countries, especially the least developed ones.

The poor of the world, as also the more enlightened sections of the rich around the world, would like the United Nations to spearhead efforts to end the systemic indifference towards poverty. The agenda of action that would achieve this objective is clear:

- One, asymmetry in trading relations between developing and developed nations; the problem of declining prices for commodities from developing countries; and all unjustified barriers to their exports must be removed.

- Two, extreme volatility in global energy markets has been causing havoc with the trade and fiscal balances of developing countries. This must end.
- Three, unpredictability in global capital movements, which periodically devastate the economies of developing countries, must be controlled.
- Four, malfeasant corporate practices, which drain off the natural resources and traditional knowledge base of developing countries without fair compensation, must be dealt with sternly.

Casting an even longer shadow over this grim developmental canvas is global climate change—from which the poor will suffer the most, though they contributed the least to it. The recent floods and forest fires in Europe are a forewarning that the countries of Asia and Africa are not the only victims of the fury of a degraded environment. The Earth's atmosphere and biosphere know no national boundaries. The choice before the global community is stark: Either we take urgent steps to protect the environment, or be prepared for far worse natural calamities.

Early this month, the Johannesburg Summit for Sustainable Development debated some of the linkages between poverty, trade, environment, national, international and corporate governance and global financial flows. We emerged from the Summit with some encouraging outcomes, but these fell well short of the demands of our time.

It has become a categorical imperative to understand, and address, man's developmental needs in their totality – and not in isolated parts. It is disconcerting that the highways of development are jammed by the noisy and unruly traffic of materialism and its brash cousin, consumerism. Human values have become mute bystanders in most political, economic and social activities.

The result of this imbalance between our material and non-material needs can never be happy for mankind. On the contrary, by placing compassion, care, fellow feeling, cooperation and other human values in the driver's seat, we are bound to get the right solutions to every problem on our planet.

Humanity is crying out for a harmonious integration of the economic, social, political, environmental and spiritual dimensions of development. This task calls for the closest possible cooperation among nations and communities, with a readiness to accept the best from every cultural and spiritual tradition around the globe. The United Nations needs to take up newer and bigger initiatives in this direction.

In this Assembly, less than a year ago—and in the US Congress the year before—I had extended India's offer to coordinate a Comprehensive Global Development Dialogue. I reiterate that offer today. If we are to achieve the development goals we have promised ourselves by 2015, we need such a dialogue urgently.

Mr. President,

As we come together once again at the United Nations, at a time of new and varied challenges, we should reflect on our collective commitment to the UN Charter, its purposes and principles. There is a growing perception – particularly among the weaker and poorer countries – that responses to issues of far-reaching impact often seem arbitrary or contradictory.

A common destiny is at stake. The world needs collective multilateralism. It needs the United Nations – the coming together and working together of all its nations in the development of a common and collective perspective.

Conflicts arise when there is no spirit of democracy within and among nations. A genuinely democratic framework enables us to respect alternative points of view, to value diversity, and to fashion solutions responsive to the aspirations of the people.

India's own experience as a hugely populated and diverse nation shows how complex problems can be addressed within a constitutional and democratic framework.

These values need to be assiduously nurtured in our societies, so that at least a future generation is rid of the scourge of poverty, intolerance, obscurantism and religious extremism.

Democratic societies are far less prone to ideologies based on violence or militarist yearnings, since they do not have their fingers permanently on the trigger of a gun. We have to be vigilant against threats to democracy worldwide arising from forces that are opposed to it, be they rooted in fundamentalist political dogmas or extremist religious ideologies.

Mr. President,

All of us are aware of the challenges. Most of us are agreed that a stable global order has to rest on the four strong pillars of peace, security, sustainable development and democracy. We have to ensure that each of these pillars is strong and resilient.

We are conscious of our collective responsibility. It is the leap from this theoretical understanding to its practical realization, which we have often failed to execute. We should not fail again. Our future generations will not forgive us if we do.

Thank you.

Speech in Millennium Summit at the United Nations

New York, September 8, 2000

"Standing at the gates of an important epoch at a point in our history that joins the past and the present and the future we the representatives of six billion people must ensure that this Millennium Summit and the General Assembly session that follows will transcend issues of narrow concerns and chart a new course for humanity. And that will lead to enduring peace, development and security for all."

Mr. President,

It is apt that the Millennium Summit of the United Nations, which symbolises the confluence of the developed and the developing worlds, should be jointly presided over by the leaders of two vibrant democracies, Finland and Namibia one a developed country from Europe, the other, a developing country from Africa.

In your joint presidency, on which I congratulate you, you symbolise the partnership between diversity and the sharing of fundamental values that lie at the core of the United Nations; indeed the very strength on which the United Nations must build itself in the new century.

This unique summit marks the formal entry of the United Nations into the 21st century and the new millennium. Mote importantly, it reflects the collective desire of peoples living in 189 countries spread across the world to forge a future free of the blemishes of the past.

A future that will guarantee equitable development of all nations East and West, North and South.

A future that will guarantee freedom from want for nearly a quarter of the world's peoples living in abject poverty.

A future that will guarantee freedom from fear of war among nations and conflicts within societies.

And a future in which nations will work together as equals for a new world order based on justice and equality.

Let there be no doubt that the journey to our future, which we begin at the Millennium Summit, is over a very long and winding road. At every turn, we will be challenged by doubts. Overcoming that challenge and forging ahead will be the real test of the resolve that we voice at this Summit.

In spite of human endeavour for peace, prosperity and cooperation among nations in the century gone by, the world is not free of conflict, often with terrible consequences. Much of this conflict is attributable to hostile aggression, lust for territory or, simply, hegemony.

But conflict is also born in failure of equitable development among and within nations. For long it has been established that poverty threatens peace and social cohesiveness within nations. It now needs to be recognised that the continuing poverty of some nations, even while others prosper, not only taunts our conscience; it also threatens peace among nations.

Poverty can neither be wished away, nor accepted as a reality beyond redemption. This affliction that strikes at the core of human dignity has to be cured through the collective will and effort of all nations, rich and poor.

The century we have just left behind is littered with many a turning point in the history of humanity. The last 100 years were both the best of times and the worst of times. There were moments of utter despair and flashes of soaring hope.

In the 20th century we have seen colonialism peak and collapse. We have seen totalitarian and racist regimes rule with an iron fist, only to crumble in the face of assertive desire for liberty and human dignity. We have seen death and destruction caused by wars rekindle humankind's urge for lasting and durable peace.

It has been a century of contrasts. Giant strides in science and technology marking the conquest of new frontiers of knowledge have helped us grow more food, produce life saving drugs and send satellites into space. Yet, millions still go hungry, die of easily curable diseases and are deprived of the enlightenment and empowerment that education ensures.

The emergence of a global economy has led to undeniable benefits like faster growth, higher living standards and new opportunities. The rapid spread of Information Technology, riding the crest of a Knowledge Revolution, has virtually led to the creation of a digital world where the click of a mouse can span vast distances in less than a fraction of a second. A 'New Economy' drives the world today.

Yet, nearly a quarter of the people this Assembly represents have neither prospered nor gained from these developments. Often, they find themselves further marginalised and more vulnerable as development economics gives way to unbridled market economics and social objectives are erased by profit motives.

Mr. President,

Globalisation was supposed to deliver economic equality among all nations through free flow of goods, services and capital. The reality we see today is an asymmetry in the benefits from globalisation between the developing and developed worlds. This asymmetry has further accentuated income disparities, thus increasing the scope of conflict and strife.

If one in four of the world's people still live in severe poverty, there is something wrong somewhere in the manner in which we have been managing global development issues. The situation is made worse by the fact that developing countries with decreasing resources, both natural and financial, are finding it increasingly difficult to meet their social obligations.

Therefore, removing economic inequality, both between and within nations, and ensuring that development does not suffer for want of funds, are two of the challenges that we have to collectively meet in the new century.

We also need to actively consider a fresh global initiative to fight poverty. In a globalised economy, poverty eradication cannot be treated as the exclusive responsibility of individual nations. Therefore, a new global strategy against poverty is called for.

Even as poverty severely inhibits the socio-economic progress of developing countries, the alarming spread of HIV/AIDS drains their productive capacities. The co-relation between HIV incidence and poverty is too compelling to ignore.

It should be the concern of all humanity to generate the resources for concerted awareness campaigns for HIV prevention; for making preventive, palliative and curative drugs affordable; and, for the scientific quest for definitive prophylaxis and cure for the various strains of the dreaded virus. These tasks should not be allowed to add to the already onerous burden that developing countries are carrying today.

Another issue that should be of universal concern is the debt burden of many a developing nation. This burden grows yearly with new debts being contracted to pay off current interest charges. This results in a continual haemorrhage of wealth that further debilitates the developing world.

The United Nations has a signal role to play in this global effort: by focusing attention on equitable development, by ensuring that development is not the preserve of a few.

In the last decade of the last century, we have seen a series of world conferences on various aspects of development —social development, women's issues, population and environment. We now look forward to the conference on financing for development.

Indeed, it is time that we looked at assurance of economic development, growth and distribution together in a high-level UN conference. And, we urge that development be made a cross cutting issue in the work of a reformed United Nations.

But economic inter-dependence is best when it is based on the principle of nondiscrimination. Only then can nations benefit equitably from global trade and commerce. To achieve this, and to ensure genuine economic multilateralism, the tendency of some to rely on non-tariff barriers to preserve markets and perpetuate current balance of trade should be resisted by all. This can be best guaranteed by ensuring, especially for developing countries, free access to markets and services through more transparent and predictable standards and requirements.

Mr. President,

Global financial integration has encouraged an unregulated and volatile capital mobility across national boundaries and currency zones. This has exposed many developing countries to tremendous risks.

Part of the problem is that we have moved towards an integrated international financial market without fully realising the potential turbulence which could result in weaker economies. Indeed, the 1990s are replete with financial crises striking developing countries and revealing the economically destabilising impact of an uncontrolled global flight of money on developing and transition economics.

The resources of the International Monetary Fund should be augmented to deal with economic crisis created by the globalisation policy being pursued by member countries. Its role in anticipating major crises through improved disclosure standards and enhanced information systems also needs to be strengthened. This would be applicable equally to both developed and developing countries.

The new century needs a new financial architecture to strengthen the role of multilateral institutions responsible for ensuring the stability of the international financial system. Multilateral cooperation should focus more clearly on the need for better policy co-ordination among developed countries to avoid policy misalignment, which can have a destabilising effect on international capital movements.

An inter-dependent world calls for greater participation by developing countries in the major forums of decision making. There is need to increase the share of developing countries in decision-making in international forums dealing with the international financial system.

Mr. President,

We cannot have true development without peace between nations and democracy within them. Indeed, democracy and peace continue to remain the best guarantors for unhindered development each secures the other.

The continued existence of nuclear weapons is a threat to global security in this new century, as in the century gone by which not only saw the development but also the tragic use of weapons of mass destruction. The international community has successfully diminished, if not entirely removed, the threat posed by chemical and biological weapons. But not so with nuclear weapons.

In fact, despite all the talk of nuclear disarmament from various forums, the stockpiles of weapons of mass destruction, in the custody of those who were the first to build up such a deadly arsenal, remain virtually untouched. It would seem that we are still far away from achieving a goal that can assure the survival of humanity in the new millennium.

India was forced to acquire these weapons in 1998 because the principal nuclear weapon states refused to accept the almost universal demand for nuclear disarmament. Moreover, the spread of nuclear weapons in our neighbourhood made us especially vulnerable.

Nevertheless, our policy is based on responsibility and restraint and we continue to press for universal, verifiable nuclear disarmament with undiminished commitment, even while safeguarding our strategic space and autonomy in decision-making. International peace cannot be divorced from the need for equal and legitimate security for all. We support the Secretary General's proposal for an international conference to address nuclear dangers.

In the interregnum, India continues with its voluntary moratorium on further underground nuclear test explosions. India remains committed to working for the successful conclusion of her security dialogue with key interlocutors on the CTBT. I reiterate our position that we will not prevent the entry into force of the CTBT. At the same time, all other countries which must ratify the CTBT under Article XIV of the Treaty, should do so without condition.

India also remains committed to participate in negotiations on a Treaty that will prohibit the production of fissile materials for nuclear weapons or other nuclear explosive devices. We will participate in these discussions in good faith and in order to ensure a Treaty that is non—discriminatory and meets India's security imperatives.

Mr. President,

Of the many other threats to peace, democracy and development, none has become as dangerous as international terrorism, with its links to religious extremism, drug trafficking and the commerce in illicit arms. ?lural and open democracies are the target of the scourge of terrorism that strikes at very root of tolerance, the mainstay of civil society in a free world.

For more than a decade now India has been a victim of cross-border terrorism that has claimed thousands of innocent lives. We have been fighting this crime against humanity with the weapons available to a responsible democracy.

India calls for united global action against these dangers. We urge the international community to quickly adopt and implement the Comprehensive Convention Against Terrorism that will be negotiated at the UN General Assembly session that follows this Summit.

Many statesman-like words have been delivered from this high tribune. Unfortunately, some of them are an Orwellian mockery. Those who have stifled democracy at home speak of freedom from this forum. Those who have engaged in the clandestine acquisition of nuclear weapons and delivery systems talk of ridding South Asia of these. Those who have repudiated solemn covenants talk of new agreements to prevent war. The authors of a vicious terrorist campaign that has claimed more than 30,000 innocent lives in India, who actively sabotaged a historic peace initiative, are now offering new initiatives for dialogue.

The world must see the reality as it is. The acid test of sincerity of purpose is not words, but deeds. Terrorism and dialogue do not go together.

We also urge the international community to act collectively against the indiscriminate proliferation of, and illegal trafficking in, small arms and light weapons. Countries should cooperate and work closely to prevent, combat and eradicate the illicit trade in small arms and light weapons by adopting an International Programme of Action of Agreed Measures.

Mr. President,

Because there can, by definition, be no equitable development without democracy, it is essential that the United Nations promote democratic norms. And the United Nations should do so not only by monitoring elections or by promoting standards of effective governance, but by example.

The United Nations is a symbol of the aspirations of the peoples of the free world to achieve the noble objectives of peace, equality and honour. The UN Charter envisaged a balance between the three major inter-governmental organs of the United Nations—the General Assembly, the Security Council and the Economic and Social Council.

Over the years, this balance has tilted rather heavily towards the Security Council. It is important that the central role of the General Assembly be respected; this Millennium Summit is a good first step, and we thank the Secretary General for proposing it. We are glad that the Economic and Social Council has again become active in the promotion of development; we trust that the momentum will be maintained.

However, in a world in flux, it is understandable that the Security Council will continue to have a rather special role to play. It is, therefore, all the more necessary that it be made more representative of the large membership.

We hope this Millennium Summit will commit itself to an early expansion and reform of the Security Council, particularly bringing in new permanent members from developed and developing countries, so that it reflects the new realities of the 21st century. This will also strengthen this world body to function more purposefully in the services of all peoples who, as the UN Charter says, constitute the United Nations.

As member States will recall, India has let it be known for some years that we believe ourselves qualified by objective criteria for responsibilities of permanent membership. Indeed, as the world's largest democracy, enormous potential, a rapidly growing economic power and a major contributor to peace-keeping operations, India has a natural claim to a permanent seat in the Security Council.

Finally, Mr. President, at this rare moment of the Millennium, when we touch history, let us pledge to work towards bringing the vast human family closer together. Let us believe in spirit that our destiny is joined. I end with an ancient Indian invocation:

Sarve bhavantu sukinah
Sarve santu nirmayah
Sarve bhadranipasyantu
Ma Kaschit dukha bhag bhavet!
(May all live happily
May all enjoy good health
May all see auspiciousness
May none experience distress
May peace prevail everywhere!)

Thank you.

Address to the 53rd UN General Assembly on September 24, 1998

Mr. President,

May I congratulate you on your election to the Presidency of the 53rd UN General Assembly? We wish you well in our shared endeavours in the United Nations and offer you our full cooperation we would like to thank your predecessor for his engagement and contribution and to compliment him for the work throughout the last year.

I first addressed this august Assembly of the UN as Foreign Minister in 1977. Since then I have had the privilege to come for the General Assembly sessions for many years but it was without ministerial responsibility. I acknowledge with gratitude the confidence of successive Prime Ministers. To me it also signifies the consensus on national interests and the foreign policy of India. When I addressed the General Assembly in 1977, it was the turning point in many ways in the history of India. The Janata Government was a coalition of many factions who united in the restoration of our people's faith in democracy. Since then we have had many changes of Government but the people's political awareness and their faith in the institutions which uphold our constitutional system has been unwavering. Today, when I come to this podium as Prime Minister I come on behalf of another coalition. India has demonstrated that democracy can take root in a developing country. I am confident that the Indian experience will prove that democracy can also provide the basis for stable, long-term economic growth in developing societies. This is the path that the people of India have chosen and I stand before you today as the symbol of this new resurgent India.

Mr. President, the world of the 1970's has receded into history. The shackling constraints of the Cold War are gone. The distinguishing feature of the last two decades has been the spread of democracy worldwide. By force of example, we have been one of the authors of the triumph of democracy. From this flows our desire to see democratization of the UN itself. An International body that does not reflect, and change with, the changing international realities, will inevitably face a credibility deficit. We, therefore, support a revitalized and effective UN, one that is more responsive to the concerns of the vast majority of its member States and is better equipped to meet the challenges ahead of us in the 21st century.

The Security Council does not represent contemporary reality; it does not represent democracy in international relations. Following the end of the Cold War, it has acquired the freedom to act but experience shows that the Council has acted only when it was convenient for its permanent members. The experience of Somalia does not do credit to the Security Council and there are other examples too. Peacekeeping operations cannot be a reflection of ulterior political priorities and perceptions.

There is only one cure—to bring in fresh blood. The Security Council must be made representative of the membership of the United Nations, developing countries must be made permanent members. It is a right to which the developing world is entitled.

Presence of some developing countries as permanent members is inescapable for effectively discharging the responsibilities of the Security Council particularly when we see that the Council acts almost exclusively in the developing world. It is only natural that on decisions affecting the developing world, these countries have say, on equal terms. Along with other measures, the Security Council too must be reformed, expanding its non-permanent membership so that more developing countries can serve on it. But this alone is not enough. Because as long as effective power in the Council rests with the permanent membership, the interests of the developing world will not be promoted or protected unless developing countries are made permanent members, on par with the present permanent members. Only this will make the Council an effective instrument for the international community in dealing with current and future challenges. The new permanent members must of course have the ability to discharge the responsibilities that come with permanent membership. India believes it can, and, as we had said before from this rostrum, we are prepared to accept the responsibilities of permanent membership, and believe we are qualified for it.

It will be a great day when democracy becomes the universal norm, and when the UN reflects this democracy in its institutions and functioning. However, open democratic societies have one scourge to contend with—terrorism. The challenge before countries like mine and other democracies is to maintain our openness, safeguard individual rights, and, at the same time, give no quarter to terrorists. Several speakers before me have recounted the terrible toll, worldwide, that terrorists have exacted, taking advantage of the trust that characterizes open societies. I recall that the G-7 Summit almost two decades back had identified terrorism as one of the most serious threats to civilised societies. Events since then including the blowing up of Air India Kanishka, the Pan Am Airlines over Lockerbie, to the recent bombings in Nairobi and Dar-es-Salaam—have only established the correctness of that judgment.

Mr. President, terrorism is one threat that affects us all equally. Terrorism takes a daily toll across the world. It is the most vicious among international crimes, the most pervasive, pernicious and ruthless threat to the lives of men and women in open societies, and to international peace and security. In India, we have had to cope with terrorism, aided and abetted by a neighbouring country, for nearly two decades. We have borne this with patience, but none should doubt the strength of our resolve to crush this challenge, its tentacles have spread across the world. Today, it has linkages with illicit trade in drugs, arms and money laundering. In short, terrorism has gone global and it can only be defeated by organized international action.

Let us make up our minds once and for all – terrorism is a crime against humanity. Unilateral steps can hardly stand scrutiny in an open society, let alone in the eyes of the international community. It should be the primary task of all open and plural societies to develop collective means for tackling this menace. At the summit meeting in Durban, the Non-Aligned Movement has called for an international conference in 1999 to develop such a collective response. We urge that the 1999 conference launch the process of negotiations for an international convention to provide for collective action against States and organizations which initiate or aid and abet terrorism.

In this fiftieth anniversary of the Universal Declaration of Human Rights, there is a growing realization that economic, social, cultural, civil and political rights form a seamless web. Analyses carried out in recent years by the UN High Commissioner for Refugees amply reflect the vicious cycle of how violations of economic, social and cultural rights inevitably lead to violations of civil and political rights. In defining its index, the Human Development Report gives a higher weightage to economic criterion for developing countries; this weightage is reduced for developed countries, highlighting the importance of the right to development for developing societies. It is therefore a matter of concern that the absolutism sought to be advocated in the promotion of human rights is often at the cost of the right to development.

India has ratified both the Covenant on Economic, Social and Cultural Rights and the Covenant of Civil and Political Rights. Other institutions in our country—the National Human Rights Commission, a free media, an independent judiciary—all serve to assure that the international human rights statutes are enjoyed by all citizens. We also remained convinced that unless progress is made on economic, social and cultural rights including the right to development, the world will continue to witness international conflict leading to migrations, displacement of people and human rights abuses.

In the closing years of the 20th century, the challenge of nuclear disarmament is another of the priorities facing the international community. We have successfully prohibited chemical and biological weapons in recent decades. The present century has witnessed the development and the tragic use of nuclear weapons. We must ensure that the legacy of this weapon of mass destruction is not carried into the next century.

For the last half-century, India has consistently pursued the objectives of international peace along with equal and legitimate security for all through global disarmament. These concepts are among the basic tenets of our national security. India has, over the years, sought to enhance its national security by promoting global nuclear disarmament, convinced that a world free of nuclear weapons enhances both global and India's national security.

The negotiations on a Comprehensive Test Ban Treaty (CTBT) began in 1993 with a mandate that such a treaty would "contribute effectively to the non-proliferation of nuclear weapons in all aspects, to the process of nuclear disarmament and therefore, to the enhancement of international peace and security". India participated actively and constructively in the negotiations, and sought to place the Treaty in a disarmament framework by proposing its linkage with a time-bound programme for the universal elimination of all nuclear weapons.

It is a matter of history that India's proposals were not accepted. The treaty, as it emerged, was not accepted by India on grounds of national security. We made explicit our objection that despite our stand having been made clear, the treaty text made India's signature and ratification a pre-condition for its entry into force.

Mindful of its deteriorating security environment which has obliged us to stand apart from the CTBT in 1996, India undertook a limited series of five underground tests, conducted on 11 and 13 May, 1998. These tests were essential for ensuring a credible nuclear deterrent for India's national security in the foreseeable future.

These tests do not signal a dilution of India's commitment to the pursuit of global nuclear disarmament. Accordingly, after concluding this limited testing programme, India announced a voluntary moratorium on further underground nuclear test explosions. We conveyed our willingness to move towards a de jure formalization of this obligation. In announcing a moratorium, India has already accepted the basic obligation of the CTBT. In 1996, India could not have accepted the obligation as such a restraint would have eroded our capability and compromised our national security.

Mr. President, India, having harmonized its national imperatives and security obligations and desirous of continuing to cooperate with the international community is now engaged in discussions with key interlocutors on a range of issues, including the CTBT. We are prepared to bring these discussions to a successful conclusion, so that the entry into force of the CTBT is not delayed beyond September 1999. We expect that other countries, as indicated in Article XIV of the CTBT, will adhere to this Treaty without conditions.

After protracted discussions, the Conference on Disarmament in Geneva is now in a position to begin negotiations on a treaty that will prohibit the production of fissile materials for nuclear weapons or other nuclear explosive devices. Once again, we are conscious that this is a partial step. Such a treaty, as and when it is concluded and enters into force, will not eliminate existing nuclear arsenals. Yet, we will participate in these negotiations in good faith in order to ensure a treaty that is non-discriminatory and meets India's security imperatives. India will pay serious attention to any other multilateral initiatives in this area, during the course of the negotiations in the CD.

As a responsible state committed to non-proliferation, India has undertaken that it shall not transfer these weapons or related know-how to other countries. We have an effective system of export controls and shall make it more stringent where necessary, including by expanding control lists of equipment and technology to make them more contemporary and effective in the context of a nuclear India. At the same time, as a developing country, we are conscious that nuclear technology has a number of peaceful applications and we shall continue to cooperate actively with other countries in this regard, in keeping with our international responsibilities.

A few weeks ago, at the Non-Aligned Summit in Durban, India proposed and the Movement agreed that an international conference be held, preferably in 1999, with the objective of arriving at an agreement, before the end of this millennium on a phased program for the complete elimination of all nuclear weapons. I call upon all members of the international community, and particularly the other nuclear weapon states to join in this endeavour. Let us pledge that when we assemble here in the new millennium, it shall be to welcome the commitment that mankind shall never again be subjected to the use of threat of use of nuclear weapons.

Mr. President, the decade of the 1990s has fallen far short of expectations; nowhere is this more apparent than on the global economic scene. The sense of triumphalism that heralded the wave of global capitalism is now giving way to caution and realism. What was initially seen as an Asian flu is now spreading to other continents.

The hypothesis that unfettered capital flows would foster economic development with the global financial markets adjusting the exchange rates stands falsified. What we have seen is the growth of a large volume of "virtual money" that has not been generated by productive economic activity. But the power of the "virtual money" is real, evident in the fact that national regulatory mechanisms are unable to cope with the impact of its rapid movement in and out of currencies. Its volatility in the short run does not follow economic logic but rumor and sentiment with results that are self-reinforcing. In developing countries and in western financial capitals, there is now a growing acceptance that premature liberalization of capital markets has been a primary cause of the current crisis.

Does it mean that the world should turn back from globalization? Our answer is an emphatic NO. Rising economic inter-dependence is a phenomenon driven by the technological imperative, but we must learn how to manage the change, India has not been affected as severely as some other countries, largely because we adopted policies that were more prudent. But a drop in commodity prices, by 30 per cent in a year and a reduction in net capital flows by 50 per cent to the emerging markets will have a negative impact on growth everywhere, including in the developed world.

I must emphasize that democratically elected leadership in open developing societies, such as India, also faces another challenge. We cannot let an unbridled free market system aggravate existing economic and social disparities. In fact, we need policy instruments to reduce disparities thus creating a more stable environment in the long term. Such policies are necessary in accountable democracies and in no way inconsistent with managed liberalization.

It is high time, Mr. President, that we begin a new international dialogue, on the future of a global and inter-dependent economy. This is a task for the sovereign states represented here and cannot be left solely to the dynamics of an unregulated market place.

Ladies and Gentlemen, Friends, I think I speak for all of us when I say that we are on the threshold of a new age. This is an over-used phrase, but we are all aware trial an exciting new universe is within our reach. Several centuries ago, Isaac Newton described his scientific discoveries as pebbles on the beach, while the Ocean of Truth lay undiscovered. It was modest of that great scientist to so describe his work, but I believe that we are now actually sailing in the Ocean of Truth. We have made exciting discoveries and will make many more which will move humankind forward.

And yet there is also an uneasy feeling that all is not well. The world is not at ease with itself. Forces are bubbling under the surface tranquility in almost all parts of the world that threaten the gains of the last century, and which seek to lead the world towards, bigotry, violence and unhealthy exclusivism.

India has a message: not a new one, for almost all religions have expressed the thought before. But we have preserved the tenets—of freedom, equality and tolerance in our daily lives. If the world of the 21st century is to be a better place than the world we have seen so far, these values must prevail. History also shows that these are easier to prescribe than to observe. And yet, as we move towards ever-closer interdependence, there is no alternative. The world and its leaders must summon the will to rise to the occasion and enter the new age with a new outlook. This is the task before us and I declare India's readiness to make its full contribution in the testing times ahead.

I close with an ancient *sloka* from the *Rig Veda* composed thousands of years ago in Sanskrit, the oldest language in the World:

> *"Svastir manushebhyaha*
> *Oordhvam Jugatu beshajam*
> *Sam no astu dvipathe*
> *Sam chathusthpate*
> *Om Shanti, Shanti, Shanti".*

Meaning:

> Let all human beings be blessed with prosperity,
> Let all flora and fauna which are life line of all creatures, grow abundantly,
> Let there be harmony with all two-legged creations,
> Let there be harmony with all four-legged creations,
> Let there be peace, peace, peace.
> (OM Shanti, Shanti, Shanti.)

Thank you, Mr. President.

19
Views on Child Labour

Prime Minister Vajpayee's Speech at the National Conference on Child Labour

New Delhi, January 22, 2001

It gives me great pleasure to be here at the National Conference on Elimination of Child Labour.

UNICEF, in one of its annual reports, has evocatively observed: *The day will come when nations will be judged not by their military or economic strength, nor by the splendor of their capital cities and public buildings but by the well being of their people; ... by the provision that is made for those who are vulnerable and disadvantaged, and by the protection that is afforded to the growing minds and bodies of their children.*

India fully subscribes to this ideal, this universal aspiration. We believe that the right to a joyful childhood, leading to a life full of opportunities, is the fundamental right of every child. Our children are the future of our nation. We are committed to nurture them through their childhood and their most impressionable and formative years, so that they can realize their full potential and contribute richly to the development of their motherland.

However, the continued existence of millions of working children in our society is a reminder of the extent of the task that lies ahead of us. As per the 1991 census, their number is 11.28 million. This is a staggering figure. It is also a pointer that the responsibility for elimination of child labour cannot be compartmentalized and left to any one Ministry or Department of Government. I am happy that this conference shows a close collaboration between the Ministries of Labour and Human Resource Development.

The sheer magnitude of the problem, as also its multifaceted nature, makes it imperative that we adopt a holistic approach, involving the entire society. This alone can make a difference.

Since Independence, our country has overcome many problems through the combined efforts of the Central and State Governments, private sector, and non-governmental organizations. Infant mortality rate has declined by half from 146 per thousand in 1951 to 72 per thousand or below now. Life expectancy has also grown from 32 years in 1951 to 63 years.

We have reached a literacy rate of over 60 per cent, which was just 18 per cent in 1951. However, there is great imbalance across the country in the area of children's education and welfare. We have States like Kerala, where nearly all the children in the age group of six to fourteen years are attending schools. Himachal Pradesh, too, is moving towards this distinction. This contrasts starkly with the poor performance in several other States in the north and the east. Even in these States, wherever educational reform programmes are implemented, we see a progressively higher enrolment in schools. There is also a visible decline in the school drop out rate.

These are positive signals. They show that, with collective and committed efforts, we can certainly achieve universal education and 100 percent literacy. Doing so would be a big step towards elimination of child labour.

Hence, my sincere appeal to all the District Collectors who have gathered here is this: Go all out to strengthen the partnership between the Government, non-governmental educational institutions, voluntary organizations, and business establishments in your respective districts. Expand and improve the network of both formal and non-formal educational activities, so that no family with a working child is left out.

Concentrate, especially, on working girls. Her educational needs are usually neglected both by her family and by the society at large. Education of girls and young women is critical for achieving many of our important goals in social development. By investing in them, we invest in India's future.

Friends, 2001 is the Year for Women's Empowerment. It would be befitting that, at this juncture, the programmes are restructured to pay special attention to working girls.

We should ensure that working children not only come to schools, but are also retained in the formal system. The enforcement machinery will have to gear itself with great vigilance and sensitivity.

I appeal to the employers to join the national efforts by actively and voluntarily discouraging the employment of children in industries and other economic activities. Their visible presence in this effort will keep middlemen at bay.

Even though elimination of child labour is our goal, in the transition period our effort should be to create adequate and easily accessible educational opportunities for working children. For example, restaurants and other such clusters of economic activity in the unorganized sector employ many children. These children live far away from their homes, with little social security. We should make it the responsibility of the employers to create, with the help of NGOs, suitable educational facilities for such children. They could, for instance, set aside their own premises for conducting classes in evening hours.

Many poor children, especially girls, work as domestic help in our country. It should be made the responsibility of the families that employ them to take care of their education. They should be given leave for a few hours each day, so that they can attend classes in nearby schools. There are some NGOs in our cities, which have set up non-formal neighbourhood schools specifically to cater to the educational needs of such children. Many socially conscious housewives have been working in such neighbourhood schools in their spare time in the afternoons. These NGOs should be supported fully.

Friends, working children need not only education, but also protection of their dignity, which is one of the few personal possessions they can have. Unfortunately, they are frequently robbed of this. Sometimes, even the police do not behave properly with them. It is an experience that leaves almost a permanent scar on their psyche. What we need at all levels is greater sensitivity and compassion; a humane and helpful attitude that recognizes that these children are a precious asset of our society who, with proper help, can have a bright future ahead of them.

I would like that National Awards be instituted to encourage and recognize the efforts being made by various organizations in the field of elimination and rehabilitation of child labour. Such awards could be instituted even in districts.

The will of the nation and the commitment of the Central and State governments to eliminate child labour are abundantly reflected in the Constitution and in several other laws of the land. In keeping with the National Child Labour Policy, we have been both active and proactive in tackling this problem. We have launched the National Child Labour Projects in areas of high concentration of this problem. Further, our various anti-poverty policies have also focussed attention on these areas.

The problem of child labour is fundamentally a problem of poverty. The principal aim of economic reforms is to eradicate poverty, so that we can also eradicate several problems of underdevelopment, including child labour. Our Government has taken many initiatives to accelerate and broaden economic reforms. I am confident that these reforms will enable India to achieve faster economic growth and to remove both regional and social imbalances in development. I urge all sections of our society to further strengthen the consensus behind the process of economic reforms.

Friends, I would like to use this occasion to share my thoughts on some other subjects with District Collectors who have gathered here today. It is not often that we call them to New Delhi. This conference, therefore, is an opportunity for me to have a direct interaction with them.

A district collector is a very important link between our people and the Government. Indeed, he or she is the face of the administration at the local level. Most of the Government's policies and programmes, especially in the social sector, are implemented through district administration. Besides the onerous responsibility of law and order, you are also required to facilitate and assist trade, business, and industry in your respective districts. From polio eradication to population control, from investment promotion to orderly management of mega-events like the Kumbh — a district collector is expected to carry out a hundred different tasks, like a true all-rounder.

I really admire district collectors for their ability to carry the burden of so many tasks on their shoulders. Often, these are young shoulders. A civil servant's posting usually begins from the sub-district level. I have met with many young officers as district collectors, and their energy, enthusiasm, and idealism always impresses me. These qualities should be retained throughout your career.

I applaud you for your good work. However, I would also like you to know that both the Government and the people have very high expectations from the district administration. There is a tremendous hunger for development all across the country, especially among those who have been deprived of even the basic benefits of development.

Our people are no longer satisfied with promises from their elected representatives and governments. They want good governance and performance. It would not be wrong to say that they are impatient for performance. As election after election in recent times have shown, they reward those who perform and show the door to non-performers. All political parties have had this experience in India's increasingly demanding democracy.

I know that elected representatives and their governments have their own specific responsibilities to deliver good governance. At the same time, all governments, irrespective of which party or coalition runs them, depend on the district administration to improve their performance. I, therefore, urge you to gear up the administration at the district level to both meet unfulfilled targets and goals, and also to face new challenges emerging on the horizon.

In discharging your responsibilities, you should actively enlist the participation of the people and their elected responsibilities. Work in close concert with Zilla Parishads, Rope in NGOs, voluntary organizations, and religious establishments. There is a tremendous potential in them to do constructive work.

As Vinoba Bhave used to say, *"Asarakari, asarkari hota hai"* — which means, non-Governmental work is effective work. I would only add that, when *sarakari* and *asarakari* efforts are combined, they become ten times more *asarkari*.

Dear District Collectors, you are an influential person in your district; therefore, lead by personal example. A good district collector is fondly remembered by the people long after he leaves. People's admiration and regard is the highest recognition for a civil servant.

With these words, I inaugurate this national conference on child labour and wish it all success.

Thank you.

20
India's Participation in SAARC at Islamabad; 2004

Symbolic Indo-Pak Bilateral Decided before Summit

The Indian government had decided in December that circumstances were right for a face-to-face meeting between Prime Minister Atal Bihari Vajpayee and Pakistani President Pervez Musharraf at the SAARC summit in Islamabad.

Just before he flew to Pakistan on January 1, national security advisor Brajesh Mishra briefed Deputy Prime Minister L.K. Advani on the summit.

Mishra stressed the meeting would be largely ceremonial, without any substantive agenda.

The BJP government feels it would not be possible to go beyond that with Musharraf, especially a bilateral dialogue that includes Kashmir, until general elections are held.

In addition, New Delhi would prefer to wait until the spring, when the mountain passes along the Line of Control become usable, to see if Pakistan will continue its clamp down on infiltration. India has been telling Western governments not to expect more than a "courtesy call" between the two South Asian leaders.

In fact, India referred to the meeting between Vajpayee and Jamali on Sunday as a "courtesy call". Monday's meeting with President Musharraf, scheduled to be held in the morning, too is likely to be described in a similar manner.

One Western diplomat said, "It's a moot question when a courtesy call becomes a bilateral." A bilateral would normally include a formal agenda, which will be lacking this time.

India may have held back on announcing the face to face because it wanted Pakistan to publicly declare its support for agreements on trade, terrorism and an extension of the ceasefire along the Line on Control.

Vajpayee, Musharraf Urged to Involve Kashmiris in Talks
Srinagar, Dec. 31

The Jammu and Kashmir Liberation Front chairman, Mohammad Yasin Malik, today appealed to the Prime Minister, Atal Bihari Vajpayee, and the Pakistan President, Gen. Pervez Musharraf, to make a "bold move" to resolve the Kashmir issue forever.

At a press conference here, Mr. Malik said –in his New Year message he had sent to the two – he had urged them to take a sympathetic view of the Kashmir problem and save the people of the State from the strife.

"I believe that both of you have firmly grasped the pressing need to initiate a peace process on Kashmir and have voiced statesmen-like wisdom on this," he said, adding "while there are extremists on all sides that may oppose such a bold move on your part, I urge both of you to seize this opportunity to now translate your visionary words into visionary deeds'.

Emphasising the participation of the Kashmiris in any negotiation process, he said, "No solution on Kashmir will be lasting unless it is legitimate in the eyes of the people of Kashmir". He said, "It is my firm belief that the principle of the inclusion of the people of Kashmir is the missing ingredient for a complete vision for a workable peace process". He urged both the leaders to "evolve a new mechanism for involving Kashmiris in the peace process'.

Mr. Malik reminded both the leaders of their statements in which they committed themselves to find a peaceful and durable solution. "Mr. Vajpayee, I would like to recall your reflection from Kumarakom on January 2, 2001 in which you firmly committed yourself to finding a durable solution," he said.

In the message to Gen. Musharraf, he said, " I deeply appreciate the statesmanship evident in your bold calling for a wise peace process which would yield a win-win solution acceptable to India, Pakistan and Kashmiris." The JKLF chairman, who has been leading a signature campaign in the Valley since June 11, said, "Eight lakhs people have signed and sought peaceful resolution to the Kashmir issue".

The Hurriyat Conference (Abbas), in a statement has urged the militant groups to announce a ceasefire to make the peace process a success.

"It is imperative upon the security forces to stop the repression against people, at the same time, it is obligatory upon militants to stop their activities in the larger interest of the success of the peace process," said a spokesman for the faction.

India and Pakistan must keep talking: Vajpayee

Islamadab, January, 3

The Prime Minister, Atal Bihari Vajpayee, confirmed today that he would interact with his Pakistani hosts during his three-day stay in Islamabad for the 12th SAARC summit that begins on Sunday.

Mr. Vajpayee, who arrived here in a special Indian Air Force aircraft, said in an interview to Pakistan Television this evening that he believed that India could talk to the Pakistan President, Pervez Musharraf, and expressed the hope that this would lead to concrete achievements.

He described Gen. Musharraf as the "biggest leader" of Pakistan, with whom he had been interacting since his February 1999 visit to Lahore. The Prime Minister wanted him to play a role in promoting peace with India.

Mr. Vajpayee, who was received at the airport by his Pakistani counterpart, Mir Zafarullah Khan Jamali, said that India and Pakistan must keep talking. "We have never shied away from a dialogue on Kashmir" even though India believed that Kashmir was an integral part of its territory.

The two countries had never really got down to serious discussions on the Kashmir issue, but had been reiterating their positions. Any serious dialogue aimed at resolving this issue would take time.

Pakistan, he pointed out, was a neighbour and India needed to live with it. The choice was between living in peace and a continued state of tension. There was, however, a realization that "we should live in peace."

Mr. Vajpayee said that it had been his endeavour to make peace with Pakistan ever since his first visit to Islamabad 25 years ago as the External Affairs Minister in the Janata Party Government.

Expressing regret at the massacre of the Muslims in Gujarat in 2002, he denied that the Bharatiya Janata Party had used it for electoral gains. Also, Pakistan-bashing was not an issue in the recent Assembly elections.

The Prime Minister dismissed a suggestion that India was acting as a "junior partner" of the United States and pointed out that the allegation was also levelled against Pakistan. India had relations of equality with the US and had no hesitation differing with it on issues.

The Prime Minister, who arrived a few hours earlier than scheduled (at 4 p.m. IST), was accorded a ceremonial welcome and guard of honour at the Chakala air base, near here. He then left the air base in a bullet-proof BMW car, specially flown in from India.

The Pakistan Foreign Minister, Khurshid Mahmud Kasuri, the Finance Minister, Shaukat Aziz, the Foreign Secretary, Riaz Khokhar, and the

Director-General (South Asia), Jalil Abbas Jilani, who had been expelled from India in 2003, were at hand to greet Mr.Vajpayee. The External Affairs Minister, Yashwant Sinha, the National Security Adviser, Brajesh Mishra, and the Indian High Commissioner to Pakistan, Shivshankar Menon, were also present.

Mr. Vajpayee exchanged pleasantries with Mr.Jamali at the airport, holding hands and waving to photographers. He drove to the highly-protected Serena Hotel, opposite the Jinah Convention Centre, venue of the SAARC summit.

The Prime Miniser's willingness to do business with Gen. Musharraf hardly comes as a surprise and is in line with his remarks on December 4, before he left for Abuja, Nigeria. Asked whom he would like to meet in Islamabad—Gen. Musharraf or Mr. Jamali—he said it was okay whoever he met.

In a statement before his SAARC visit, Mr.Vajpayee said, "While in Islamabad, I will take the opportunity of bilateral meetings with other SAARC leaders, besides interacting with our hosts. I hope all discussions, bilateral and regional, would proceed in the spirit of friendship, cooperation and good neighbourliness."

Just before Mr. Vajpayee's arrival here Pakistan, as chair of the SAARC summit, formally announced that there had been agreement on the text of the South Asian Free Trade Area draft, the SAARC social charter and the additional protocol to the existing convention on terrorism.

Announcing this at a press conference, Mr. Kasuri said that Kashmir was a bilateral issue between India and Pakistan and had nothing to do with the additional protocol on terrorism. He was responding to a question whether the additional protocol would impact the "freedom struggle" in Kashmir.

Mr. Kasuri said one could only be optimistic on India-Pakistan relations and his Prime Minister had tried hard to bring about a dialogue between the two countries. "The general assumption is that this opportunity provided by SAARC should not be missed [for a bilateral meeting between India and Pakistan]," he added.

SAARC Summit Preparatory Meetings Begin Today

Islamabad, December 28, 2003

As Pakistan gears up to provide foolproof security to the visiting SAARC heads of state and delegates, a programming committee consisting of senior officials will meet here tomorrow and the day after to lay the ground for other preparatory conferences at various levels leading to the summit from January 4 to 6.

It is the meetings at the level of Foreign Secretaries on December 31 and January 1 and at the level of Foreign Ministers on January 2 and 3 that would be watched with interest in view of the desire by Several members for a political settlement on the South Asia Free Trade Agreement.

The SAARC Commerce Ministers met here on December 23 and 24 but failed to finalise the accord in view of the reservations expressed by Bangladesh. The Pakistan Foreign Secretary, Riaz Khokar, told a news conference here that SAFTA negotiations were still continuing and he was optimistic about its outcome. He said its finalisation was on hold due to insistence by a member state for enhanced special and differential treatment for the Less Developed Countries.

Other areas of focus included agreements and conventions on suppressing terrorism, narcotics and psychotropic substances, trafficking in women and children for prostitution, and child welfare. It is immediately not clear whether there will be an agreement on suppressing terrorism as India and Pakistan have serious differences on its definition in the context of Jammu and Kashmir.

Three comprehensive reports on poverty alleviation will be submitted to the 12th SAARC summit for approval. These reports have been prepared by the Independent South Asian Commission on Poverty Alleviation, the SAARC Secretary-General and Finance Ministers.

No Bugs Found in PM's Hotel Suite, but Officials are Cautious

Islamabad, January, 4

Not much is known about what transpired at the meeting between Vajpayee and his Pak counterpart Mir Zafarullah Khan Jamali. But at the summit's inaugural, Jamali treated Vajpayee with utmost respect. The Pak premier ensured that other SAARC leaders were a step behind Vajpayee while being escorted to the dais. Jamali later introduced him as a visionary, a poet, a prolific writer and an able politician. "All these are qualities of a true leader," he observed after Vajpayee's speech.

The audience clapped, not once but twice, while Vajpayee was on his feet. He struck an instant rapport with his audience by driving home the relevance of a slogan on a hoarding that had caught his attention near Islamabad airport: "Together we stand a better chance in the world." In his view, that wasn't just a slogan, but the profound truth in the context of South Asia. There was applause again when the PM talked about a bold transition from mistrust to trust.

Among those accompanying the PM is his foster son-in-law, Ranjan Bhattacharya. Housed in the sprawling Serina hotel, the Indian entourage also includes the PM's Principal Secretary Brajesh Mishra, External Affairs

Minister Yashwant Sinha and Foreign Secretary Shashank. A cook from the Taj Group is at hand to prepare Indian cuisine for the premier and his team.

The VVIP suite of Hotel Serina was turned upside down days before the PM's arrival. Insiders say the hotel, which has been taken over by the Indian delegation, was debugged. Sleuths scanned the VVIP suite and the rooms meant for Yashwant Sinha, Brajesh Mishra and other senior officials. Although no electronic bugs were found, the Indian delegation has been advised not to discuss sensitive issues on the phone or in the room.

Islamabad is abuzz with the talk of oil diplomacy steering the current round of peace moves between India and Pakistan. Jamali also referred to the need for a gas pipeline in his inaugural address at the summit. The idea of a gas pipeline is a practical one given the growing energy needs of the region. However, the current round of back-channel diplomacy is being linked to an earlier attempt involving an Indian company having a big stake in the petrochemical sector.

With their better halves busy with the SAARC summit, Ayesha Khan, the wife of Pakistan's High Commissioner to India, indulged in a different kind of diplomacy.

Ayesha accompanied Neelima Sinha, wife of External Affairs Minister Yashwant Sinha, and Kalpana, wife of Foreign Secretary Shashank, to a guided tour of Lahore and Islamabad. The two women were so charmed by Lahore and Pakistani hospitality that they endorsed the need for early peace in the region.

SAARC Nations Strive for Trade Accord

Islamabad, December 31, 2003

Bilateral contacts between India and Pakistan on the sidelines of the SAARC summit are possible if the regional grouping succeeds in adopting the South Asia Free Trade Agreement (SAFTA) framework and the additional protocol to the Regional Convention on Suppression of Terrorism.

Highly-placed sources said this evening that these were the two issues that dominated the opening day of the standing committee meeting of the Foreign Secretaries of the South Asian Association for Regional Cooperation. At the end of the first day, official-level discussions continued in the hope of a possible agreement.

Indications are that as the host country Pakistan is keen on achieving a consensus on both the free trade framework and the additional protocol on terrorism. Most countries assembled here are aware that without a pact on SAFTA, the summit would not be much of a success.

As for the additional protocol on terrorism, the differences are mainly between India and Pakistan on the definition of terrorism. While Pakistan wants a distinction made between "freedom struggles" and terrorism in the context of Kashmir, India is opposed to any such categorization.

India, it appears, is not against showing flexibility in trying to reach an accord on the additional protocol on terrorism. The discussions will continue tomorrow.

Officials sources said that experts from member countries met separately to complement the efforts to the Foreign Secretaries in an attempt to narrow down the differences on SAFTA. As things stand, Bangladesh has reservations about the treaty and wants the Least Developed Countries (LDCs) to be given preferential treatment.

"It is not correct to be over-optimistic on the trade agreement at this juncture though in our informal consultations once again special efforts would be made for an agreement. If the Foreign Secretaries fail, another effort would be made at the meeting of Foreign Ministers beginning January 2 as there is a feeling that we should not let the summit happen without SAFTA," a senior official told *The Hindu.*

The additional protocol on terrorism mainly deals with measures to curb the financing of terrorism in the context of 9/11. While there is no disagreement on the objective, India and Pakistan differ on the approach. India is for bringing the convention in line with a series of post 9/11 UN Resolution and Pakistan favours the adoption of the 2003 NAM Declaration.

The regional convention on terrorism came into force in 1988 following its ratification by the SAARC member-states. On a proposal made by Sri Lanka after 9/11, the member-states had decided that an additional protocol would be included in the convention on suppression of terrorism. A draft of the protocol was prepared by Sri Lanka in May 2002. While there was general agreement on it, an impasse was created as Pakistan and India called for certain modifications in the preamble.

Terrorism: India hopes for a 'strong message'

No bilateral talks planned with Pakistan leaders at SAARC summit

New Delhi, December 27, 2003

India today expressed the hope for a "strong message" on terrorism and clinching of the elusive South Asian Free Trade Area (SAFTA) framework agreement at the January 4-6 South Asian Association for Regional Cooperation (SAARC) summit in Islamabad.

Briefing presspersons on the summit, the Foreign Secretary,

Shashank, reaffirmed that the Prime Minister, Atal Bihari Vajpayee, would travel to Islamabad despite the recent assassination attempts on the life of the Pakistani President, Pervez Musharraf.

He said no "bilateral meetings" with Pakistani leaders had been fixed so far, but Mr. Vajpayee would certainly interact with his counterpart, Mir Zafarullah Khan Jamali, during the SAARC sessions, and attend a dinner being hosted by Gen. Musharraf.

Asked how safe it was for the Prime Minister to go to Islamabad, Mr.Shashank said that everyone, naturally had to be concerned about the safety of leaders.

"President Musharraf has himself said that he is the target of the terrorists. They [the Pakistanis] are making foolproof security arrangements. We are going on that basis."

He said Pakistan was the "epicentre" of terrorism, adding that the country itself was suffering the consequences of the menace. However, this did not mean that security arrangements could not be made for the summit.

Asked if Mr. Vajpayee would make the "customary call" on President Musharraf, Mr. Shashank said the Prime Minister would go by whatever programme had been agreed to for the summit meeting.

On resumption of a composite bilateral dialogue between India and Pakistan, the Foreign Secretary linked this to the overall issue of cross-border terrorism and infiltration.

"We need to make an assessment on a longer-term basis," he said, adding that this should include the dismantling of the terrorism infrastructure.

To a question on the reported statement made by the Defence Minister, George Fernandes, that infiltration continued at the same level as before, Mr. Shashank said: "This has been our feeling. Also that cross-border infiltration has not stopped."

On SAFTA, he has hopeful that the issue could be clinched despite the differences that marked the last around of talks among the Commerce Secretaries in Islamabad. Mr. Shashank also referred to a recent speech by the Prime Minister, where he spoke of closer South Asian interaction and integration.

Once SAFTA was in place, South Asia could move towards a customs union, an agreement on banking and some kind of common currency as well. Pakistan could also accord the Most Favoured Nation (MFN) status as far as trade relations were concerned. Mr. Shashank was hopeful that an additional protocol to an existing agreement on terrorism could be agreed upon at the Islamabad summit.

Asked about Pakistan's draft circulated on the issue of terrorism, he said this was still a draft and would be subject to the "cycle" of negotiations.

Admitting that there was difference of opinion on the definition of terrorism between India and Pakistan, he said issues such as Palestine could be placed in a separate category in order to make progress.

Would the recent cooperation extended by Bhutan in tackling the anti-India insurgents figure in the SAARC declaration, he was asked. He said this could be included if there was consensus.

India was ready to help Pakistan to deal with the issue of cross-border terrorism. It had made a proposal to Pakistan in this regard and was awaiting Islamabad's response.

Would India-Pakistan issues derail the larger SAARC summit? Mr. Shashank said that New Delhi's intention was to concentrate on the SAARC agenda.

SAARC must take up Bilateral Issues: Pervez

Islamabad, January, 4, 2004

Pakistan President Pervez Musharraf on Sunday called for an amendment to the SAARC charter to discuss bilateral issues among member countries but refrained from directly mentioning Jammu and Kashmir.

Speaking at a banquet he hosted for Prime Minister Atal Bihari Vajpayee and other SAARC leaders at the Presidential House here, Musharraf emphasised, "We must expand the SAARC character to discuss bilateral issues at regional level. If we fail, cynicism will take over."

Vajpayee and Musharraf shook hands in the presence of other SAARC leaders before all of them moved into the banquet hall where the Pakistani President welcomed his guests in a 10-minute speech.

This was the first time in two years that Vajpayee and Musharraf came face-to-face after the famous handshake at previous SAARC summit in Kathmandu in January 2002.

Musharraf said, "South Asia will never achieve its full potential unless disputes and tensions are resolved peacefully."

Elimination of the root cause of tensions and resolutions of disputes were essential steps to a cohesive and integrated South Asia, he said. "If we fail, cynicism will take over and the SAARC will lose its credibility and momentum," he added.

"The biter truth is that SAARC will never achieve its full potential unless disputes and tensions that draws apart are resolved peacefully with justice and equity," he said.

The leaders of SAARC should move towards solving the disputes boldly with the objective of seeking honourable solutions (to disputes) with mutual respect and in the spirit of accommodation, the Pakistani President said.

"We must put behind the mistrust, bitterness and tension and expand our charter and even discuss bilateral issues at the regional level. We owe it to our people," he said, adding, "let us pledge not to disappoint them".

Musharraf said there could be no development in the absence of peace. "There can be no peace so long as political issues and disputes continue to fester".

Vajpayee Delivers Inspiring Speech

Regretting continued "mutual suspicions and petty rivalries", Prime Minister Atal Bihari Vajpayee on Sunday asked the SAARC countries to be sensitive to each other's security concerns and make bold transition from mistrust to trust to ensure development and peace in the region.

"Mutual suspicions and petty rivalries have continued to haunt us. As a result, the peace dividend has bypassed our region," Vajpayee said, addressing the 12th SAARC summit at Jinnah Convention Centre here.

Asserting that any joint endeavour needed mutual trust and confidence, he said, "For many decades, South Asian countries, which have a complex and troubled colonial legacies, have been unable to forge an integrated economic understanding circumventing political differences."

He observed that history "should not shackle us" and "we have to look forward now with a collective approach in mind". "We have to change South Asia's image and standing in the world. We must make the bold transition from mistrust to trust, from discord to concord and from tension to peace."

He said because of mutual rivalries and inadequate coordination, smuggling, drug trafficking, money-laundering and gun-running flourished across our borders.

He made a special mention of the "courageous action" by Bhutan against Indian insurgents operating from its soil. "I would like to draw attention to the courageous action taken by His Majesty the King of Bhutan and his government against insurgent groups which were trying to use Bhutanese territory to launch terrorist activities in India.

Vajpayee for Joint Celebration of 1857 Anniversary

Prime Minister Atal Bihari Vajpayee on Sunday suggested that India,

Pakistan and Bangladesh could together celebrate the 150th anniversary of the uprising of 1857 against the British colonial rule in the sub-continent.

"Perhaps India, Pakistan and Bangladesh can together celebrate that anniversary, in remembrance of our joint struggle against a common adversary," Vajpayee told the SAARC summit here.

"Not not very long ago, I had visited the Andaman islands, where during our colonial days, political prisoners were kept in confinement. On the inscription in the cellular jail there, I found many names of brave martyrs and freedom fighters from what are today three South Asian countries ," he added.

He said, "Our forefathers had fought side by side, transcending religious, regional and linguistic differences against a common colonial oppressor in our first war of Independence in 1857.

It reminds us that many of us have a shared history, which predates our more recent divisions."

SAARC Apart, the Real Breakthrough is in SAFTA

The breakthrough has already taken place, but those covering the summit are not quite seeing it right. The Indian media is focused on Prime Minister Atal Bihari Vajpayee's meetings with Pakistani President Pervez Musharraf and Prime Minister Jamali while the Pakistani media is looking for signs of Indian concessions on Kashmir.

But the breakthrough lies is the framework agreement on South Asian Free Trade Area to be signed on Monday. Looked at any way, this will, over the next decade, sharply boost economic cooperation between countries of the region, primarily, India and Pakistan. This in turn will lead to closer people-to-people ties and create a network of friendly relationships in which the Kashmir issue can be meaningfully addressed. There is no other option. India will not discuss Kashmir as long as it has a Pakistani-aided gun pointing at its head.

A focus on economic relations will also bring a measure of realism in Pakistani thinking about India. Many in Pakistan worry about this. At the SAARC inaugural, Jamali, too declared that economic union could not take off unless political disputes were settled in a just manner.

But external realities are propelling Pakistan along another course. Pakistan had blocked SAFTA for as long as it could, and now the realities of its economic situation has compelled it to change track. India already has Free Trade Agreement with Nepal and Sri Lanka and is negotiating one with Bangladesh. External Affairs Minister Yashwant Sinha has been telling audiences of business people in Pakistan that these are win-win agreements that have ensured that the smaller markets have not been swamped by Indian goods, on the other hand, Nepal holds a trade surplus with India and Sri Lanka's trade has grown 137 per cent in 2002,m the year in which the FTA came into operation.

Pakistan situation is unenviable. Despite a massive emotional and financial investment in militancy in Kashmir, it is no nearer to seeing India off from the state than it was in 1989. But in the period since then, the Indian economy has grown at a handsome pace and it has a GDP of $2.7 trillion (Purchasing power parity) as compared to Pakistan's $295 billion (PPP) or just 11 per cent of India's. Pakistan's economy is growing at a sluggish four per cent while India's growth rate is double of that. Poverty is declining in India currently 25 per cent people are considered below the poverty line, but Pakistan which had one of the strongest economies in SAARC is now witnessing a growth of absolute poverty which currently accounts for 35 per cent of its population. Pakistan's dream of maintaining parity with India are now confined to the nuclear and military fields a debased currency of power. Even there India spending a mere 2.3 per cent of its GDP on defence is outspending Pakistan which spends five per cent by a factor of four. It was able to achieve some parity by the use of terrorism, but even that instrument has had its day.

Treaty Implementation will Help Reduce Tariff

SAARC countries' historic decision to implement the SAFTA on January 1, 2006 will see a reduction of tariffs between the seven member nations to between 0-5 per cent by the time the agreement is fully implemented on December 31, 2015. The agreement is expected to be signed on Monday, January 5, by all the heads of governments.

In the period between now and the implementation of the agreement, member countries will complete four procedural formalities: Formation of sensitive lists, rules of origin, revenue loss compensation mechanism for the lesser developed countries and an arbitration council or dispute settlement body.

Under the agreement, India and Pakistan get seven years to achieve the 0-5 per cent goal, Sri Lanka gets 8, and lesser developed Bangladesh, Nepal, Maldives and Bhutan get 10 years. Under the treaty, each of the countries will create two sensitive list one for the more and the other for the less developed countries outlining the products whose tariffs will not be reduced. Anti-dumping issues, countervailing duties will be decided on by WTO rules.

SAFTA will be guided by the ministerial council of commerce ministers of all states and this will be its highest decision-making body.

My Last Attempt at Peace, says Vajpayee

Islamabad, January, 2, 2004

The Prime Minister, Atal Bihari Vajpayee, has again said that this will be his last attempt at making peace with Pakistan a point that he made in the middle of 2003 in an interview to German magazine.

In an interview to the *Dawn*, the Prime Minister said the entire spectrum of political opinions in India was for peace, cooperation, and friendship with Pakistan.

On whether his Cabinet colleagues shared his views, Mr. Vajpayee responded: "The main question that is raised by critics of my peace initiative is whether it is getting—and will get in the future–a matching and sustained response from Pakistan.

If such a response was coming, the Prime Minister said that he saw no problem putting behind violence, terrorism and can see no obstacle to [the] establishment of a climate of friendship and cordiality in which we can discuss and resolve all our outstanding bilateral issues, including Jammu & Kashmir." In Mr. Vajpayee's view the Agra summit failed because Pakistan was insisting on the centrality of the Kashmir issue and India could not accept that.

The Prime Minister was quoted as saying that he did not want to repeat his frequently-stated views on terrorism.

Referring to the period since his April 18, 2003, hand of friendship speech in Srinagar, Mr. Vajpayee stressed: "These eight months have witnessed the ground swell of popular enthusiasm in the people of both our countries—parliamentarians and political workers, business and professionals, artists and social activities—for a normal, peaceful, and cooperative bilateral relationship. We should buildup the momentum and on the recent positive developments in constructive manner."

Peace Meets Progress

Islamabad, January 5, 2004

A significant narrowing of differences appears to have occurred when the Prime Minister met the Pakistan President this morning, resulting not just in "progress"—that was how the Indian side described it – but even the likelihood of a breakthrough in bilateral relations, leading to the start of composite dialogue process.

The talks lasted "about an hour" (considerably more than a normal "courtesy call"), but there was no one-on-one interaction between the two leaders. The talks were held in the presence of respective delegations-Mr. Atal Bihari Vajpayee accompanied by foreign minister Mr. Yashwant Sinha, national security adviser Mr. Brijesh Mishra, foreign, secretary

Mr. Shashank , and India's high commissioner to Islamabad Mr. Shiv Shankar Menon; and General Pervez Musharraf with his chief of staff and security adviser Lt-Gen. Hsmid Javed, Foreign Minister Mr. Khurshid Mahmud Kasuri, Foreign Secretary Mr. Riaz Khokhar, and Pakistan's High Commissioner in India Mr. Aziz Ahmed Khan.

Sources said the talks would initiate a comprehensive dialogue, including "detailed discussions" on Kashmir. The proposed Srinagar-Muzaffarabad (J&K and PoK) bus service might be of "immense significance" and indicative of a movement towards a "soft border" option between parts of the divided state.

There is almost a complete clampdown on the substance of the hour-long "courtesy call" because, as Mr. Sinha said while briefing the media later, " it is not in the interest of the cause to share the details."

"The cause," Mr. Sinha explained, was "furtherance of the process started by Mr. Vajpayee on 18 April when he extended a hand of friendship to Pakistan in a speech at Srinagar." "We are interested in the success of a certain process." Asked to elaborate on the meeting, he said, "both leaders welcomed the steps towards normalization of relations and expressed hope that the process will continue." However, the issue of extending an invitation to either Gen Pervez Musharraf or "Mr. Atal Bihari Vajpayee" did not figure," Mr. Sinha said.

The Pakistan leadership, will today, has kept its promise of not raising Kashmir at the SAARC summit, but its information minister did harp on it today, telling a TV channel that " the way leading to normalcy is passing through Kashmir". Shiekh Ahmed Rashid maintained Kashmir and terrorism figured in the talks today, even as he told PTV that there is a "changed atmosphere (now)". India had raised the issue of terrorism, Pakistan Kashmir, he said and hinted at a joint declarations. But Mr. Sinha said: "I have said what I had to say" and the rest was "mere speculation" as the issues involved were "very sensitive". Mr. Rashid was incidentally dropped a minister-in-waiting on Mr . Vajpayee's arrival, for issuing strong statements against India recently.

Discordant notes were also sounded by the extremist Hizbul Mujahideen chief, Syed Salahuddin, who denounced SAARC as a " failed organisation" because it failed to deal with Kashmir's "reality" in a statement issued from Muzaffarabad in Pak-occupied- Kashmir.

But the refrain at the end of the day was best summed up by Mr. Vajpayee's statement, made before todays, meeting, at the foundation stone laying ceremony for an extension of the Indian high commission chancery complex. "Today the weather has slightly changed" he said, though in the context of today's rain. The chill in the air belied the progress made in ties. Minutes later, Mr. Vajpayee elaborated: "Dialogue should continue and we should attempt to understand each others, difficulties as we work together to find a way out (*Samvad lagataar chalta rahe aur ek doosre ki mushkil ko samajh kar hum mil kar kam karne ka rasta nikale*)."

SAARC Nations Sign Social Charter

The South Asian Association for Regional Cooperation countries have signed a social charter to reaffirm its principal goal of promoting the welfare of people of South Asia in all fields.

The charter aims to improve the quality of life, accelerate economic growth, social progress and cultural development and to provide all individuals an opportunity to live with dignity and realize their full potential.

The member-countries agreed to establish a people-centred framework for the social development and to build as culture of operation and partnership, and to respond to the immediate needs of those affected by human tragedy. The provisions of the charter shall complement the national processes of policy-making, their implementation and evaluation, while providing broad parameters and principles for addressing common social issues and developing and implementing result-oriented programmes in specific social areas.

Its implementation shall be facilitated by a national coordination committee or any appropriate mechanism as may be decided in each country.

The charter particularly deals with poverty alleviation, health issues, education, human resource development and youth mobilization, promotion of the status of women, promotion of the rights and well being of the child, population stabilization and drug de-addiction, rehabilitation and re-integration.

The member-states can amend the charter through an agreement between all the parties.

The Pakistan Prime Minister, Mir Zafarullah Khan Jamali, signed the charter on behalf of his country while the Bangladesh Prime Minister, Khaleda Zia, the Bhutanese Prime Minister, Lyonpo Jigme Yaeser Thinley, the Prime Minister, Atal Bihari Vajpayee, the Maldives President, Maummon Abdul Gayoom, the Nepalese Prime Minister, Surya Bahadur Thapa and the Sri Lankan Prisident, Chandrika Kumaratunga, signed on behalf of their countries on Sunday.

The charter urges all the member-states to attach importance to social development and economic growth. It stresses that legislative, executive and administrative frameworks should be provided for the progressive realization of social and economic goals.

It asks the SAARC states to maintain a social policy and strategy to ensure an overall and a balanced social uplift of their people.

The states agree that the obligations under the social charter shall be respected, protected, and fulfilled without any reservations and that the enforcement thereon at the national level shall be continuously reviewed through an agreed regional arrangement and mechanism.

Vajpayee meets Jamali as ties are put on track

Ending a nearly three-year-long drought in bilateral meetings between India and Pakistan, the Prime Minister , Atal Bihari Vajpayee, today met his Pakistani counterpart, Mir Zafarullah Khan Jamali, soon after the 12th summit of the South Asian Association for Regional Cooperation got off to a satisfactory start.

As the two countries agreed to carry forward the peace process, the Prime Minister, who sought a "courtesy call" on the Pakistan President, Pervez Musharraf today, will meet him tomorrow. Speaking at a banquet attended by the SAARC leaders tonight, Gen. Musharraf introduced a jarring note in an otherwise positive atmosphere when he called for the expansion of the SAARC Charter to include discussions on bilateral issues, a viewpoint that India has consistently opposed.

The banquet, attended by Mr. Vajpayee, saw Gen. Musharraf calling for the elimination of the "root causes" of tension in South Asia, a known Pakistani euphemism for the Kashmir issue.

Suggesting that all issues be addressed in a spirit of boldness and accommodation, Gen. Musharraf said that Islamabad was ready to play a role in seizing the opportunity to live in peace. He did not, however, refer to the Kashmir issue directly.

Earlier, reflecting a degree of rare agreement between India and Pakistan, the official accounts of todays meeting between Mr. Vajpayee and Mr. Jamali and the two Foreign Ministers, Yashwant Sinha and Khurshid Mahmud Kasuri, used identical language.

"They [the two Prime Ministers] met in a warm and friendly atmosphere. The meeting [with officials present] lasted for about half-an-hour out of which about 15 minutes was a one-on-one between the two Prime Ministers," Mr. Sinha told presspersons.

Referring to his meeting with Mr. Kasuri, Mr. Sinha said: " Both of us expressed our satisfaction at the progress in our bilateral relations. We discussed various ways of maintaining the momentum and agreed on the need to do so."

Accounts gleaned from a variety of sources show that the bilateral relationship has been put on track and a new degree of confidence appears to have emerged.

The sources said that a range of preparatory contract between the sides, including In the days before the arrival of Mr. Vajpayee to Islamabad, had taken place. In order to maintain the sanctity of the process, officials are reluctant to reveal the exact nature of the contacts.

Conscious of the possible fallout of Mr. Jamali's decision to skip a reference to the Kashmir issue in his SAARC address, the Pakistan Foreign Office spokesman made it a point this evening to stress that Kashmir was a dispute and did not constitute an integral part of India.

However, in a prepared response on Kashmir, the spokesman said that the Indian leadership was aware of the Pakistani position that Kashmir was a dispute that had to be resolved.

Pakistan, he said, welcomed Mr. Vajpayee's remarks to Pakistan Television that the two countries had to have a long-term engagement for the resolution of the Kashmir issue. The dispute, he maintained, must be resolved through peaceful means and its resolution was in the interest of both nations.

India Proposes Poverty Alleviation Fund

The Prime Minister, Atal Bihari Vajpayee, today proposed the creation of a Poverty Alleviation Fund and offered $ 100 million as initial contribution for poverty alleviation programmes and projects outside India.

Making the proposal in his address to the 12th SAARC Summit here, Vajpayee said the fund could be professionally managed and could fund specific poverty-alleviation programmes and projects in SAARC.

" Once we have agreed on the modalities of the creation of such a fund and on its charter, India would be willing to make an initial contribution of $ 100 million to this fund on the understanding that this money would be used entirely on projects within SAARC, but outside India," he said.

'Vajpayee asked me to take care'

The Pakistan President, Pervez Musharraf, disclosed here this evening that the Prime Minister, Atal Bihari Vajpayee, asked him to take care of himself from terrorists when the latter called him up to congratulate him on the success of the SAARC summit.

At a news conference where he gave details of his telephonic talk with Mr. Vajpayee, Gen. Musharraf could not control his laughter while disclosing that Mr. Vajpayee wished him protection.

"This morning I received a call from him. He wished me a long life. We also congratulated each other on the successful joint statement," he said.

Asked whether he feared more threats to his life on account of the latest "deal" with India, Gen. Musharraf said he had nine lives and he had not " consumed" all of them.

He said the ceasefire in Kashmir was not under his control and maintained that the Line of Control (LOC) was in the command of Pakistan where the Government can order a ceasefire with "a blow of a whistle." "We cannot guarantee a ceasefire in Kashmir. But I think my words carry weight and they [Kashmiris] can consider my proposals."

He said the India-Pakistan joint statement was a victory for the people of the region. "Moderates of the region are victor," he said, adding that extremists from both sides of the border may try to sabotage the process. "This is a good beginning. We will move forward with hard work, sincerity," he said. The need was not to touch on divergences. "The time has come to leave the old divergences [behind]." He denied that India and Pakistan had reached any " secret deal."

Asked why India should believe his assurance on dealing with terrorism, he said: " I only say what I mean."

On the composite dialogue, he stressed that its "when and where" would be finalized over a period of time. At some stage, he said, the people of Kashmir would have to be taken into confidence. " We must have the Kashmiris involved in one way or the other."

The Pakistan Prime Minister, Mir Zafarullah Khan Jamali, said Pakistan was for "peace" and was not interested in the "peace" process. "We want good relations with all. Our talks with Atal Bihari Vajpayee have been fruitful. We are hopeful of stability and peace in South Asia."

"Musharraf and Vajpayee hold the key to success," Mr. Jamali said. The "courtesy calls" among him, Gen. Musharraf and Mr. Vajpayee lasted longer than expected. "I took half-an-hour and Musharraf took and hour." On Mr. Vajpayee's proposal that India, Pakistan and Bangladesh should jointly celebrate the 150th anniversary of the 1857 war of independence, Mr. Jamali said the war had a different connotation for Pakistan. "We can consider it," he said.

Text of PM, Musharraf Statement

The following is the text of the joint press statement issued by the External Affairs Minister, Yashwant Sinha, on Monday's meeting between the Prime Minister, Atal Bihari Vajpayee, and the Pakistan President, Pervez Musharraf:

The President of Pakistan and the Prime Minister of India met during the SAARC Summit in Islamabad.

The Indian Prime Minister while expressing satisfaction over the successful conclusion of the SAARC Summit appreciated the excellent arrangements made by the host country.

Both leaders welcomed the recent steps towards normalisation of relations between the two countries and expressed the hope that the positive trends set by the CBMs would be consolidated.

Prime Minister Vajpayee said that in order to take forward and sustain the dialogue process, violence, hostility and terrorism must be prevented. President Musharraf reassured Prime Minister Vajpayee that he will not permit any territory under Pakistan's control to be used to support terrorism is in any manner. President Musharraf emphasized that a sustained and productive dialogue addressing all issues would lead to positive results.

To carry the process of normalisation forward, the President of Pakistan and the Prime Minister of India agreed to commence the process of the composite dialogue in February 2004. The two leaders are confident that the resumption of the composite dialogue will lead to peaceful settlement of all bilateral issues, including Jammu and Kashmir, to the satisfaction of both sides.

The two leaders agreed that constructive dialogue would promote progress towards the common objectives of peace, security and economic development for our peoples and for future generations.

Leaders adopt Islamabad Declaration

In a major concession to Pakistani sensibilities, the Islamabad Declaration adopted by the SAARC Heads of State/Government today said the creation of a "suitable political and economic environment" would help the birth of the proposed South Asian Economic Union.

Other than the declaration, the 12th SAARC Summit also adopted the South Asian Free Trade Area (SAFTA) Agreements as well as an additional protocol to the existing convention on the suppression of terrorism.

As per the Agreement, SAFTA will come into force from January 1, 2006, and the "developing countries" in SAARC will reduce their tariffs to between zero and five per cent for Least Developed Countries (LDCs) beginning from January 1, 2006.

The declaration said the SAARC nations condemned terrorism in all its forms and manifestations, is a challenge to all states and to all of humanity, and cannot be justified on any ground, whatsoever.

"Terrorism violates the fundamentals values of the United Nations and the SAARC Charter and constitutes one of the most serious threats to internationals peace and security. We agree to fully implement the relevant international conventions to which we are parties," the declaration said.

It reaffirmed the commitment of SAARC to the Regional Convention on Suppression of Terrorism, which, among others, recognized the seriousness of the problem as it affected the security, stability and development of the region.

"The signing of the Additional Protocol... to the Regional Convention...to deal effectively with financing of terrorism is a flutter manifestation of our determination to eliminate all forms and manifestations of terrorism from South Asia," the document said.

Interestingly, concerns on national security have been extended to the SAFTA Agreement, which allows member states to taken action and adopt measures in the interests of national security.

The SAFTA accord also allows any contracting state to pull out of the treaty at any time after it comes into force on January 1, 2006. "Such withdrawal shall be effective on the expiry of six months from the date on which a written notice thereof is received by the Secretary – General of SAARC....."

A SAFTA Ministerial Council comprising Commerce/Trade Ministers and a Committee of Experts have been envisaged in SAFTA for the administration and implementation of the agreement.

The accord envisages that states shall " give special regard" to the situation of LDCs when considering there application of anti-dumping and/or countervailing measures and allow a consultations with LDCs in this regard.

The SAFTA Agreement also "suggests" a number of measures that members may adopt, including the removal of barriers to intra-SAARC investment, harmonization of custom facilities, transit facilities for efficient in intra-SAARC trade and simplification of procedures for business visas.

"Any dispute that may arise among the contracting States regarding the interpretation and application of the provisions of this [SAFTA] Agreements or any instrument adopted within its framework concerning the rights and obligations of the.... States will be amicably settled through a process initiated by a request for bilateral consultations," the document said.

Describing SAFTA as a major milestone, the Declaration said: "It is important to maintain this momentum and move towards further broadening of economic cooperations and to ensure equitable distribution of benefits of trade...."

On enhancing political cooperation among SAARC nations, it said: "We envision South Asia to be a peaceful and stable region where each nation is at peace with itself and its neighbours and where conflicts, differences and disputes are addressed through peaceful means and dialogue."

India, Pakistan to start Dialogue in February

In a giant step forward, India and Pakistan today announced that they had agreed to "commence" the process of "composite dialogue" in February. The level of the dialogue is still to be decided, according to both sides.

A joint press statement issued just before the Prime Minister Atal Bihari Vajpayee, returned to New Delhi late this afternoon, saw the Pakistan President, Pervez Musharraf, reassure India that he "will not permit any territory under Pakistan's control to be used to support terrorism in any manner."

The accord raised expectations of a rapid improvement in bilateral relations with both sides stressing that there were no "winners and losers". A "win-win" situation had been created for both.

However, Gen. Musharraf went as far as to say that "history had been made," suggesting that the two countries may have agreed on a long-term trajectory to resolve contentious issues.

Asked whether there had been some back-channel diplomacy, he said : "I don't think so. We [have] never reached in the past where we have reached now. With [the] passage of time and developments around the world, there is a realization [of geo-economic realities]."

From the statements made by India and Pakistan, it appeared that the formal dialogue is not as important as testing the sincerity of both countries in adhering to the letter and spirit of today's agreement in the coming weeks. The statement continued: "The two leaders are confident that the resumption of the composite dialogue will lead to a peaceful settlement of all bilateral issues, including Jammu and Kashmir, to the satisfaction of all sides."

At the end of several days of hard negotiations on the text of the statement, the two countries seemed to have ended a long period of acrimony and non-contact that had marked their relationship since the December 13, 2001 attack on India's Parliament.

The six-paragraph statement said: "Prime Minister Vajpayee said that in order to take forward and sustain the dialogue process, violence, hostility and terrorism must be prevented.... President Musharraf emphasized that a sustained and productive dialogue addressing all issues would lead to positive results."

"Both leaders welcomed the recent steps towards normalization of relations between the two countries and expressed the hope that the positive trends set by the CBMs (confidence-building measures) would be consolidated."

On the question of India's wanted "list of 20", Gen. Musharraf said that this should be looked at in an environment of trust and harmony "later." He counselled presspersons that Pakistan and India should leave aside contentious issues and concentrate on steps that could be taken easily.

Sounding like a man India could do business with, he said that a "thaw" had taken place in bilateral relations owing to the positive actions taken by both countries – Gen. Musharraf was open in praising Mr. Vajpayee's "vision and statesmanship."

Gen. Musharraf said the two countries had arrived at an "agreement to take the [peace] process to its logical end" and added in a matter- of-fact fashion that Kashmir was an issue that had to be resolved.

21

Announcement of Lok Sabha Elections

It became official when Prime Minister Atal Bihari Vajpayee told Finance Minister Jaswant Singh to prepare for a Vote-on-Account so that the process of the General Election could be completed and a new government was in place by April-end.

Responding to the party's appeal for holding an early Lok Sabha poll, he said, "I hereby direct Finance Minister Jaswant Singh to present a Vote-on-Account in Parliament at an early date" and hoped that "a new government would be in place by April".

Sources said the Finance Minister could present a Vote-on-Account by the end of this month. Immediately after Mr. Vajpayee's return to the country after attending the BIMSTEC summit in Thailand in the second week of February, the Union Cabinet would meet and recommend the dissolution of the Lok Sabha which would set the electoral process in motion by the middle of February.

The Cabinet could recommend the dissolution on February 13, a date considered lucky for the party, sources said adding that Vajpayee wants a new government in place by the beginning of April. Since, the present Chief Election Commissioner J.M. Lyngdoh would retire on February 7, the party is confident that the new CEC would work out the election dates in such a way that a new government was installed by the first week of April. Sources added that the multi-phased election would also take care of objections of the NDA partners.

The two-day meeting of the Bharatiya Janata Party National Executive, at Hyderabad authorised the Prime Minister to decide on the dates of the early Lok Sabha elections.

Delegate after delegate spoke on the advantage of an early election which should be held as early as possible. But the views of the various constituents of the National Democratic Alliance should be taken into consideration while deciding the exact dates of the Lok Sabha poll.

Briefing newspersons about the political resolution, Mission 2004, the Prime Minister's address and Deputy Prime Minister L.K. Advani's intervention, BJP president M. Venkaiah Naidu said a calendar of the campaign would be ready by tomorrow.

The party's campaign would begin on January 23, the birth anniversary of Netaji Subhas Chandra Bose, and at least 100 rallies would be held across the country by the time the official notification of the General Election comes out.

Naidu also announced the setting up of three committees. The campaign committee convener would be general secretary Pramod Mahajan. The second committee, headed by former BJP treasurer Ved Prakash Goel, would try to mobilise resources for the election and another committee, headed by Commerce Minister Arun Jaitley, would prepare a vision document that would inform about the country's future in the next five years. The other members of these committees would be announced later, the BJP president said.

In reply to a question, Naidu said the BJP would prefer simultaneous elections for the Assembly and the Lok Sabha. The Andhra Pradesh Assembly election should also be held along with the Lok Sabha as there was no point in holding separate elections since the time gap was too short.

The four-page political resolution has praised Vajpayee's leadership, saying, "Destiny has placed the responsibility of shaping India's future in BJP's hands."

The resolution also indulges in Congress bashing, saying that a victory of the Congress would mean a return to instability. While the NDA victory would mean a faster economic growth, its defeat would result in stagnation and regression, the resolution said.

To a question on the BJP's action plan for the minorities, Naidu said a sustained effort would be undertaken to have a dialogue with these sections so that any misconception about the party could be removed.

Earlier, the Prime Minister told the meeting that the "world has come to recognise us as the dominant and guiding constituent of Indian politics" and "all misconceptions and motivated propaganda about our party have been belied".

"The BJP is not merely a political party, but a movement for social transformation", he said adding, "we will seek a renewed and larger mandate to build a strong and prosperous India".

Get Ready for Battle, PM Tells Party

New Delhi, Jan. 28. The Prime Minister, Atal Bihari Vajpayee, today said the people of the country had already decided to give another term to the BJP and the NDA and the task ahead was to translate this overwhelming mood into votes.

"Get ready for the battle", he told BJP MPs at the parliamentary party meeting and stressed, "We have to win." He painted a rosy picture, saying the atmosphere was conducive because of the feel good factor and the "Opposition being in disarray."

To those MPs asking for more sops for the electorate such as increasing the limit of small-scale industries, he reportedly said this was not possible but assured sympathetic consideration after the NDA's return to power. "We will do these after we return to power," he said.

The Deputy Prime Minister, LK Advani, while expressing similar optimism said that this was the first time that incumbency was an asset for the government. "Go and win the elections," he directed.

The Parliamentary Affairs minister, Mrs Sushma Swaraj, urged members to be present in both Houses from tomorrow so that the government was not caught off guard. She told them that Parliament would be adjourned tomorrow after which it would meet on Friday. Parliament would have a three-day holiday from 31 January after which it would meet for three days from 3 February for the vote-on-account formality.

She explained to them that the government had done the correct thing by deciding to dissolve the House before going to Parliament for a vote-on-account. The government must go to Parliament with a proper reasoning for seeking the vote-on-account, she reportedly explained.

Stage Set for General Elections (13th Lok Sabha Dissolved)

New Delhi Feb.6. The President, A.P.J. Kalam today dissolved the 13th Lok Sabha on the advice of the Prime Minister, Atal Bihari Vajpayee, setting the stage for the next parliamentary elections.

A Rashtrapati Bhavan communique, issued this morning, said that Vajpayee had called on the President on January 27, 2004 and conveyed to him the advice of the Union Cabinet that the Lok Sabha be dissolved on February 6.

Vajpayee met the President again on Thursday (February 5) and informed him that the votes-on-account (railways and general) 2004-2005 and the Finance Bill, 2004, had been passed.

The communique went on: "As necessary financial and other business have since been transacted by Parliament, the President has now accepted the recommendation and, in exercise of the powers conferred upon him by sub-clause (b) of clause (2) of Article 85 of the Constitution of India, has signed an Order today dissolving the 13th Lok Sabha with immediate effect."

Today's dissolution of the Lok Sabha is the sixth time the President has invoked Article 85. There were early dissolutions in the past on December 27, 1970 (Fourth Lok Sabha), August 22, 1979 (Sixth Lok Sabha), March 13,1991 (Ninth Lok Sabha); December 4, 1997 (Eleventh Lok Sabha), and April 26,1999 (Twelfth Lok Sabha).

The dissolutions in 1979, 1991, 1997 and 1999 became necessary because the Government of the day had lost its majority and no alternative government could take its place.

Index

H

I

N

O

P

Q

R